LONGMAN REVISE GUIDES

Series editors: Geoff Black and Stuart Wall

TITLES AVAILABLE:
Art and Design
Biology
British and European History
Business Studies
C. D. T. – Design and Realisation
Chemistry
Computer Studies
Economics
English
English Literature
French
Geography
German
Mathematics
Mathematics: Higher Level and Extension
Physics
Religious Studies
Science
Social and Economic History
World History

FORTHCOMING:
C. D. T. – Technology
Commerce
Home Economics
Human Biology
Integrated Humanities
Music
Office Studies and Information Technology

GCSE

RELIGIOUS STUDIES

J Glyn Harris

LONGMAN
REVISE
GUIDES

Longman

ACKNOWLEDGEMENTS

The author is indebted to the following Examination Groups for permission to reproduce past examination questions. Whilst permission has been granted to reproduce their questions, the answers, or hints on answers are solely the responsibility of the author and have not been provided or approved by the Groups. The Groups accept no responsibility whatsoever for the accuracy or method of working in the answers given.

London and East Anglian Group (LEAG)
Northern Ireland Schools Examination Council (NISEC)
Southern Examining Group (SEG)
Welsh Joint Examination Committee (WJEC)

The author further acknowledges the permission given by Brenda Lealman to reproduce the photograph in chapter 5.

Longman Group UK Limited,
Longman House, Burnt Mill, Harlow,
Essex CM20 2JE, England
and Associated Companies throughout the world.

© Longman Group UK Limited 1989
All rights reserved; no part of this publication
may be reproduced, stored in a retrieval system,
or transmitted in any form or by any means, electronic,
mechanical, photocopying, recording, or otherwise,
without the prior written permission of the Publishers.

First published 1989

British Library Cataloguing in Publication Data

Harris, J. G. (John Glyndwr), *1918–*
  GCSE religious studies
  1. England. Secondary schools. Curriculum subjects: Religion
  G.C.S.E. examinations
  I. Title
  200′.76

ISBN 0–582–03851–0

Produced by The Pen and Ink Book Company, Huntingdon, Cambridgeshire.

Set in 10/12pt Century Old Style

Printed and bound in Great Britain by
Wm. Clowes Limited, Beccles, Suffolk.

CONTENTS

EDITORS' PREFACE

Longman Revise Guides are written by experienced examiners and teachers, and aim to give you the best possible foundation of success in examinations and other modes of assessment. Examiners are well aware that the performance of many candidates falls well short of their true potential, and this series of books aims to remedy this, by encouraging thorough study and a full understanding of the concepts involved. The Revise Guides should be seen as course companions and study aids to be used throughout the year, not just for last minute revision.

Examiners are in no doubt that a structured approach in preparing for examinations and in presenting coursework can, together with hard work and diligent application, substantially improve performance.

The largely self-contained nature of each chapter gives the book a useful degree of flexibility. After starting with the opening general chapters on the background to the GCSE, and the syllabus coverage, all other chapters can be read selectively, in any order appropriate to the stage you have reached in your course.

We believe that this book, and the series as a whole, will help you establish a solid platform of basic knowledge and examination techniques on which to build.

Geoff Black and Stuart Wall

AUTHOR'S PREFACE

This Revise Guide has been prepared for the benefit of students who will study Religious Studies for the GCSE examination. It's not a text book or a complete covering of the syllabus content of the six examining groups. Instead it is a guide to the main areas of study specified by the syllabuses in each of the six religions and directs attention to the basic knowledge that is essential for understanding each religion in its own right.

I wish to thank Blake Hemmings for his comments, and to express my appreciation to the editors for their skilful and careful production. On a personal level I am indebted to my wife for her patience and her practical help throughout the period of preparation.

J. Glyn Harris

1

THE EXAMINATION AND ASSESSED COURSEWORK

AIMS

ASSESSMENT OBJECTIVES

CONTENT

GRADES

MODES OF EXAMINING

HOW TO USE THIS GUIDE

INTRODUCTION

The GCSE is a single system of examining at 16+ based on nationally agreed criteria. It introduces several important changes in examining.

In religious studies you will study aspects of one, two or three of the following major religions: Buddhism, Christianity, Hinduism, Islam, Judaism and Sikhism. The examination is open to candidates of any religious persuasion, or none, and will emphasise the educational base for the study of religion. Of critical importance is the *coursework* which will be given greater emphasis than before.

The study will provide opportunities for:

- exploring the world of beliefs and practices and the link between the way religious people think and act;

- thinking about your *own* responses to what each religion says about moral and social issues, based on appropriate evidence and argument;

- expressing your knowledge, understanding and what you can do in a positive way.

RELIGIOUS STUDIES CRITERIA

The syllabus and examination is based on General and Subject Specific Criteria. It will be helpful if you have a copy of *your* particular syllabus which gives information about the content and methods of assessment of your examining group. The examination is set and marked by the six examining groups:

London and East Anglia (LEAG)
Midland (MEG)
Northern (NEA)
Northern Ireland (NISEC)
Southern (SEG)
Wales (WJEC)

The addresses of these groups are provided on page 5.

AIMS AND ASSESSMENT OBJECTIVES

There are five general aims for religious studies. These are the educational basis for studying religion and they apply to whatever religion you study. You must bear this in mind as it is from these aims that the *assessment objectives* are derived. The five aims are:

- to promote an enquiring, critical and sympathetic approach to the study of religion, especially in its individual and corporate expression in the contemporary world;
- to introduce candidates to the challenging and varied nature of religion, and to the ways in which this is reflected in experience, belief and practice;
- to help candidates to identify and explore questions about the meaning of life, and to consider such questions in relation to religious traditions;
- to encourage candidates to reflect on religious and on non-religious responses to moral issues;
- to enable candidates to recognise and appreciate the contribution of religion in the formation of patterns of belief and behaviour.

These aims ensure that you will:

66 How religions express their beliefs and practices today. 99

- study the *observable features* of religion as it is believed and practised in the contemporary world; you will learn about how different religions encounter each other in Britain and across the world;
- consider the *challenging and varied nature of religion* through exploring its inner vitality and the claims it makes;
- encounter questions about the *meaning of life* that arise whenever we study how human beings think and act as they do;
- confront *moral issues* that arise out of the cut and thrust of everyday living;
- learn about the *life style* of religion and the distinctive features of each major religion.

The National Criteria specify three **assessment objectives** for religious studies. These are *knowledge, understanding* and *evaluation*. These objectives are precise and *your learning must be geared to them*. They are not special to religious studies as they can be shared with other subjects, but they offer the opportunity for you to maximise your performance in positive ways. They are a valid and reliable way of testing what you know, understand and can do in religious studies. This means that no-one will be disadvantaged or unfairly favoured.

At the beginning, you should realise that knowledge, understanding and evaluation are *not* three entirely separate objectives. In practice they will often overlap so as to make your study more coherent. Consider this question:

What do you think makes a young man or woman choose to enter a closed religious order?

66 Select and present relevant factual information in an organised manner. 99

66 Show understanding through explaining the beliefs and practices. 99

In order to answer this question you must first show that you *know* what 'a closed religious order' is. You may do this by giving an example(s). Then you must show that you *understand* why a religion may have 'closed orders'. Finally, you will be expected to say *what you think* about the young person's decision. In a complete answer the three assessment objectives have been tested. You should refer to the next chapter for further information about each of the three assessment objectives.

Six major world religions (Buddhism, Christianity, Hinduism, Islam, Judaism and Sikhism) form the **content** of the syllabus. You will study at least one of these, possibly two or three, but no more. Each examining group also ensures that at least one syllabus is concerned *wholly* with Christianity under the Mode 1 arrangements.

You will study religion through a variety of **approaches**, such as origins, teachings, history, contemporary issues, sacred texts or the study of the traditions of a voluntary authority. A further choice is a study of **themes** from three major world religions, which may include founders and leaders, sacred writings, festivals, fasts, solemn days, worship and ritual, community life, personal experience and moral teaching.

You are advised to read carefully the *title* of the syllabus option you choose and the *introduction* to it. This will inform you about the aim and scope of the option. This is an introduction to a syllabus on Judaism:

- The intention is to offer an introductory study of Judaism as a living religion. It provides for an investigation of the historical basis and development of Judaism, together with a study of the main beliefs, practices and institutions, achievements and way of life of the Jewish people.   (WJEC)

The syllabus defines the *weighting* of the assessment objectives and the aggregate marks you will earn (including coursework and final examination). The weighting of the objectives is:

> **Evaluate issues of belief and practice arising from the study of religion.**

- knowledge 35–45%
- understanding 35–45%
- evaluation 15–25%

4 ▷ GRADES

On the basis of your performance you will be awarded a grade which will show what standard you have achieved. All aspects of the examination (including coursework) will be taken into account when awarding a grade. To achieve a grade F or grade C you will be likely to have demonstrated the following:

Grade F

- a partial knowledge of the syllabus content; this implies an ability to select some of the relevant information required, and to set it down with an attempt at organising the material;
- such understanding of some of the areas concerned with the study of religion as will demonstrate, for example, an ability to
  1 recognise particular uses of language in religion,
  2 explain in simple terms the influence of special people, writings or traditions,
  3 state a principal religious belief in your own words,
  4 recognise a moral issue and to relate an appropriate religious belief to it,
  5 recognise a question about the meaning of life and link it to the study of religion;
- express clearly a personal opinion directly related to an issue raised and offer an argument in support of it.

Grade C

- a wide knowledge of the syllabus content: this implies an ability to select some of the salient features of the information required, to identify contexts and to show some skill in organising and presenting the material;
- a reasonable understanding of most of the areas concerned with the study of religion, and in particular
  1 a correct understanding of some uses of language in religion, including a simple understanding of basic concepts,
  2 some understanding of the influence of at least one of the examples (special people, writings, traditions) on individuals or religious communities,
  3 an ability to explain principal beliefs clearly and to trace a relationship between belief and practice,
  4 a clear understanding of at least one moral issue and the application of a religious belief to it,
  5 an ability to identify and to respond independently to a question about the fundamental meaning of life which might evoke faith responses;
- an ability to recognise some of the significance of an issue raised, to express in a clear statement a personal opinion directly related to it, and to support that opinion with some use of evidence and argument.

There are three *modes* of examining at GCSE and you may enter for any one of them:

MODE 1

In this mode, the *syllabus* is drawn up by the examining group and approved by the Secondary Examinations Council. The *examination papers* are prepared by the group in accordance with the National Criteria (General and Subject Specific). The *examination work* is then marked by the examining group, which also awards the grades.

MODE 2

In Mode 2, the *syllabus* is drawn up by the school or centre, though it still has to meet the requirements of the National Criteria. The syllabus must be approved by the examining group and the Secondary Examinations Council. The *examination papers*, however, are produced by the examining group and the *examination work* is then marked in the first instance by the examining group. Afterwards the work is compared with the group's own Mode 1 candidates so as to ensure equivalence of standards between the two modes. The examining group also awards the grades for the Mode 2 candidates.

MODE 3

Preparation of the *syllabus* for Mode 3 is the responsibility of the school or centre. It has to conform to the National Criteria and be approved by the examining group and the Secondary Examinations Council. The school or centre prepares the *examination papers* which also have to be approved. The *examination work* is marked by the school or centre and then submitted to the examining group to be moderated. In this instance too the work is compared with that of all other candidates, so as to ensure uniform standards. Once again the examining group determines the grades to be awarded.

This Revise Guide sets out to offer you help in developing the skills you need as a student of the GCSE examination in Religious Studies.

The first three chapters inform you about the examination and how you should organise your study.

The chapters on each of the six major religions set out the essential knowledge and the concepts you need to understand. Each chapter tells you what you need to know, understand and be able to do in order to achieve a satisfactory grade.

No matter what religion or religions you study you will find the chapters on those religions relate to the syllabus of whatever examination group you will be taking.

There are questions for you to discuss and specimen questions for you to answer. The student answers and tutor's comments will show you how you should answer examination questions.

EXAMINATION GROUP ADDRESSES

London and East Anglian Group
LEAG   'The Lindens', Lexden Road, Colchester CO3 3RL

Midland Examining Group
MEG   Robins Wood House, Robins Wood Road, Aspley, Nottingham
                     NG8 3NR

Northern Examining Association
NEA   Devas Street, Manchester M15 6EU

Northern Ireland Schools Examinations Council
NISEC   Beechill House, 42 Beechill Road, Belfast BT8 4RS

Southern Examining Group
SEG   Stag Hill House, Guildford GU2 5XJ

Welsh Joint Education Committee
WJEC   245 Western Avenue, Cardiff CF5 2YX

International General Certificate of Secondary Education
IGCSE   1 Hills Road, Cambridge CB1 2EU

EXAMINATION TECHNIQUES

PREPARING FOR THE EXAMINATION

Your syllabus will give you a complete description of *what* is to be examined and *how* it will be examined. With regard to the syllabus, the National Criteria (General) state that the 'title must give a clear indication of the content'. This applies also to any *option* you may choose. The syllabus is presented in sections which contain a number of items for study. Here is an illustration:

Syllabus title: Jesus and the Foundations of Christianity
Sections:
    1 What do we know about Jesus?
    2 What do the records tell us?
    3 Responses to Jesus

The *items* in each section tell you what aspects you will study. Some of the items are general and others specific. Ask yourself at an early stage . . . . How should I study this item? . . . . What must I focus on? . . . . How much time must I spend on it? . . . . In what depth should I study it?

When you read a syllabus, you will focus on individual words or clusters of words which describe its content. Some words will be familiar, but others may be new or be terms used in religion. Pay attention to the *context* in which the words or terms are used, so that you learn their meaning in that particular context.

As you read your syllabus, you will get an overall impression of it and you will be conditioning yourself for your study.

1 ▷ ACHIEVING THE OBJECTIVES

❝ ❝ Assessment measures how far the assessment objectives are achieved. ❞ ❞

There is no one way of learning that suits everyone. But there are some things that affect our learning, whoever we are. In this examination these are the assessment objectives of *knowledge*, *understanding* and *evaluation*. Is there a technique for achieving these?

KNOWLEDGE

One technique of acquiring **knowledge** is to ask a series of simple questions such as these:

- WHAT do I need to know?

If you ask this question it will lead on to asking WHAT knowledge is important? You will soon be asking WHAT interests me about this topic? Suppose the topic is the Five Pillars of Islam. Ask WHAT *do I need to know about the Five Pillars?* WHAT *knowledge of them is important?* WHAT *interests me about the Five Pillars?*

- WHY do I need to know?

WHY is one of the most important questions we can ask. Asking it will help to clarify the way you learn. Once you know WHY you need the knowledge you will find it is easier to remember it and later on to use it correctly.
Ask WHY *do I need knowledge of the Five Pillars of Islam?*

- HOW can I know?

If you ask this question it will direct you to *sources* of knowledge. You may get your knowledge from books or pictures or from contact with members of a faith or visits to places of worship. Ask HOW *can I get knowledge of the Five Pillars of Islam?*
Asking WHAT do I need to know? WHY do I need to know? HOW can I know? is a sure way of stimulating interest and curiosity about a topic. It will help you think about it and see why the knowledge is important.

UNDERSTANDING

Is there a similar technique for developing **understanding**? Ask the following questions as you study ideas or statements:

- WHAT is the meaning of . . . ?

We all ask this question, either consciously or unconsciously as we learn. At first it may be simply questions about the meaning of terms or concepts or statements such as WHAT *is the meaning of* 'covenant' or 're-incarnation' or 'Saturday is the Jewish Sabbath'.
As you learn more about a subject you will ask more complex questions which require more thought and the ability to understand things from more than one point of view. You may be asked to show your understanding of the Christian teaching on divorce and why Christians do not always agree about it.

- HOW can I explain . . . ?

Examiners often ask candidates to explain or interpret a saying, or an action, or a piece of evidence. Explaining is one way of showing understanding. Suppose you were given this passage to read:

> The Hijrah, or emigration from Mecca is the hinge of the Muslim story and the beginning of the Islamic calendar. After the death of Abu Talib and Khadijah Muhammad had visited Taif, an important centre south east of Mecca. But his reception had been hostile. All the more timely then was the interest of a group of pilgrims from Yathrib, a city to the north, in his message. They asked for further enlightenment and he sent them a teacher.

Now answer this question:

> Explain carefully the meaning of (a) 'the hinge of the Muslim story'; (b) 'the interest in his message'.

In order to show understanding you need to select any relevant knowledge or facts about the 'Muslim story' and 'his message'. You need to see whether there is any other information that is important. You can then proceed to explain the meaning of the two phrases. You could treat explaining a passage like this as a piece of detective work!

EVALUATION

When it comes to **evaluation** ask:

- WHAT do I think?

By asking this question, what you learn (knowledge) and understand become part of your own thinking. You will be on the way to making 'a reasoned personal response'.

Attempt this question:

> You are taken by a friend to Friday prayer in a mosque. As this is your first visit, your friend explains the proceedings to you.

(a) Would an explanation help you to enter into the spirit of what is happening? Or would you prefer to follow the proceedings without any explanation?

(b) Do you think worship in one religion should be open to members of another faith? State clearly the reasons for your opinion.

Evaluation of evidence

It is difficult to be completely objective when we study any subject. We all have our ideas about what is valuable and worthwhile. In this examination you will learn to evaluate 'on the basis of evidence or argument'. In this case you must not allow your prejudices to come in the way of your evaluation, and therefore to distort it. You may give your own views and the reasons for your opinion. You may argue 'how far' you agree or disagree with a point of view. You will *not* be tested on whether your opinion is right or wrong but on whether you understand what is asked and can back up your opinions with reasons and evidence.

Attempt this question:

> The walls of a mosque are decorated with texts from the Qur'an but there are no images.

> Write three sentences *for* and three sentences *against* the use of images in worship.

A PRACTICAL NOTE

The techniques already described will help to develop skills of *knowing, understanding,* and *evaluating*. They do not prescribe a method for everyone. They encourage you to be an *active learner*, but you must discover your own learning style. There are no tricks or short cuts that make learning easy! Here are ten hints that will help you further in preparing for the examination:

1 Draw up a schedule of work on each of the topics you will study; find out how much work you need to do on each.
2 Allocate your time sensibly between the sections of your syllabus and leave time for the other subjects you will be studying.
3 Balance the work you do in class with what you do on your own.
4 Concentrate on what you are doing during your study time. You may study best in short spurts, or for a longer period. Make the best use of your time by keeping your mind on what you need to know, understand and can do.
5 Learn to profit from your reading by picking out the main ideas and important points.
6 Make notes as you study – this will keep your mind active, and the notes will be useful when you come to revise.
7 Set aside regular time to revise what you learn as you go along. Don't leave it all till the end.
8 When you are given a task, make sure that you understand what it is and follow the instructions carefully; try to complete every task on time so that you do not have a backlog to worry you.
9 Remember your teachers are there to advise and help with any problems. Use whatever services you can to help with your learning.
10 Make time for relaxation – this is most important!

THE EXAMINATIONS

2 > THE WRITTEN EXAMINATION

The National Criteria in Religious Studies offer two points of useful guidance:

- The techniques of assessment must make provision for testing candidates of different levels of ability.
- The assessment scheme shall be representative of the syllabus as a whole, and candidates shall be assessed on each of the major parts of the syllabus.

Your examining group will prepare a written examination at the end of the course as *one* of the components of the final assessment. The test will be

- valid . . . . it will test what it sets out to test;
- reliable . . . . it will test in an accurate and consistent way.

The test will also

- discriminate . . . . it will award marks for each part of the test which will detect the differences between the performance of the candidates.

The examining group will design a scheme of assessment for the written paper(s) that will show how one candidate's performance deviates from others who have sat the same test. This will place the candidates in the correct order and identify the different levels of attainment. This will determine the award of the final grades.

COMMON PAPERS

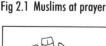
A variety of question types and how to achieve differentiation.

In the GCSE examination in religious studies, candidates will sit a *common* paper(s). All components of the written examination will be taken by *all* the candidates and everyone will be assessed on the same basis.

The common papers are designed for candidates of all abilities and the different components within the paper will show how differentiation is to be achieved. You should find out how many *written* papers your examining group requires and how each paper is to be *structured* and the *types of questions* that will be asked.

3 > TYPES OF QUESTIONS

Every examining group will use a variety of *question types* in the written examination. This is in accordance with the National Criteria:

- These may include the use of stimulus material, multiple choice, short answer, structured and extended essay questions, including the use of open texts . . . .
- The principle of an incline of difficulty may be built into appropriate questions in order to ensure that the examination provides an adequate test . . . .

STIMULUS MATERIAL

Stimulus material may be written or visual, a piece of primary or secondary evidence, a symbol or diagram, an illustration or map, a simulated or a contrived situation.
Here is a question with a visual stimulus:

1 What is the name for the different positions or postures shown in the picture?
2 Why do Muslims all face in the same direction?
3 Prayer is a communal act. Explain this.
4 Offer three reasons why daily prayer is important to a Muslim.

Fig 2.1 Muslims at prayer

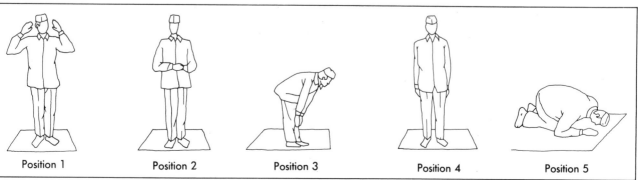

Position 1   Position 2   Position 3   Position 4   Position 5

Answers:

1 The name for the postures is rakah (it means 'unit').
2 The Muslims all face Mecca and the ka'aba; this gives prayer a common focus.
3 The worshippers join together to pray; this creates a sense of belonging and unity; it shows the solidarity of believers in Islam.
4 Prayer five times a day is commanded in the Qur'an; it brings the Muslim into touch with God and fellow Muslims; it is source of spirituality; it affirms faith.

MULTIPLE CHOICE QUESTIONS

A **multiple choice** question is composed of a *stem* and a number of *responses* or distractors. The stem may be an incomplete statement or a question. Only one of the responses or distractors is correct.

Your task is to identify the correct response. Each of the responses stands on its own and each is plausible but only *one* is correct. Work out these examples:

- Jesus called his first disciples
  1 to be his followers;
  2 to be his prayer partners;
  3 to be his servants;
  4 to be his co-workshippers.
- When did Jesus declare that he is lord of the Sabbath?
  1 in the synagogue at Nazareth;
  2 after going through the cornfields;
  3 in reply to Caiaphas's question;
  4 in the temple in Jerusalem.

OBJECTIVE QUESTIONS

Objective questions will test recall and give you the chance to present facts and knowledge. They do not ask for understanding or analysis or the evaluation of the knowledge. Objective questions may be any of the following:

- simple recall . . . .
- sentence completion . . . .
- matching items . . . .
- true or false statements . . . .
- antonym (opposites) . . . .
- analogies . . . .

Objective questions may stand as separate items in a section of the examination paper or may be part of a composite question, as in this example:

a) Muslims meet for prayer in a mosque. What is a mosque?
b) Only male Muslims pray in the prayer hall. Why is this?
c) Explain the importance of Friday prayer to a Muslim.
d) Describe how individual Muslims contribute to Friday prayer.

The first part is an objective question; the second part tests your understanding of the custom; the third part asks you to say what you think of the importance of prayer to a Muslim. In the final part you may show 'empathy' with the feelings and attitude of the individual Muslim.

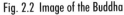

Fig. 2.2 Image of the Buddha

STRUCTURED QUESTIONS

A **structured question** provides guidance about how you should answer it. It gives a framework for your answer. It includes a number of pointers or signposts for composing an answer. The base from which to launch the answer is the *stimulus*. There may be an incline of difficulty in the structure and different objectives may be tested. Here is a structured question based on a visual stimulus:

1 What is the religious meaning of the following aspects: the 'halo' often shown round the head; the ears; the hands?
2 The position of the figure is also important. Explain your understanding of its importance.
3 Where did Guatama first preach after his enlightenment? To whom did he preach?
4 What important Buddhist ideas are represented in the celebration of Wesak?
5 How far is Buddha's moral behaviour designed to help himself or help others?

(LEAG)

Here is an example of a structured question without the use of a visual stimulus:

A young coloured woman was attacked early one evening as she was on her way home along a poorly lit road. She was robbed of her purse, which contained about £20, her credit cards, house keys and small personal items. In the attack she was badly beaten about her head and was left with serious facial injuries and lost the sight of one eye.

Develop an argument that expresses your view of the action that might be taken:

1 by the community to protect such people from attack;
2 to compensate victims of such attacks;
3 to deal with the attacker after he/she is caught;
4 to explain religious attitudes towards the victim *and* her attacker.

(WJEC)

ESSAY QUESTIONS

You may be asked to write an essay during the course as well as in the final examination. There are many ways of writing an essay, but the wrong way can get anyone into trouble! So what are the guidelines?

1 **Give your essay a target**. Make sure that you know what you want to say. It's a good idea to jot down some of the things you want to say *before* you begin your essay. When you have done this you can settle to writing it and when you have finished you can look back to see if you have said what you wanted to say.
2 **Keep to the point**. Say what you want to say in the right place. Avoid including what is not relevant. Structure your points in an ordered way. Don't try to say everything in one go.
3 **Organise your material**. Do this first by collecting the materials you wish to use. You can do this in a number of ways, depending on the subject of the essay. Once you have got the materials together you can begin to organise your essay.
4 **Think carefully about how you begin**. Your opening sentence or paragraph should make the reader want to read on. You might tell the reader how you are going to approach the subject.
5 **Keep to the right length** if this is given, otherwise use your common sense. Make your writing clear as if you are reading it on the radio, or to an audience.
6 **Pay attention to your style**. Paragraph your essay. Check the grammar and spelling. Use words and language that *you* understand.
7 **Think about the conclusion** as a summary or final comment. Try to conclude by leaving a good impression on the reader. Perhaps refer back to the question and give a balanced judgement in the light of the evidence you have presented.

You must be sure that you know the precise subject of the essay and how you intend to write it. The same applies to every examination question!

4 ANSWERING THE EXAMINATION PAPER

The following points may help you in answering the examination paper(s) in a relaxed manner. Before you begin answering the paper, take the following steps:

1 *Allow yourself time to read each question carefully*. Focus on what the question asks and note any information given. If the question asks you to 'describe' or 'explain' or 'relate' or 'say what you think' or 'give reasons' then follow the instructions carefully and do not waste time by giving answers to other kinds of questions.
2 *Decide which questions you intend to answer*. Tick the questions you think you can answer best (if you have a choice). Also decide which questions you will answer first and how much time you will spend on each question.
3 *Plan your answers*. Do your best to answer the whole paper. Try to leave time to read back over the answers. It can make a difference if you detect any mistakes. After analysing a question it will help to jot down some key points and put them in order. These will be memory aids to help answer the question fully.
4 *Follow the instructions*. Read the instructions about the length of the examination, the number of questions to be answered, and the value of each.
5 *Finally* . . . Make sure that you arrive in the examination room on time and that you take with you all the things you think you will need, pen, pencil, eraser, ruler, crayons, etc.

5〉   **REVISION**

5〉   **REVISION**

Revision is the final stage in preparing for the examination. It is very important and to make the most of this:

1 *Plan your revision*. Prepare a simple revision programme; write out a list of topics you wish to revise during the time; plan to revise when you are most likely to be able to give all your attention to it.

❝ Preparing for the written examination. ❞

2 *Techniques*. Concentrate on key elements or central ideas, the major personalities and themes; revise these in relation to the assessment objectives (knowledge, understanding, evaluation); work out how your revision applies to each of these; check through the syllabus to make sure you cover all the crucial points.

3 *Procedures*. Try to minimise distractions; give special attention to any parts of the course you may find difficult or uninteresting; ask for help with any parts you are not sure about or with any problems.

C O U R S E W O R K

You will be asked to submit a folio of **coursework** as part of the final assessment. The coursework will test the same assessment objectives as the written examination, namely, *knowledge*, *understanding* and *evaluation*.

6〉   **WHAT IS COURSEWORK?**

Obviously this is work done during the course which will be assessed in a systematic way. The marks you earn will be aggregated into a final grade. You may prepare your coursework either in class or as homework.

There are aspects of religious studies that are particularly appropriate to assessment by coursework. It extends your study of religion in a number of interesting ways. It gives you an opportunity to gain marks for work that may not be tested in a written examination. In particular, you may *use a variety of skills* in different contexts. For example:

❝ Preparing and presenting folios of coursework. ❞

1 *observing* religious rites, celebrations, festivals and movements;

2 *making personal responses* to religious expression through a variety of media such as art, music, architecture, symbols, artefacts, dance and movement;

3 *reflecting about religious issues* in public life, in personal and social behaviour;

4 *designing, conducting and evaluating simple surveys* which test a religious point of view or the impact of a piece of religious teaching.

Be sure to study carefully the *guidelines* for coursework in your particular syllabus. These will tell you about any special requirements of your examining group.

In coursework you will become familiar with a number of terms whose meaning you should know. These include:

■ **Assignment.** This is an 'assigned' task given you to do. It may be a written task or a piece of investigation or practical fieldwork.
You will need to know how many assignments you are expected to present for assessment and the regulations about length, content and presentation.

■ **Folio of work.** This is the final package of work which you will present for assessment. You will receive information about how many pieces of work make up a folio.

Every piece of coursework you are asked to do will be assessed in its own right. It will help if you find out *which* of the assessment objectives is being tested and *what weighting* is being given. You will also be told whether the coursework task is of the 'closed variety' (requiring only one response or a limited number of responses) or whether it is of the 'open' kind (allowing for a more wide ranging set of responses).

The table (Fig 2.3) shows how each assignment tested a *particular* assessment objective, and the *weighting* of each objective over the whole coursework programme. You can see here that half the total marks were available for 'understanding'.

TITLE OF COURSEWORK	ASSESSMENT OBJECTIVE		
	Knowledge	*Understanding*	*Evaluation*
1 *Classwork Test on content of Genesis*	14/20		
2 *Classwork Essay on Passover and Easter*		13/20	
3 *Review of TV film on divorce*			15/20
4 *Homework Essay on Last Supper*		14/20	
5 *Letter writing in class on death*		Not handed in	
6 *Classwork Test on First Revelation to Muhammad*	16/20		
7 *Classwork Essay on Islamic Revival*	5/20		
8 *Letter to school Governors about disregard of Muslim rules re girl's education.*			13/20
9 *Homework Essay on Hajj*		12/20	
10 *Prayer for use during Ramadan*		12/20	
TOTALS	35/60	51/100	28/40
			(LEAG)

Fig. 2.3 A Student's Coursework Performance.

7 STYLES OF COURSEWORK

You will probably be given a *variety* of coursework tasks and it will be useful to know why this is the case. Varying the tasks you are set gives you a better chance of achieving the different assessment objectives and of using different skills. Here are three examples of types of coursework in Religious Studies:

INVESTIGATION

Investigation implies that you will *locate* and *select* information from readily available sources that are relevant to your coursework task. It also means that you can *use* the information as evidence for substantiating a point of view or showing that you understand religious teaching or practices.

Skills

Investigation will involve using skills of research, analysis and description, exploring events and issues in the light of evidence, stimulating the search for further knowledge and understanding.

Topics

Any number of topics may be investigated. Some of these may be a piece of religious evidence (for example, the Israelites and their exodus from Egypt, or the founding of the Sikh dharmasala). You may investigate the life and work of a significant religious leader from any period. Or again, you may investigate the relation between religion and any living situation.

INTERPRETATION

Coursework tasks that focus on interpretation will allow you to *explain* the meaning of different religious ideas and practices. You will be able to look at these from a number of perspectives. You will also be able to assess the value of any evidence or ideas and present your own conclusions.

Skills

Interpretation will give you scope to use your skills of critical thinking and analysis. You will be able to probe the reasons for holding religious beliefs or practising them in particular ways. You will also be able to explain the importance of religion in different contexts.

Topics

The task may be that of interpreting some religious teaching or beliefs (for example, the resurrection in Christianity, or re-incarnation in Hinduism). It may be to interpret a scene from religious art, or images and symbols from various religions. The interpretation may be from the point of view of a member of a religious group, or a non-religious person.

REFLECTION

A coursework task that fits under this heading will require mainly evaluation. It will allow you to *reflect* upon a religious topic or activity from a personal point of view.

Skills

Reflection will require applying your mind to the subject and questioning the meaning. It will involve looking at it from a number of points of view. It will also give the opportunity to discriminate between different parts of the subject and use affective skills.

Topics

You may be asked to listen to a piece of religious music, or view a religious ceremony, or the performance of religious dance. You will reflect upon the stimulus and make your response to it. Or the task may be to reflect upon a situation of conflict between two racial groups and then to express your conclusions.

The following topics of a distinctive nature have been presented for GCSE. In your opinion, which of them could best be treated through investigation, interpretation or reflection?

Poverty and deprivation
Kosher food and dietary laws
Yamulka and Tefillin
Christian denominations
Visits to various religious buildings, such as a Hindu Temple
Parables of Jesus
Discipleship
Work of the Parish Priest
The Jerusalem Temple
Jesus' teaching on forgiveness and judgement
The 'work ethic' and its Christian rationale
Divorce and marriage
Discrimination
Addiction
Resurrection narratives
Birth stories
Christianity in action

PRESENTING COURSEWORK

Your teachers will give you instructions about presenting coursework. The *amount* of coursework and how it is to be presented is important as you must fulfil the regulations of your examining group. You will be expected to submit your coursework at the time announced. It will then be assessed along with the work of all other candidates.

8 ⟩ ASSESSING COURSEWORK

Your coursework will be assessed in two stages. First, it will be assessed by your own teacher(s) and then by assessors from your examining group. In GCSE, teacher assessment is required in all cases. The teacher is in a unique position of being able to marshall evidence of everyone's performance during the whole period of preparation for the examination. In some cases only the teacher is able to assess the work. The teacher will know *how* you have produced the coursework and all the activities and skills that have been used. The 'process' of producing the coursework as well as the final 'product' can be assessed by your teacher. However, to ensure fairness and reliability the marks given to you by your teacher are subject to checking by an external moderator.

GETTING STARTED

This chapter looks at five topics that are common to the syllabuses of the six religions. It looks at some fundamental aspects that will help you in your study of the topics.

It will be helpful to have a copy of your syllabus. The syllabus is sub-divided into a number of *sections*. Within each section a number of *topics* are specified that are central to the particular syllabus. Take for example the section **Religious Expression** in the LEAG syllabus. It is divided into two main topics (themes): 'Contemporary Worship and Ritual', *and* 'Fast, Festival and Pilgrimage'. The syllabus then gives a number of *examples* of each topic as well as the *key concepts* you need to understand.

It will be useful if you begin your work on a topic by writing down *your* initial definition of the topic or your first thoughts about it. Afterwards you will be able to outline some of the main points in more detail and to suggest how you will deal with them. If you have any difficulty in defining the topic area discuss it with your teacher. You can avoid many pitfalls if you keep your definition of the topic constantly in view and remember the purpose for studying it.

You will find help in understanding the *purpose* for studying the topic by looking at the *introduction* to the syllabus or section of the syllabus. For example the introduction to the section of the syllabus on **Religious Expression** states that the purpose is 'to show a general knowledge of the outward forms of religious expression, and of their meaning and significance for believers'.

ESSENTIAL PRINCIPLES

1 ▷ TOPICS AND COURSES

You will see from the grid in Fig. 3.1 that the following five topics are *common* to the six religions, although the terms used to express these topics differ from syllabus to syllabus. The topics are: *origins* (historical background); *growth*; *beliefs*; *worship*; *sacred writings*.

This grid will help you to identify precisely which of the topic areas are appropriate to your particular syllabus.

RELIGION	TOPIC	LEAG	MEG	NEA	NISEC	SEG	WJEC
Buddhism	Origins	+		+		+	+
	Growth and Spread	+		+		+	+
	Major Beliefs	+		+		+	+
	Worship	+				+	+
	Festivals and Celebrations	+		+		+	+
	Rites of Passage	+				+	+
	Sacred Writings	+		+		+	+
Christianity	Historical Context	+	+	+	+		+
	The Church	+	+	+	+	+	+
	Beliefs		+	+	+	+	+
	Scriptures	+	+	+	+	+	+
	Worship	+	+	+		+	+
	Festivals and Plgrimages	+	+	+		+	+
	Leaders	+					+
	The Christian Life	+	+	+	+		+
	Moral Issues	+	+	+	+	+	+
Hinduism	Historical	+				+	+
	Sacred Writings	+	+		+	+	+
	Major Beliefs	+	+	+	+	+	+
	Worship	+	+	+	+	+	+
	Festivals and Pilgrimage	+	+	+		+	+
	Rites of Passage	+		+		+	+
	Major Movements		+	+			+
	Moral Values	+		+			
	Hinduism Today		+		+		+
Islam	The Five Pillars	+	+	+		+	+
	Sacred Writings	+	+	+	+	+	+
	Major Beliefs	+	+	+	+	+	+
	Worship		+	+	+	+	+
	Festivals and Pilgrimage		+	+	+	+	+
	Home and Family			+			+
	Rites of Passage	+				+	+
	Sects	+	+		+		+
	Moral Values	+			+		
	Islam Today		+	+	+		+
Judaism	Historical Context	+		+	+		+
	Scriptures	+	+	+	+	+	+
	Major Beliefs	+	+	+	+	+	+
	Worship	+	+	+	+	+	+
	Festivals	+	+	+	+	+	+
	Home Life				+		+
	Rites of Passage	+		+		+	+
	Sects	+	+	+			+
	Moral Values	+					+

Fig. 3.1 Topics covered by the major syllabuses.

RELIGION	TOPIC	LEAG	MEG	NEA	NISEC	SEG	WJEC
Sikhism	Origins	+		+		+	
	The Ten Gurus	+		+		+	
	The Khalsa	+		+		+	
	Scripture	+	+	+		+	
	Worship	+	+	+		+	
	Major Beliefs	+	+	+		+	
	Festivals and Pilgrimage	+	+	+		+	
	Rites of Passage			+		+	
	Sikhism Today	+	+				

2 > ORIGINS AND FOUNDERS

ORIGINS

Why study the *origins* of religion? Each of the six religions (with the exception possibly of Hinduism) have known historical origins. Knowledge of the origin is often crucial for understanding the religion. You will need to know about:

> It is necessary to know about the date and origin of a religion.

a) the *date* of origin;
b) *how* the religion originated;
c) *where* it originated;
d) any *special features* concerning its origins.

Knowing the *date* of the origin of a religion sheds light on the historical circumstances in which it emerged. For this you will need reliable sources of information. You can get this from studying the sacred writings of the religion or books or evidence from archaeology. Piecing together all the information is like piecing together a complex jigsaw puzzle. Fortunately, many scholars have sifted the evidence and given us reliable information on the date of origin of the religions of your study. Here is a table:

- Buddhism   6th century BCE (Before the Christian Era)
- Christianity   1st century CE (Christian Era)
- Hinduism   undated
- Islam   7th century CE
- Judaism   13th century BCE
- Sikhism   15th century CE

You will notice that Hinduism is undated. Modern Hinduism has emerged over many many centuries and Hindus say that its origins are lost 'in the mists of time'. They speak of it as the 'eternal dharma' (law or teaching). It is safe to say on this basis that Hinduism is the earliest of the six religions. You will hear more about the circumstances in which these religions emerged when you study them individually. In the meantime, note the date of the beginnings of the religions as this will help to explain some of their special characteristics.

FOUNDERS

In the course of learning about the origins of religion, you will learn also about their *founders*. Some religions have a historical founder, others do not. Hinduism does not have a named founder. Islam refers to Muhammad as God's messenger (rasul) rather than the founder. Jews refer to Abraham as their 'father' and to Moses as the founder of Judaism. Buddhism takes its name from Gautama Buddha, Christianity from Christ, and Sikhism has Guru Nanak.

In the eyes of their followers, the founders are persons of special qualities. They have powers to inspire and lead, and possess authority and spiritual energies beyond the lot of ordinary people. Believers say that the character and work of the founders determine the character of the religion.

You will learn to *understand* these faiths through learning about their founders. It is not possible to understand them in any other way. A Buddhist believes that Buddhism *is* the Buddha; it is not an abstract principle but a way of life centred on the Buddha. Christians believe that Christianity *is* Christ; it is not a doctrine but a life centred on Christ. Sikhs honour Guru Nanak as the first guru or teacher who founded their religion.

3 > GROWTH OF RELIGION

When you learn about the date of a religion you will also learn about its place of origin. This too will help you understand it more fully. The six religions of the GCSE are divided geographically between eastern and near eastern:

- Buddhism
- Hinduism   } **Eastern**
- Sikhism

- Christianity
- Islam   } **Near Eastern**
- Judaism

As you learn about individual religions you will discover the influence of the country and culture of their origin. The three *eastern* religions have the imprint of the language, thought forms and symbols of the east stamped upon them. The same is true of the *near eastern* religions. Here are some *differences* that are striking:

	Eastern	*Near Eastern*
TIME	Moves in circles.	Moves from point to point.
LIFE	Cycle round the 'wheel of existence'.	Moves from birth to death.
	Life is not an entity that begins at a specific moment in time.	Life begins with birth at a specific moment in time.
DEATH	The individual may endure many lives.	Death is the termination of physical life.
	After death there is reincarnation or re-birth.	The soul may continue to exist through eternity.
	The state and condition of the new life depends on behaviour in the present.	Belief in heaven and hell.
		Religions that believe in resurrection.
GOD	God is conceived in many ways and forms.	God is known through personal revelation.
	Belief in many gods.	Only one God.
	God may be personal or impersonal.	God is personal.
		God will intervene to establish his rule throughout the world at the end of time.

You will learn a number of *terms* that relate to these differences between eastern religions and the others. You will learn the meaning of these terms and how to use religious language. You could underline the religious terms in the above account of religions and begin to compile a list of terms.

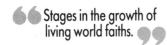
Stages in the growth of living world faiths.

By today, these religions have spread far beyond their homeland and are often strongest in other parts of the world. You may check this from the following table as well as from the maps of the present spread of individual religions.

Religion	*Country of origin*	*Present spread*
■ Buddhism	India (Nepal)	South east Asia, China, Japan and Tibet
■ Christianity	Israel (Palestine)	Throughout the world
■ Hinduism	India	Mainly India
■ Islam	Arabia	Gulf states, Africa, Bangledesh
■ Judaism	Israel	Israel, Russia, USA, Western Europe
■ Sikhism	India (Punjab)	Punjab, Africa, Europe

In the course of their growth and spread, the religions have changed and it is sometimes difficult to compare their present character with their original forms. Christianity, for example, looks very different today from what it did in the first century CE. As religion has spread it has been influenced by different customs and cultures, divided into groups or sects, and has changed its forms of worship and organisation. This is evidence of the fact that religion is a living phenomenon.

4 ▷ BELIEFS

There are many ways of defining religion but most make reference to *beliefs*. Here are three that are fairly common:

- religion means belief in a supreme being;
- religion is a unified system of beliefs about life and death;
- religion is a system of intellectual beliefs and feelings.

Belief is a central core of religion; some religions, for example Islam, have a structured system of beliefs; others, such as Hinduism, do not have a formal system of beliefs. Where religion prescribes a creed, its members accept this as the norm and abide by it.

❝ The belief patterns of religion. ❞

As you study different religions you will see that they can be *classified* according to their beliefs. Christianity, Islam, Judaism and Sikhism are all 'theistic' religions. That is, they are dominated by belief in God. They believe in God as a *living* being who is all powerful and all present. They believe in God as a *personal* being so they address him in a personal way as 'my God' or 'your God' or the 'God of Jesus' or 'God the gracious and compassionate' or the 'God of Abraham, Isaac and Jacob'.

On the other hand, Theravada Buddhism is 'non-theistic'. It does not have a belief in a personal or all mighty being called God. It does not deny his existence, but does not mention it either.

One way of classifying religions is on the basis of their beliefs about God.

Another aspect that you will come across is the division between beliefs in *many* gods and belief in *one* God only. You will learn about how Hinduism has from time to time acknowledged many gods or a supreme god manifested in many forms. On the other hand, Christianity, Islam, Judaism and Sikhism are all *monotheistic* faiths, though they differ in the ways they interpret this. Jews and Muslims, for example, do not believe that God is a trinity of persons (Father, Son and Holy Spirit) united in one supreme being. Sikhs believe in one God, but do not express this in any way that might limit him.

If you scan your syllabus under the topic 'Beliefs' you will see how wide ranging religious beliefs are. There are variations *within* a single religion as well as *between* religions. You will find yourself asking questions such as *why* do members of the same religion sometimes hold *different* beliefs? Jews have different beliefs about the Messiah, and Christians have different beliefs about the meaning of the death of Jesus.

In this examination you will *not* be expected to pass judgement for or against any beliefs, or on the use that is made of them. You will learn that beliefs may be put to different uses by different religious groups. Beliefs about hygiene or dietary laws or dress may be applied differently by religious adherents. Nor will you be asked to prove or disprove the validity of any belief. You *will* however be expected to show understanding and sympathy in learning *why* beliefs matter to the people who hold them and to show 'openness' in the way you treat them.

In the GCSE you will *not* be asked to decide whether some beliefs are true and others untrue, or whether some are more true than others, or whether some are more useful than others. Christians and Jews believe that God made a covenant or solemn agreement, but you will not be asked to decide whether one covenant is superior to the other. Buddhism and Hinduism have beliefs about what happens when a person dies, but you will not have to adjudicate between them. *You will only be tested on your knowledge and understanding of religious beliefs, and not on whether you own or disown them.*

But you should heed this warning about studying religious beliefs. The examiners will expect you to show *understanding* of their meaning and significance. You will not be learning about the 'external shell' of the beliefs which religious people hold but *what the belief is and what it means*. All beliefs have meaning and are intelligible to the people who hold them.

Religious beliefs are in most cases enlivened by religious *action*. You will not study religious beliefs in a vacuum, or as theories. The beliefs provide a guide for action and a particular life style. They produce codes of moral behaviour and values which govern the way people behave. You may think of religious belief as a commitment to truth *and* a way of life. Religious people do not as a rule divorce their beliefs from their practice.

5 ▷ WORSHIP

❝ The varied content and styles of worship. ❞

Why do all religions practise worship? You will probably find that religious people answer the question in a variety of ways. Some worship because it gives peace and quiet to think and meditate, others because they enjoy being with other people. But worship has a deeper meaning. What might this be?

Here are three ideas for you to consider:

■ worship is homage paid to a superior being;

■ worship engages in a relationship with a superior being;

■ worship is a response to a superior being.

If you question Christians about worship they will say that when they worship God they pay homage to God, and that through worship they enter into a relationship with God. They *use* prayers, hymns, sacraments, and the Bible to help do this. They also say that they respond to God through their worship. Worship (from an old English word 'weorthscripe') means 'recognising worth'. Worship is recognising the 'worth' of the superior being (God). Buddhists who do not use the word God pay homage before the Buddha image. In other religions, to offer worship to any thing other than the Supreme Being is considered idolatry.

Worshippers *express* their feelings of awe or reverence as they worship through the *gestures* they perform. Buddhists remove their shoes in the presence of the Buddha image and never point their feet in his direction; Hindus bow before the image of the god; Christians kneel before the altar and make the sign of the cross; Muslims prostrate themselves facing towards Mecca; Jews cover the head and face the Ark; Sikhs remove their shoes and bow before the Adi Granth (their holy book). These gestures express the inner feelings and response in worship.

STYLES OF WORSHIP

One feature of worship is its varied *styles* even within the same religion. Both form and content vary, as you will learn. Nevertheless, every act of worship is a unity even though it may include a number of elements. A useful comparison is with the body which has many parts but is a unity. The secret of the unity is in the body itself. So it is with worship; it may include processing, singing, praying, meditating, praising, speaking, reading, yet the whole is a unity. The secret of the unity is *in* the worship itself to which each part contributes.

Broadly speaking you will meet two styles of worship, either 'sacramental' and non-sacramental, or 'liturgical' and non-liturgical.

■ **sacramental**   the use of outward visible signs which express spiritual grace. Sacramental worship is worship which centres on sacraments, such as the eucharist in Christianity;

■ **liturgical**   the use of prescribed forms of worship or regular ritual, such as regulated prayer in Islam.

You will gather that, firstly, sacraments and liturgy depend on the nature of the individual religion – worship in Christianity is 'sacramental' when the worshippers share in the eucharist in 'remembrance of Christ'. Islam is a religion of submission to Allah (God) and the 'liturgy' of worship expresses this. Secondly, sacramental and liturgical worship is communal. This form of worship must involve other worshippers, no sacrament or liturgy may be observed by an individual in private.

Not all worship, by any means, is of this style. You will learn about religious groups who worship without any set liturgy or ritual. They believe they can worship without any external aids. One such group is the Quakers. Can you think of others?

RITUAL, SYMBOLS AND IMAGES

These are three concepts you will learn about religious worship. What do they mean?

■ 1 **Ritual**   a formal religious ceremony or set of ceremonies that give a regular pattern to worship. The ritual may comprise words or music or other set forms.

Ritual performs *three functions*:

a) it forges links between the worshipper and the object of worship (God);
b) it focuses the attention on the object of worship;
c) it depicts an aspect of the nature or history of the religion.

Here is an illustration of these three functions:

A company of Hindus attend the worship of the goddess Lackshmi in their temple. The Brahmin priest arrives and takes his place in front of the altar. All is silent until the priest begins to chant a hymn to the sound of a bell. A clay pitcher filled with water and covered with a coconut is placed near the image of the goddess. The priest ties a length of cotton thread to four corner posts to enclose the pitcher. *The link is forged with the goddess*. The priest sprinkles the worshippers and the image with water from the pitcher as he recites verses from the scriptures. All minds *are concentrated on the image* as prayers are said. The priest brings the goddess to life and the image is elevated. *Aspects of the myths and character of the goddess are told* until the priest finally chants a mantra (sacred formulae or syllables).

Ritual worship, where it is practised, performs these three functions. You will find it helpful and interesting to answer the following question:

To which of the three functions of ritual do the following ritual acts refer:

a) the Buddhist dressing the Buddha image;
b) the Christian standing during the reciting of the creed;
c) the Hindu fire ritual;
d) the Muslim reciting the creed;
e) the Jew parading the Torah scroll;
f) the Sikh walking backward away from the Adi Granth;
g) the Buddhist reciting the three Jewels;
h) the Christian kneeling before the altar;
i) the Hindu burning incense;
j) the Muslims sitting in rows in the mosque;
k) the Jew standing for the final prayer;
l) the Sikh standing as the Adi Granth is put away.

■ 2 **Symbol** a sign by which something is known or used to represent something else.

Symbols have a special function in worship:

a) they may represent the object of worship;
b) they express the meaning of worship at different levels;
c) they identify the worshipper with aspects of the nature and history of the religion.

Here is an illustration of the use of symbols in Sikh worship:

The worshippers sit in the Sikh temple facing the platform which holds the Adi Granth. As this is read a fan (chauri) made from animal hair or peacock feathers is waved over the sacred book. This is a symbol of *the sovereignty of the Adi Granth*. The book is the voice of the Guru (God).

During the prayers the kara prashad (holy food), which is contained in a large iron bowl, placed near the Adi Granth is stirred with a kirpan (a short knife), which is a *symbol of the resistance to evil*. This custom goes back to the time of Guru Gobind Singh and the formation of the Sikh Khalsa. Later the kara prashad is served to everyone present as a *symbol of God's provision*, the unity of the faith and charity to all.

These are among the symbols you will learn about if you study any of these religions:

■ the symbol of placing the hands together before the forehead and pointing them upward toward the Buddha image;

■ the symbol of bread and wine in the Christian eucharist;

■ the symbol of five lights before the image of the Hindu god;

■ the symbol of washing before entering the mosque in Islam;

■ the symbol of the perpetual light in Judaism;

■ the symbol of offering food in Sikhism.

How would you explain the function of each of these symbols in the worship of the different religions?

■ 3 **Image** a likeness such as a statue, picture, idea or representation in the mind.

Images often have a function in worship, especially of:

a) stirring depths of feeling and thinking;
b) conveying the spiritual reality present in worship;
c) depicting truths in a visual form.

The images in view may be a picture or painting, a statue or carving, a sculpture or frescoe, an icon or embroidery.

Here is an illustration of the use of images in Christian worship:

Members of the Greek Orthodox Church assemble for the liturgy. They stand before an icon and light a candle. They look at the image of the virgin and child or the saint and *they feel deeply moved*. They kiss the icon and handle it with affection. They feel *drawn into the presence* of the person whose image the icon portrays. They think of the significance of the image and receive its spiritual power.

You will learn more about the role of images in religion as they are frequently used in worship. Even so, you may consider them as part of the ritual or symbolism of worship. Or you may think that paying reverence to an image of the Buddha, a Christian saint or Christ belongs to the 'affective' (feeling) dimension of worship. In this case you will need to 'put yourself in the shoes' of the worshippers if you are going to appreciate their feelings in the presence of these images.

Look carefully at this image of the Buddha:

Fig. 3.1 Homage before Buddha

a) What feelings might paying reverence in the presence of this image inspire in a Buddhist?

Look at this image of the Hindu god Ganesha:

Fig. 3.2 Ganesha

How might paying reverence before this image inspire lovable and generous thoughts in the Hindu?

The image symbolises the power and wisdom of an elephant and the swiftness of a mouse.

Do you think that having the image of Ganesha is a help to the Hindu to worship?

Look at this figure of Christ on the cross:

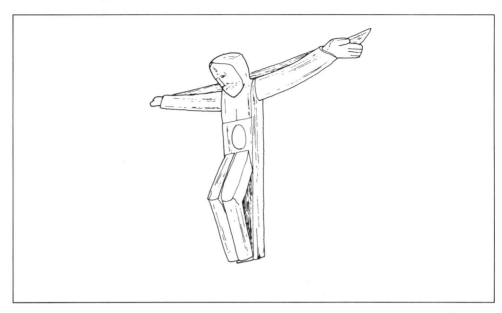

Fig. 3.3 Christ on the cross

How does seeing the figure on the cross help a Christian in worship?

SACRED PERSONS

In many religions communal worship requires *special people* to conduct it. Their status and role differ from one religion to another and in some instances worship may *only* be conducted by a priest or minister or bishop.

Persons who are appointed officially to conduct worship are 'ordained' or 'set apart' for this special task. They have special spiritual gifts and knowledge of worship and are trained to conduct it. They act as spiritual guides to the worshippers. Only they have authority to conduct certain forms of worship. Only a bishop or priest may conduct the eucharist in some churches, and only a priest leads worship in a Hindu temple. Such people exert a great influence on worship.

6 SACRED WRITINGS

❝ The authority, use and significance of sacred writings in religion. ❞

There are many *reasons* for learning about the scriptures and sacred writings of religion. Here are four for you to consider:

1 The *authority* of scripture and sacred writings. Some religions believe they are revealed or spoken directly by God.
2 The *practical guidance* the scriptures and sacred writings give.
They instruct believers about their beliefs and how they should practise them.
3 They provide *answers to questions* about the mystery of life and the goal of religion.
4 They are *used in corporate worship* and private devotions.

You need to know a number of things about the scriptures and sacred writings.

1 The names given to them

- **In Buddhism** *The Three Baskets* (this is the best known Buddhist scripture; you will learn about others if you study this religion).

- **In Christianity** *The Bible* = the Book. The part which relates specifically to Christianity is called the New Testament (Testament = covenant or agreement)

- **In Hinduism** *'Revealed'* writings, this is, in principle, a source of their authority; *'Remembered'* writings, this is, in principle, a source of knowledge. If you study Hinduism you will learn more about these.

- **In Islam** The *Qur'an*

- **In Judaism** *TaNaK*

- **In Sikhism** *Adi Granth* or *Guru Granth Sahib*

2   The content and authorship

Your particular syllabus may prescribe some content for study but you will not be expected to know *all* about the content and authorship of the sacred writings. To introduce you to these here are some points:

a) **content:**   this is complex as the writings are made up of a variety of religious and moral teaching, stories, myths and legends, history, letters and sermons, prose and poetry;

b) **authorship:**   you will discover this depends on how members of different religions look upon their sacred writings. These are the main alternatives:

       i) the author is God who revealed the writings directly;

      ii) God inspired human authors to write these sacred works;

      iii) the sacred writings were composed by members of religion from choice.

3   Compiling the sacred writings

The sacred writings were compiled into book form years after they were first spoken. For years they were handed down in a spoken form as sayings, stories, teachings, or (as in the case of the Qur'an) recited as received from God. In later times they were compiled into the book form.

They were collected and written down for the practical purpose of serving the faith. Those who did so knew *what* they were doing and *why* they needed to do it. The religions needed their sacred writings in a permanent form for the sake of the faithful. Here is a breakdown of how the sacred writings were compiled:

- **Buddhism**   the Buddha's teachings were handed on from person to person until a beginning was made in the 1st century BCE in a monastery in Matale in Sri Lanka to compile them in writing. This refers to the Buddhist Pali canon.

- **Christianity**   information about Christ was first passed on orally and later written in the gospels. In 365 CE the church decided on the twenty-seven books of the New Testament.

- **Hinduism**   the vast Hindu sacred writings were collected into a written form over many years; behind them there is a long period when they were passed on in an oral form.

- **Islam**   the Qur'an was revealed to Muhammad and recited as received and later written down.

- **Judaism**   the books of the TaNaK first circulated in an oral form and were compiled at a council at Jamnia in 90 CE.

- **Sikhism**   the Adi Granth was first compiled by the fifth guru in 1604. The final edition was compiled in the time of the last of the personal gurus in 1710.

You need to *understand* a number of things about the sacred writings. The two most important aspects are i) *how believers regard* their sacred writings, that is, their authority; and ii) *how they use* their sacred writings in worship and daily life.

Here is a selection of views by members of different faiths:

- **A Buddhist**   they are the 'word of the Buddha';
- **A Christian** 'the authority of the New Testament is that God speaks through it';
- **A Hindu**   'all Hindus believe in the truth of the Vedas' (the earliest Hindu scriptures);
- **A Jew**   'Torah is the unceasing revelation of God as grasped and recorded by man'; (Torah is the first part of TaNaK);
- **A Muslim**   'Read the Qur'an and you'll find the answers to all your questions';
- **A Sikh**   'The Guru Granth Sahib is but one song, one Idea, one Life'.

If you attempt to explain these statements you will also be able to say *what you think* about the way believers regard their sacred writings.

BUDDHISM

GETTING STARTED

Buddhism is the religion of the disciples of the Buddha. The historic Buddha was born near the borders of Nepal in India in the sixth century BCE. Today, most Buddhists live outside India as you can see from this map.

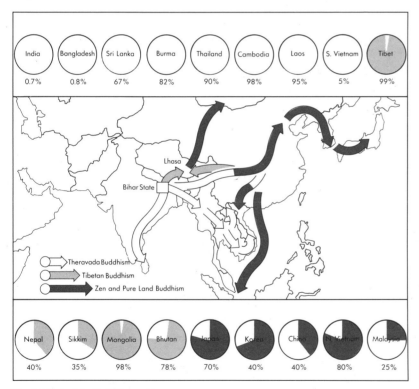

Fig. 4.1 Map of the Buddhist world

Buddhism is a major missionary religion, with about 300 million followers.

ESSENTIAL PRINCIPLES

1 ▶ **IMAGES OF THE BUDDHA**

❝❝Why the Buddha image is significant to the Buddhist.❞❞

You have probably seen pictures of the Buddha which show him either standing, sitting or lying down. You may find the shape or form of the image striking, especially the very tall images or the image of a fat laughing figure like a character from a comic opera. Buddhism is permeated with these images. They are all different, yet significant to the Buddhist.

Here are three images for you to study:

THE SITTING BUDDHA

This image represents the Buddha in the lotus or meditation posture. Notice the expression of calm and peace. Also how each foot is placed on the opposite thigh in a meditation position. The stem of the lotus flower points upward from the mud and will blossom into a flower of exceptional beauty. The lotus position is the basic position of meditation and is highly symbolic.

THE TEACHING BUDDHA

Notice how in this image the fingers of the Buddha's right hand point to the earth. This is a symbol of the Buddha's call to the whole earth to share his message until everyone shares its blessing. He once said:

Let each burning human tear drop on my heart and there remain, nor ever be brushed off until the pain that caused it is removed.

His message is:

Friendliness for the whole world,
All embracing.

THE WHEEL OF THE LAW

This image is of the Buddha setting the wheel of the Law in motion. The forefinger and thumb of the right hand are joined to form a circle, which represents the wheel of the Law, while the finger on the left hand points to it as though it is being set in motion.

Buddhists do *not* worship the image or rupa but may sit and meditate in its presence. It is the *impression* the image creates that matters. The image is the incarnate 'principle of enlightenment' and Buddhists carry the impression of the image as they seek for enlightenment by following the Buddha's rule.

Fig.4.2 The Sitting Buddha

Fig.4.3 The Teaching Buddha

Fig.4.4 The Wheel of the Law

2 THE BUDDHA'S SEARCH

The historic Buddha searched for an answer to the problem of life. Buddhists engage in the same search and are helped to an answer by following the way of the Buddha. It is important to understand this search.

Imagine that you are looking at the splendour of a sunset on a calm summer's evening. You may wonder at its beauty and ask why the sun rises and sets. You may wonder why the world needs the sun, or what kind of world this is. Then you go on to ask, Why am I here standing and looking at the sunset? This may lead you to ask, *Who am I?* You are now making an inward journey. No-one else can make this journey, only you.

Write down quickly some of your thoughts and feelings as you look at the sun setting. What are your thoughts and ideas about it? Are your feelings pleasant or happy? Exciting or puzzling? What questions do you want to ask? Put all your thoughts and feelings together and you may say 'This is me' or 'My thoughts and feelings are what I am'. Now suppose you look at the sun setting in a month or a year's time, do you think you would have the same thoughts or feelings? Would your ideas of the sun and the world be the same? The answer is probably no – but only you yourself know this; only *you* can answer the question because only *you* can make the inward journey.

Making this journey is like stepping into the unknown. The historic Buddha made such a journey and he found answers to the problem of human life. He taught his followers to make the journey for themselves:

Be ye lamps unto yourselves;
Rely on yourselves;
Do not rely on any external help.

Hold fast to the Truth as a lamp;
Seek salvation alone in the Truth;
Look not for assistance to anyone besides yourself.

3 THE THREE REFUGES (OR JEWELS)

Buddhists make a vow of allegiance to *the Buddha, the teaching* and *the Sangha* (Buddhist order). They do not respect the Buddha as a personal god or as if he acts on their behalf. They make their vow of allegiance personally in the presence of the Buddha image and repeat it often. Every gathering of Buddhists opens with reciting the The Three Refuges, although individuals may make the vow on their own. The vow is precise:

I go to the **Buddha** for my refuge
I go to the **teaching** as my refuge
I go to the **order** for my refuge

4 THE BUDDHA AS REFUGE

Siddhartha Gautama (who became the Buddha) was born in Kapilavastu in the border country of Nepal in India. There is some uncertainty about the exact date of his birth, most probably it was either 563 or 560 BCE. His family belonged to the Sakya clan and the warrior class (kshatriya) of the Hindus. He is sometimes referred to as Sakyamuni (the wise man of the Sakyas).

Many legends are told about his birth in the Jataka, which highlight how with the birth of Siddhartha Gautama the path of enlightenment became visible to the whole world.

His mother Maya dreamt before his birth that she was standing near a tree on the slopes of the Himalayas when a white elephant danced before her, holding a lotus flower in its trunk. The elephant danced three times, and when she told her strange dream to her husband Suddhodana he called wise men together to explain its meaning. They said the dream was a sign that the child would be a great ruler. If he abided by his family duties he would have the world at his feet, but if he renounced them, he would be the saviour of the world. Later, Maya was visiting her family when she heard a voice warning her that the time of the birth of her child was near. She turned into the garden of Lumbini and as she clutched the branch of a sala tree her son was born. He was received at once by Brahma and other Hindu gods, the heavens were lit with bright lights, and a choir of angels acclaimed his birth. The child took seven steps to the north, south, east and west, as a symbol that his message would dominate the world. He also announced in a loud voice:

I am the chief of the world.
This is my last birth.

GAUTAMA IN HIS TIME

The social and political conditions of North India were passing through a time of change. The old social order was breaking down and new classes of wealthy merchants were becoming more powerful. There was much movement of population and many people felt insecure. Many were seeking for answers to human problems, especially about *what is life, has it any purpose, why do innocent people suffer*, and *what happens after death?*

When they looked to religion for satisfaction, all it could offer was refuge in ritual practices or in traditional doctrines. So some turned to living a life of self denial as hermits or ascetics. They hoped to find inner peace and an answer to the problems of life by turning away from worldly things. Siddhartha lived a comfortable and luxurious life, married and had a son. Like so many of his class (his father was the ruler of the Sakyas), he was shielded from the harsher side of life and was able to indulge in sports and a life of ease. All this changed when he came face to face with sickness, death and poverty.

A DAY'S ENCOUNTERS

According to Buddhist legend in the course of a single day Gautama met an old man leaning heavily on his stick, his body frail and his voice croaked:

'What is this', he asked his charioteer. 'Who is responsible for his condition? He himself? Or his family?'
'Not at all', replied the charioteer. 'This is old age; work and suffering are the cause of his condition. His family have turned their back on him and left him helpless to die in the forest'.
Then he added; 'Old age comes to everyone, to your father and mother; everyone will come to this'.

He then came across a man suffering from a fatal disease and felt the man's pain pierce his mind. He saw a funeral on the way to the place of cremation and was touched by the sorrow of the mourners. He saw a monk (bhikkhu) in a tattered robe, who walked with dignity and held out his alms bowl with a noble humility. He seemed perfectly happy and peaceful. Then he declared:

This is the secret of release.
I will give up the life of empty pleasure.

THE SEARCH

The memory of those meetings kept nagging at him until he confessed to his father;

O king, everything in this world changes and decays.
Let me go out alone as a hermit to beg.

When he was twenty-nine he left home to find a teacher who could point him to the answer to the problem of life. He joined a company of wandering teachers and studied the Vedas (the ancient Hindu scriptures), but they did not give him the answers he sought. He joined some hermits and fasted until his body became so weak that he nearly died. The more he suffered, the more Mara, the tempter, sought to destroy him. This only made him more determined to find the answer.

ENLIGHTENMENT

As he sat under a banyan tree in deep thought about the meaning of life and the causes of suffering, the moment of illumination came to him. The tempter gave him no peace but Gautama made a mark on the ground with his finger as a symbol that he would give the world his message. Suddenly the light dawned for him.

It was a moment of supreme elation. He felt his spirit surge into a state of 'higher consciousness' and his mind was at peace. He had found the secret of release (vimuti) and joy:

My mind was freed from sensual desire, from desire for existence, and from ignorance. In me now freed, arose the knowledge of my freedom. I realised that rebirth is destroyed . . . . Ignorance was dispelled, knowledge arose. Darkness was dispelled, light arose. So it is with him who abides vigilant, strenuous and resolute.

He was now the Buddha – the 'enlightened' one. Tradition says that this happened in Gaya in modern Bihar as he sat near a bodhi tree not far from a temple of a Hindu god Vishnu.

Today it is a place of pilgrimage for Buddhists. It is said that the Buddha remained in Gaya for four weeks in meditation before he returned to his friends to begin his mission. At first, Mara tempted him to keep the message to himself but the Buddha was resolved to share it with everyone who was ready to receive it:

> I wish now to turn the wheel of the Rule: for this purpose I will go to the city of Benares to enlighten everyone who is in darkness and to open the door of immortality to them.

5 > THE TEACHING (OR BELIEFS) AS REFUGE

The Buddhist vows:

> 'I go to the **teaching** for my refuge'

At first, some of his neighbours resisted his teaching, but he soon won them over. As he began to show them the way they could travel themselves and find for themselves the path of illumination, they began to listen and receive his message.

THE BENARES SERMON

If you think of a doctor who first diagnoses sickness and then prescribes a cure, that will give you a clue to the Buddha's method in this sermon. This sermon is the essence of his message – it is his analysis of the problem that each human being faces and how this problem can be answered.

Four noble truths

The Buddha taught *four noble truths*. The first two are his diagnosis or analysis, the second two are his prescription. The four truths are:

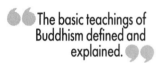
The basic teachings of Buddhism defined and explained.

a) suffering is universal;
b) the cause of suffering is universal;
c) the remedy for suffering is universal;
d) the path of release from suffering is universal.

Suffering (dukkha): suffering is universal and no-one can escape it. It is like a sickness that the Buddha diagnosed in this way:

> This, O Bhikkhus, is the Noble Truth of suffering; death is suffering; presence of objects we hate is suffering; separation from objects we love is suffering; not to obtain what we desire is suffering.
> Briefly, the fivefold clinging to existence is suffering.
> All existence is dukkha (suffering).

Desire (tanha): the universal cause of suffering is desire (tanha) or the craving for continued existence. Such desire breeds ignorance and self delusion that keeps us bound to the world and a round of innumerable rebirths:

> The cause of dukkha (suffering) is tanha (desire), that is to say, suffering is caused by one's selfish desire or attachment to life and everything associated with this life.

There is nothing permanent in life or the world. Desires change all the time and everything is subject to natural law. To remain in the grip of desire only increases suffering. *What then is the remedy?*

Release from suffering: the Buddha's remedy for the ills of life is twofold. It is firstly achieved through eliminating self desire and the craving for attachment to the world. To do this there are two extremes that must be avoided:

> There are two extremes, O monks, that should not be practised.
> And what are these two?
> That devoted to passions and luxury – which is low, unworthy, vulgar and useless; and that devoted to self mortification, which is painful, unworthy and useless.
> By avoiding these two extremes, the Perfect One (Buddha) has gained the enlightenment . . .

The Middle Path

This is the second part of the Buddha's prescription. He presented a middle way between the extremes of selfish desires and self denial. This is his 'Lotus of the True Law'. It is:
> 'like a tank for the thirsty, like a fire for those who suffer from cold, like a garment for

the naked, like a caravan leader for the merchants, like a mother for her children, like a boat for those who ferry over . . . . like a lamp for those who are wrapped in darkness'.

Buddha declared that the Middle Way (the Eightfold Path) is the way to personal enlightenment and *nibbana*:

Now this, O monks, is the noble truth of the way that leads to the cessation of suffering (dukkha).

> **Stages on the Buddhist path to *nirvana*.**

The Middle Way is basically the Buddhist way of life, it is positive and defined step by step:

i)	**Right understanding**	this consists of a) understanding the meaning of the four Noble Truths; b) understanding the true nature of the self; c) understanding the world for what it is.
ii)	**Right intention**	everyone must follow the Middle Way for the right reason and deliberately.
iii)	**Right speech**	speech is part of action; it must always be true, pure and noble; falsehood, slander and vile speech must be avoided.
iv)	**Right conduct**	right conduct involves acting morally, being considerate to all people, and showing kindness for all living creatures.
v)	**Right occupation**	only work that is proper and sets a good example should be done.
vi)	**Right endeavour**	everyone must strive after truth and avoid falsehood, seek what is good and shun evil.
vii)	**Right contemplation**	controlling the mind makes a person free from the extremes of self denial or self indulgence.
viii)	**Right concentration**	this means focusing the mind completely on the means of achieving *nibbana*.

The Middle Way is the foundation of Buddhist morality. It is a practical programme of right action and thought that leads to *wisdom* and *knowledge*, and which gives true *insight* and *inward calm*.

HUMAN LIFE

The teaching of the Buddha is distinguished from other religious teaching of his time by *his understanding of human life*. Hinduism taught that the individual soul (atman) is eternal and will survive death. This means that Hinduism believes in a permanent self. On this, the Buddha parted company with Hinduism. The Buddha denied the existence of a permanent or eternal self.

The self

The self changes all the time. Feelings, thoughts, ideas are constantly changing. Nothing remains the same in the world within or without. The self (*atta*) is constantly changing.

Refer back to the question *'Who am I?'* Your thoughts and feelings about this question change with your experience and the time at which you ask it. Mental states and physical urges are always changing. No-one can say 'I am this' or 'I am that' because there is no permanent 'I' or 'self'. The Buddha taught a message of 'No self' (*anatta*). *So what then?*

The self is a collection of five components or *skhandas*, namely:

- a physical body   (rupa)
- feelings   (vedana)
- sight   (samjna)
- consciousness   (samskara)
- thought   (vijnana)

There is no central core to these five elements, they only create an illusion of being permanent. In reality, they are in a state of constant change and may dissolve at any time. There is no permanent self – *the individual is only a collection of these ever-changing elements*.

Rebirth

If there is no permanent self, what happens when a person dies?

Natural life ends with the loss of consciousness. At the time of natural death the five components (*skhandas*) realise themselves in a fresh body. The self is then reborn into a state of 'impermanence'. Rebirth is the consequence of the operation of natural law which keeps a person bound by desire (*tanha*). For as long as this is the case, the cycle of rebirth will continue.

Rebirth is not a good thing and each new birth depends on the previous existence. It is determined by the action of *kamma* – the law of cause and effect. The only way to break free from this sequence is by eliminating desire and following the Middle Way. This promotes 'perfection' and release from the round of rebirth when the individual may pass into a state of 'higher consciousness'. But each step must be taken simultaneously, *not* consecutively.

Nibbana (Nirvana)

This word describes the end of the cycle of rebirth, but it is almost impossible to say what it means. It may mean 'extinction' as if a candle goes out when there is no more wax. In any case, Buddhists view it as the supreme good as it releases a person from the necessity of further rebirth. Beyond this, there is no need for explanation. A person passes into a state of 'higher consciousness'. When he was asked what happened beyond this, the Buddha kept a noble silence. Whether or not there is life after death does not make present suffering any less. The need for release still remains, but there is hope of achieving it:

> There is, O monks, a condition where there is neither earth nor water, nor fire, nor air, nor the sphere of infinite consciousness, nor the sphere of the void . . . . that condition, O monks, do I call neither a coming, nor a going, nor a standing still, nor a falling away . . . . Nibbana.

6 THE SANGHA (OR ORDER) AS REFUGE

'I go to the **order** for my refuge'

The five persons who first heard the Buddha's message were commissioned by him:

> Go ye forth, O disciples, for the salvation and joy of many, out of compassion for the world. Go not two together on the same path, preach, O disciples, the doctrine which is noble in its beginnings, in its course, and in its consummation.
> Proclaim the Noble Path.

Key stages in the spread of Buddhism.

The message spread first in North India and among the first to receive it were members of the Buddha's own class (the warrior class). Soon a community or order (Sangha) of Buddhists came into being.

The Sangha provided ideal conditions for those who were able to spend their whole lives in the search for salvation. This way was not open to everyone, as not all could leave their homes and families to spend all their time in meditation. But there were some who were able to follow the example of the Buddha and devote all their time to the search for enlightenment.

LIFE IN THE SANGHA

The Sangha is the community of Buddhist monks who are committed to living as a 'worthy person' (*arahat*) in the search for *nibbana*. They are completely devoted to the teaching of the Buddha and aim to practise it to the full. They follow a life style based on the Buddha's rule. They observe five precepts:

1 Refrain from destroying life.
2 Refrain from taking what is not given.
3 Refrain from unchastity.
4 Refrain from bearing false witness.
5 Refrain from strong drinks.

The outward symbol of their devotion is the yellow robe. This is a symbol of *knowledge*, *wisdom*, *concentration* and *morality*. Furthermore, it symbolises the fact that the monk has discovered the way of release from desire and the freedom to advance to the goal of *nibbana*.

Life in the Sangha is simple, but orderly. The members have no personal possessions and if they leave they have nothing to take away with them. The alms bowl and the shaven head are signs of dedication to the Buddh's rule. This is reinforced by the five other rules that monks observe:

1 To eat moderately.
2 Not to watch dancing or drama or such spectacles.
3 Not to use perfumes or ornaments.
4 Not to use comfortable beds.
5 Not to accept money.

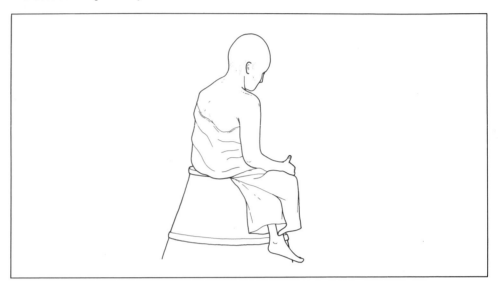

Fig. 4.5 Buddhist monk

Meditation

The monks spend a good deal of time in meditation (*samadhi*). Meditation is the practice by which the monk hopes to see clearly the inner reality of the Buddha's teaching. It is the central act of the Buddhist community. It induces direct knowledge of the Buddha's rule and focuses the mind on it; it turns the mind away from false desire (*tanha*) and illusion or false ideas and from evil thoughts. Meditation fosters feelings of love, compassion and generosity. The monks meditate together as a community, led by a meditation master. He gives guidance on the procedures and directs the mind to the focus of the meditation. Buddhists do not meditate in isolation – this is not a 'private' religion.

The stages of meditation are:

i) the monks sit on the ground in a quiet spot before a simple object on which they can focus the mind, maybe a flower or a symbol;
ii) they focus the mind on the object to the exclusion of everything else;
iii) they close their eyes and imagine the shape or form of the object, and gradually move away from its shape or form to the formless;
iv) quietly, they move away from the effort of meditating to concentration without any conscious effort;
v) in this state of effortlessness they experience a sense of inner rapture and see everything as if in unbounded space;
vi) in this state of meditation they are able to perceive directly and in an immediate way and gain insight into 'transcendental wisdom'.

It is not easy for us to understand these stages, as it is from 'within' that the state of pure consciousness is attained.

Order of nuns

It seems as if it was the Buddha's original intention to found only communities of males. However, he gave his consent to establishing an order of nuns. They too are completely devoted to the Buddha's teaching and discipline (vinaya) of the Sangha.

JOINING THE SANGHA

A young person who wishes to become a monk joins the community for a trial time before the 'period of study'. That is, before the rainy season when the monks do not travel outside the monastery. The person is free to return to his ordinary life after this trial period if he so wishes.

If he decides to join the community, he then prepares for ordination. First, he must pay off all his debts and show that he can live a life of poverty. He pays visits to his family and friends, who will support him in his life as a monk. They believe that supporting him gains them merit.

On the day before his ordination, he and his friends process through the streets, and a bell is rung to announce that one is about to become a monk. He dresses in a white robe (the symbol of purity) and music is played to create an atmosphere of joy. The *naag* (the name given to a person who wishes to become a monk) may receive gifts from his family and friends.

Before the ceremony of ordination, his head is shaved and he leaves for the monastery dressed in expensive clothes, just as Gautama was dressed when he left home in search of enlightenment. As he proceeds to the monastery, he carries a wax candle, a joss stick and a flower. When he arrives at the door he takes off his expensive clothes and enters the monastery in poverty.

Inside, his father presents him to the monks and elders who are seated and waiting to receive him. He sits before them, clutching his monk's yellow robe and asks for ordination. As soon as the monks and elders give their approval, he withdraws and returns in his monk's dress. He then asks to be instructed in the discipline of the monastery. The presiding monk asks him a number of questions, and if he answers them satisfactorily he is admitted to the Sangha. From then on his training begins.

Members of the Sangha are greatly respected by other Buddhists. They set an example by their devotion to the Buddhist rule and by teaching it to others. They live with only what they need and are supported by voluntary gifts from lay people. The giver who places the gift in the 'alms bowl' is blessed. As the monks walk with their 'alms bowl' they recite verses from the Buddhist scriptures and whatever gifts they receive they share with their fellow monks.

 **7 ▷ THE WIDER COMMUNITY**

Those Buddhists who do not live in a monastery look to the monks for guidance and inspiration to follow the Buddha's rule. But whether they belong to the Sangha or not, all Buddhists share the same convictions and hope to achieve illumination and arrive at *nibbana*. All Buddhists aim:

> To live according to the commands and to obey the teaching of Buddha.
> This is the essence of Buddhism.

THE FAMILY

The family is the basic social unit of Buddhism. It teaches a lot about the relationship between husband and wife and children and parents.

Husbands are charged to care for their wives and to treat them with kindness and affection. They must be faithful and give their wives their rights and dues. Wives should love their husbands and care for the home, be industrious and careful in the use of the family's resources.

Parents should follow these five rules in caring for a son:
1 keep him from harm; 2 show him the right way; 3 instruct him; 4 find him a good wife; 5 give him his inheritance.

In return, a son should support his parents, if necessary, just as they have provided for him. He should uphold the dignity of the family, guard his inheritance, and pay respect to departed relatives.

TEACHERS AND MASTERS

Teachers are expected to show kindness to their pupils and instruct them in the right spirit. They should teach morals to children and speak well of them. They should encourage them to learn and help them to understand things. Pupils are taught to respect their teachers, to be obedient and eager to learn.

Employers should treat their workers with respect. They should act generously and never exploit their workers. They should give them their dues and allow them time for leisure. They should pay them honourably for their work. In return, workers should be loyal to their employers and speak well of them. They should work honestly and without grudge or complaining.

Wealth that is earned honestly is a good thing. It can be used to make other people happy and to help the poor. It should never be used in a selfish way. Money should never be earned in a way that harms other people. The ideal is to use wealth for the benefit of others.

LIVING IN SOCIETY

There are Buddhists in many different countries with their own social systems. They practise their rule in these societies but do not give up the ideal of promoting universal order free from the extremes of crushing poverty and excessive wealth. By following the Buddha's rule, there is hope of uniting society in peace and harmony.

Ideally, it is a society which follows the Middle Way. Those who follow the Buddha's rule are described as 'therapy to heal sickness', 'a gem that sparkles', 'a breeze that refreshes', 'a rain cloud that waters the earth', 'a skilled teacher who shows the way to the peaceful haven'.

HARMLESSNESS

No-one who follows this rule will think of harming another person or any living thing. They avoid occupations that are harmful to anyone, including making armaments or weapons of destruction, or manufacturing drugs, tobacco or alcohol. They do not speak evil of others, or tell lies about them. They show consideration of everyone in private and in public. They do not take what belongs to someone else or encourage anyone to steal. They believe that to demean other people is harmful, therefore they avoid any unjust actions such as fighting a war, or putting people in prison. They treat strangers with kindness and never neglect people who are in need. Right thinking and right effort are the spring of social wisdom and right action.

8 SCHOOLS OF BUDDHISM

Today there are two main schools, or groupings, of Buddhism. Firstly, there is the *Theravada School*, or the *School of the Elders*. It is sometimes called the Lesser Vehicle and flourishes mainly in the Buddhist countries of South Asia. So it is also called the Southern School. Secondly, there is the *Mahayana School*, or the *Greater Vehicle*. It flourishes mainly in the countries of North Asia and is often called the Northern School.

The First Council

After the Buddha's departure, questions arose about the teaching and discipline of the faith. The Buddha did not name anyone to lead the movement after his death, nor did he leave any written instructions. He said that it was the *dhamma (dharma)*, that is, the law and teaching, that must rule. Who was to explain the teaching? Who was to instruct young monks? A council was held at Ragjir to settle the matter.

Five hundred monks met together and Kasyapa took the lead. He called two monks, Upali and Ananda, to recite the dhamma and the discipline (*vinaya*) which everyone should follow. The five hundred monks agreed to this. Then five hundred other monks joined the council. They said they were not satisfied with the rule and discipline that Upali and Ananda had recited. They preferred to follow the teaching and discipline they had received from the Buddha himself. The council was divided between two parties – the liberal party who followed Kasyapa and the more traditional party.

The Second Council

A second council was called to debate ten points on which some monks were said to be departing from the Buddha's teaching and discipline. Certain monks wished to relax parts of the discipline, so as to allow lay people to have a greater share in the movement. Other monks did not agree, as they believed this departed from the true teaching and discipline.

The monks who took the more liberal view rose and left the council. They formed the progressive wing of Buddhism, which is known as Mahayana. The others remained and formed the Theravada School.

The Third Council

About 240 BCE a third council was called by Emperor Ashoka at Pataliputra. Ashoka was a devout Buddhist and the council was held to affirm the traditional teaching and discipline as the 'orthodox' form of Buddhism. It broke with those who had departed from this. This council also agreed on the content of the Pali Canon of Buddhist scriptures, which became the authentic scriptures of the Theravada School.

COMPARING THE TWO SCHOOLS

THE BUDDHIST SCHOOLS COMPARED	
THERAVADA	MAHAYANA
Main characteristics	*Main characteristics*
1 Loyalty to the dhamma and vinaya (the rule and discipline).	1 Respect for the Buddha as an ideal enlightened person.
2 Performance of vows (the Three Refuges).	2 Every Buddhist is on the way to attaining enlightenment.
3 Devotion to the Tipitaka (the traditional scriptures).	3 Belief in the bodhisatta – a Buddhist who is on the way to Buddhahood but who (like the Buddha) remains in the world to help others achieve salvation.
4 Support for the Sangha and spiritual leaders.	4 The bodhisatta will spread the message throughout the world by showing love and compassion to all people.
5 Zeal for spreading the rule and being an example to others.	5 Devotion to scriptures not in the Tipitaka.
	6 Teaching on the Three Bodies of Gautama – the Body of Truth; – the Body of Bliss; – the Body of Appearance.
	7 Belief in the appearance of the future Buddha (metteya) who will restore the teaching where it is neglected.

Although these two schools are separate, you should not assume that there is no contact between them. They have developed certain characteristics of their own through existing in different countries. They both breathe the 'spirit' of the Buddha's teaching and discipline and share the same hopes.

AMIDA BUDDHA

There is great variety in Mahayana Buddhism. One of its best known sects is the *Pure Land Sect*, which has many followers in China and Japan.

The sect probably came into being in the fourth century CE when the Chinese ruler, O-Mi-to, decided to accept the Buddha's teaching and took a vow as a bodhisatta. He showed great devotion to the Buddha and compassion to his people. From China the sect spread to Japan, where it became known as Amida after the Japanese form of the Chinese emperor's name.

The sect developed the notion of the Pure Land, which is a kind of haven from which Buddhists can receive help to progress towards Buddhahood. They can receive help from Amida Buddha and complete happiness by repeating his name on their journey to *nibbana*. Singing the praises of Amida helps Buddhists in their meditation and assures them a place in the paradise of the Pure Land. There is a Buddha for every age, who is able to assist those who seek for true enlightenment.

This sect soon became popular in China and Japan and many temples were built. It appealed particularly to the poor and uneducated as a form of Buddhism that is open to everyone.

ZEN

Zen means meditation and is widely known in the west. It originated in China and later become popular in Japan. It is said that the Buddha once preached a sermon whilst he held a flower in his hand. He smiled on his listeners and one of them came under the spell of the smile and the flower. He realised their significance and told others about them. One of them was called Bodhidhamma and he carried the message of the sermon to China in 552 CE.

The core of the message is that the only way to salvation is through meditation. Good works alone or reading the scriptures cannot lead to salvation but true meditation can. Therefore:

Meditate upon the Mind as Supreme Dhamma and Supreme Master.
Separate yourself from noise, sloth and sleep, and make a thorough survey of all the different aspects of the self discriminating Mind.

When the Mind is disturbed, the multiplicity of things is produced; when the Mind is quieter, the multiplicity of things disappears.

He who meditates upon the Mind as Supreme Dhamma of the Buddha, as Supreme Master, obtains Nibbana.

These are some characteristic aspects of Zen meditation:

1 Sitting in meditation (*zazen*) in a central place in a simple Zen temple, usually surrounded by a garden; facing each other so as to achieve complete harmony between themselves and with the whole of nature.

2 Using the technique of question and answer to gain knowledge of the inner meaning of things. There is no logical answer to many of the questions asked, as may be seen from these examples:

   a) How many elephants are there on a blade of grass?
   b) What was your original face before your parents begot you?
   c) If clapping two hands produces a sound, what is the sound of one hand clapping?
   d) Can you take hold of empty space?

What is the aim of Zen Buddhist meditation?

The following answers may be given: i) through meditating in this way the Buddhist realises his true self and finds inner peace; ii) when the true self blossoms, the individual is freed from desire, unreality, ignorance and rebirth; iii) by seeking to know the 'inner meaning' of things, perfect knowledge is gained and everything is seen in a direct way; iv) probing a question beyond its obvious meaning, analysing it sensibly discloses its inner significance and floods the mind with light and true knowledge; by achieving enlightenment the riddle (*koan*) can be understood and the mind enjoy peace.

9 ▷ BUDDHIST SCRIPTURES

The Buddha was a skilled and attractive teacher. He used a variety of methods in teaching his message, which included parables, illustrations from nature, similes, metaphors, question and answer, discussion and debate. Yet he did not write a book, or leave any written records.

After his departure his disciples began to collect his teaching and put it into writing. Many other works have been added to the sum total of Buddhist sacred writings and it is difficult to put them into any order. The scriptures of the Theravada School are the best known, but the Mahayana School has its own scriptures, although not all have been translated into languages of the west.

THE TIPITAKA (THE THREE BASKETS)

These are the scriptures of the Theravada School. If you imagine builders at work on a building site, handing on one basket of material to another, then you will see why they are called the Three Baskets (Tipitaka). They were handed on from one to another until the time came for them to be collected in a written form. The Tipitaka is part of the Pali Canon, which was compiled in Sri Lanka in the first century BCE. The *Three Baskets* are:

Vinaya Pitaka *(Discipline)*	*Sutta Pitaka* *(Themes)*	*Abhidamma Pitaka* *(Analysis)*
The book of discipline consists of rules and explanations; instructions to monks; guidance on caring for the sick, giving charity, living peacefully; instructions to teachers and pupils; welcoming women into the order.	Contains the Dhammapada, with an account of the Four Noble Truths and the Middle Way.	Explanations of teachings from the Sutta Pitaka; knowledge about the essence of life; source of 'higher' knowledge.

Buddhists believe that the oldest part of the Tipitaka is the Vinaya Pitaka. It contains the purest collection of the Buddha's teaching and rule. The Sutta Pitaka is written in prose and poetry and Buddhists treasure it as it contains the Dhammapada. Many learn this by heart so that they can recite it regularly. The Abhidamma Pitaka is the most recent part and is important on account of its explanations and analysis of the earlier teachings.

MAHAYANA SCRIPTURES

The Mahayana School adopted much of the Pali Canon, but has also produced its own works. As more and more sects were formed so new additions were made to the scriptures. These are in a variety of languages and in many volumes. The Chinese texts alone are said to number 1,662.

Among the best known works of this School is the Diamond Sutta, which contains teaching about the *bodhisatta*. It is dated from the fourth century CE. The Lotus Sutta is best known among Buddhists in Japan as a source of teaching about social matters and the inspiration behind virtuous works. The scriptures of Tibet are extensive and remote. The Ka-gyur consists of 108 large volumes and 225 volumes of explanations. Another Tibetan work consists of 35 volumes, along with 14 volumes of explanations.

10 ▷ WORSHIP

The Buddha image is the focus of Buddhist devotion. Worship is not a condition for attaining *nibbana*, but devotion to the Buddha's rule is. *The Buddha image is not worshipped but homage is given to what the image represents.* Acts of devotion and ceremonies centre on the Buddha image, on account of what it conveys and the help the Buddhist receives from being in its presence. Buddhism does not have a holy day or set times for worship, but Buddhists gather to meditate and pay homage before the Buddha statue as part of their ritual.

WORSHIP IN THE HOME

On a visit to a Buddhist home you will see a shrine room with a statue of the Buddha. The image is decorated with flowers and maybe bowls of water. Before the image there is an incense burner and candles and a tray for offerings of food.

Families may have different customs, but they pay their homage to the Buddha in his presence. The ritual is fairly simple. The family join together before the image and recite the Three Refuges and the Five Precepts. They light the candles and offer flowers and food. Some time is spent quietly kneeling before the image and texts may be recited from the scriptures. They may use a rosary (*seikbadi*) during the devotions. If this takes place in the morning the image is dressed, or if the family gathers together in the evening the children pay homage to their elders and ask pardon for wrongs they may have done, and the parents give them their blessing. In a Mahayana Buddhist home, prayers may be said to the Buddha and the *bodhisatta* for help on the path to nibbana.

WORSHIP IN THE TEMPLE

Temples abound in Buddhist countries, some are very old and elaborate and built in a monastery precinct or a place sacred to Buddhists. Basically, the structure symbolises the five elements – fire, air, earth, water and wisdom. The square base symbolises the earth and the structure extends upward to a point or spire to symbolise wisdom.

The main part is the shrine, which contains the image of the Buddha. There are other images which aid concentration during meditation. When the worshippers assemble they sit facing the image and recite their vow of loyalty to the Buddha, the teaching and the order. Around the image there are candles, flowers and incense sticks. The worshippers place their offerings near the image and during the worship raise their hands to the forehead and upward to the image in an act of homage. They bow three times in homage to the Buddha, the teaching and the order. As they sit facing the image, with their shoes

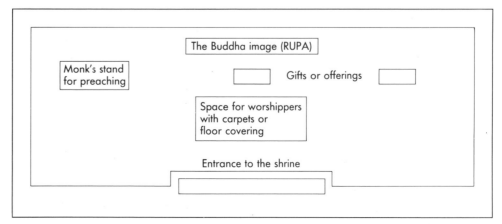

Fig. 4.6 Inside a Buddhist temple
shrine room

removed and the feet turned away, they listen to the monks chanting sacred texts or giving instruction. After the monks have left, the people may remain and talk and drink tea. The temple is a place of social gatherings as well as a place of meditation.

PAGODA AND STUPA

A *pagoda* or *stupa* is a mound of stones built over a relic or relics of the Buddha. These are the most precious remains of the Buddha and are very special to the Buddhist. Relics of the Buddha were taken from India to other countries where his teaching spread. Mahinda, the son of the Emperor Ashoka, who introduced Buddhism into Sri Lanka, was asked by the people for relics of the Buddha to help them in their devotion. It is believed that he took a collar bone of the Buddha to Sri Lanka, where it was placed in a golden box and buried under a stupa. One of the Buddha's teeth was taken to Sri Lanka and buried in Kandy, the site of the famous temple of the Golden Tooth. A part of the bodhi tree from Bodh Gaya, where the Buddha received his enlightenment, is planted in Anuradhapura, a famous Sri Lankan Buddhist centre. It is said that relics of the Buddha's hair were taken to Burma and buried in the Shwe Dagon, one of the greatest of the Buddhist shrines. When there were no relics available, a sacred text or some other object may have been buried beneath the stupa. Some stupas are quite simple structures, but others are amazingly large, such as the Golden Pagoda in Rangoon. It was built over two thousand years ago, and contains four shrines, each with a golden image of the Buddha.

11 ⟩   FESTIVALS

Buddhist festivals vary considerably from one Buddhist country to another. Theravada and Mahayana Buddhism have their own festivals, which in the main are associated with events in the life of the Buddha. It is not possible to give a complete list, as Buddhist chronology differs from country to country. The Buddhist calendars combine lunar and solar elements. For other purposes they use a western calendar.

DAYS OF OBSERVANCE

Certain days are set apart each month as days of special duty and rest. The days are sacred and may be spent in visiting monasteries and offering gifts to monks. Some Buddhists dress in white and spend the whole day with the monks.

These are days of rest from work and paying homage to the Buddha. The Buddhists listen to sermons, spend time in meditation and recite religious verses. They are days for observing the eight precepts very strictly: not to kill, lie, steal, look at dancing, use ornaments, use grand beds, eat before noon, or enjoy sexual pleasure.

NEW YEAR

The Buddhist new year begins in April and is celebrated in different ways. In Sri Lanka, for example, there is a water festival on the first two days. Sprinkling each other with water is a sign of cleansing. The following three days are days of devotion, when visits are paid to monasteries and gifts given to monks. In the temples the images of the Buddha are bathed and respect is paid to the dead. There may be processions through the streets.

In Thailand it is the custom at the new year to release birds and fish from cages. These are bought in readiness for the new year so that they can be set free as a mark of compassion to all living things. This is thought to bring happiness and reward.

ASALA PUJA

This festival celebrates the anniversary of the Buddha's first sermon. It takes place at the time of the full moon in July. It is sometimes called the 'Day of Proclamation', in remembrance of the time when the Buddha proclaimed the Middle Way. On this day, monks preach sermons on the subject of conversion and recall the conversion of the Buddha in Bodh Gaya. In Sri Lanka the festival is a national, as well as a religious event. The relic of the Buddha's tooth is processed through the streets of Kandy as a show of devotion and loyalty. Monks do not take part in the procession, but usually stand and watch.

MAGHA PUJA

This is a Theravada festival which celebrates the time when the Buddha ordained 1,200 monks and sent them out to preach his message to the world. Each monk had received enlightenment and went out to enlighten others. When he commissioned them the Buddha also preached a sermon on the subject of purity. The monks sat at his feet and once they had listened to his message they arose and began their mission. During the festival, lights are lit to symbolise the message of enlightenment. In the larger temples 1,200 candles may be lit, one candle for each of the monks.

POSON

This festival is held in Sri Lanka to commemorate the coming of Buddhism to the island. The Emperor Ashoka was keen on the spread of Buddhism in its purest form to other countries, so he sent his son Mahinda as a Buddhist missionary to Sri Lanka. His mission was highly successful and Sri Lanka is now one of the leading Buddhist countries. The celebrations centre on Minhintale, the town which Mahinda first visited.

It is a colourful and joyous festival. The main event is a procession in which some venerated person or object is carried. There is a great deal of ceremonial and noise, dancing and drumming. A central feature is the image of Mahinda, which is carried high to represent the ideal character. Large numbers of people take part in the procession, which is very popular. At the end there is a great display of fireworks.

WESAK

This is probably the best known Buddhist festival. It takes place in May at the time of the full moon. It lasts for three days and commemorates the birth, enlightenment and departure of the Buddha. The main accent is on his enlightenment and in Buddhist homes and temples lights are lit and decorations put up. There are symbols of illumination everywhere and Buddhists gather in their homes and in the temples to make offerings to the Buddha. They listen to sermons by the monks, especially about Buddha's enlightenment and teaching. Special mention is made of the Buddha's compassion and his love and care for all living creatures. Caged birds are released and special gifts are given to the poor, but without them knowing. The most solemn part of the festival is the renewing of vows and keeping the eight precepts. Buddhists visit the monasteries and offer gifts of food to the monks. They also send greeting cards with pictures from the life of the Buddha.

HANA MATSURI

This is a Mahayana Buddhist festival held in Japan to celebrate the birth of the Buddha. It is popularly known as 'the festival of flowers'. It is a happy festival, during which the Buddha image is washed with sweet tea and hydrangea leaves. This custom recalls the time when the child Gautama was bathed in the sweet-scented lake in the garden of Lumbini. Another custom is that of garlanding the image of the Buddha with flowers and then carrying it in a procession through the streets. As the procession proceeds, pieces of pink, white and yellow paper in the shape of lotus flowers are thrown along the way.

OBON

Buddhists in Japan celebrate this festival in July. It is a solemn time when they remember their ancestors. The Buddhists say that their ancestors' spirits return to their homes for the festival, guided by the light of lanterns. The spirits of the ancestors are welcomed and given offerings of food. After this the festival ends with a social gathering and folk dancing.

HIGAN

Higan is another Japanese Buddhist festival. It is held in the spring and autumn to commemorate the dead. Prayers are offered on their behalf and gifts are made to the deceased. At the same time, Buddhists gather in the temple to give thanks for the dead and to listen to sermons.

PARINIBBANA

This festival is also known as the 'Great Death'. It is kept in Mahayana countries to commemorate the Buddha's entry to *nibbana*. According to Buddhist tradition, as the Buddha approached death, his favourite disciple, Ananda, asked him for his final instructions to his followers. The Buddha replied that he had no further instructions beyond the rule he had taught. Each person must hold to the truth and follow his rule which is the only way to full enlightenment. During the festival, people remember the Buddha's last utterance:

Dissolution is the nature of all composite things.
Strive onward. Work out your own salvation with diligence.

A FINAL NOTE

For three months of the year, Buddhist monks do not travel outside the monasteries. In the early times they lived in simple huts and spent the time in meditation on the Buddha's teaching. These three months are a solemn time for monks and lay people. It was once the custom not to marry during the solemn months (July to October), or to take part in entertainment. The time was spent in helping other people and fulfilling the duties of a true follower of the Buddha. Gifts are carried by the lay people to the monasteries and offered to the monks by a leading lay person. During these months the monks depend on the gifts for their food. In return, the monks bless those who bring gifts, instruct them in the Buddha's rule and urge them to be faithful to their vows.

12 ▷ PILGRIMAGE

A conversation between the Buddha and his disciple Ananda defines the Buddha's attitude to pilgrimage:

> There are four places, Ananda, which the devoted person should visit with feelings of reverence.
> The place, Ananda, at which the devoted person can say, 'Here the Buddha was born'.
> The place, Ananda, at which the devoted person can say, 'Here the Tathagatha attained to supreme and highest wisdom'.
> The place, Ananda, at which the devoted person can say, 'Here the wheel of the Dhamma was set in motion by the Tathagatha'.
> The place, Ananda, at which the devoted person can say, 'Here the Tathagatha passed finally away'.

Each of the four places has a connection with a significant happening in the life of the Buddha . . . his birth . . . enlightenment . . . turning the wheel of the law . . . his departure. Making a pilgrimage to these places is a means of being in close spiritual affinity with the Buddha. The pilgrims share his spiritual power and deepen devotion to the Buddha's way. Visiting these four places brings them merit, helps them to have a good rebirth and is a source of blessing. Today these four places are sacred to Buddhists:

- at Kapelavastu (the place of his birth), a pillar was erected by the Emperor Ashoka to mark the spot;
- at Bodh Gaya, there is a bodhi tree by which the Buddha sat as he received his illumination. Nearby is the Mahabodhi temple;
- in the Deer Park in Benares, there is a statue of the Buddha preaching his famous sermon;
- in Kusinara, from where the Buddha departed, stands the Nibbana Temple.

Pilgrims feel that visiting these places brings their religion alive, but the Buddha intended that pilgrimage should not be made out of interest or curiosity or cold duty. He declared: 'the devoted person should visit them with feelings of devotion'.

As well as having the 'feel of the place', the pilgrims make an 'inner pilgrimage' that deepens their commitment to the Buddha's rule. Many other places are sacred to Buddhists, especially those where relics of the Buddha are buried. Some of these have already been mentioned, like the hair relic deposited in the Shwe Dagon Pagoda in Rangoon, the tooth relic in the Temple of the Sacred Tooth in Kandy, and the branch of the bodhi tree planted in Anuradhapura.

Pilgrims gather at these places during their festivals. Each year, during the Wesak festival, Buddhists gather at the Great Stupa at Boroburdur in Java. This is one of the major Buddhist monuments and pilgrims may climb the terraces to the top and have a feeling of making progress towards nibbana. Along the way there are carvings of scenes from the life of the Buddha, which are revered by pilgrims. Pilgrimage always involves paying homage before the Buddha image and presenting offerings. Time is spent in meditation at the sacred place and gifts are made to members of the Sangha.

13 ▷ RITES OF PASSAGE

Buddhists include their religion in all the important celebrations and occasions in life. The rites of passage are celebrated differently in different Buddhist countries, but they nearly always involve the monks.

BIRTH

The celebration of birth in Theravada Buddhist countries is quite simple. The child is taken by its parents to the local temple to be named. The monk sprinkles the child with water and pronounces a blessing for a happy life. A pure wax candle is burned and the molten wax left to fall into a bowl of pure water. This symbolises the union of the four elements – air, fire, wind and water. The union of the elements is a symbol of the harmony the child will achieve during his life.

MARRIAGE

In earlier times parents chose the marriage partners for their children. Today, things have changed but many old customs continue. This is how a traditional marriage ceremony is conducted in the Buddhist country of Thailand. The ceremony takes place in the home, with the monks taking a prominent part. First they bless the home by sprinkling holy water as a sign of purity. Then they read some suitable texts from the Buddhist scriptures, after which the monks are given gifts of food, that are thought to ensure a happy future for the bride and bridegroom.

In preparation for the ceremony, the Buddha image is dressed, and the couple to be married pay homage before it, light candles and burn incense. The couple bow together to receive the gift of a coral crown and greetings from the bridgeroom's friend. As he does so, he also makes a sign with his thumb on each of their foreheads. All the married people present then come forward to offer their greetings by placing a drop of water on the couple's heads as a sign of blessing. Then, the bride's friend presents everyone with a flower as a mark of respect and affection. After this, everyone is invited to sign a book with their good wishes, which the married couple can keep as a reminder of the ceremony. The whole company then enjoys a meal, dancing and toasting the newly weds.

If a marriage takes place in a temple in a Theravada Buddhist country, a cotton thread is placed around the Buddha image and links everyone together as it is passed around. The monks also are linked with the thread, and bless the marriage couple, also reading texts from the scriptures. Then two pieces of cotton thread are cut. The senior monk ties one piece round the bridegroom's wrist; the groom then ties the other piece round the bride's wrist. The marriage union is now symbolised and the bride and groom wear the cotton thread until it falls away naturally.

DEATH AND COMMEMORATION

Death has no fears for the Buddhist; it is described as 'blissful rest'. Certain customs are observed that can be traced back to the time of the Buddha, when the Buddha's body was cremated and his remains dispersed.

Cremation is common and in the case of monks, the ashes are deposited in a stupa after cremation, explaining why there are many stupas near Buddhist monasteries. But cremation is not universal in Buddhist countries; in Sri Lanka, for instance, burial is usual, while in Tibet only the body of the Dalai Lama is cremated. Other corpses are left in desolate places to be devoured by birds and wild animals. Buddhists believe that when approaching death a person's thoughts are vitally important. Sacred texts may be read, so as to fill the mind with pure thoughts in preparation for the moment of death. The name of the dying person may be written along with the words: *May he find peaceful bliss in nibbana.*

One Buddhist belief about death is that consciousness continues for three days after the death of the physical body. During the whole of this time, sacred texts are read. In China and Tibet these are usually from the Book of the Dead, and refer to the pre-existence of the Buddha and his vow to help people who suffer. In China and Japan, Buddhists believe that the *bodhisatta* prepares the way to the Pure Land or that Amida descends to meet the dying person. In Theravada Buddhist countries, the monks chant sacred texts for twelve days after a death. At the burial, those present transfer their merit to the dead person, in the hope of ensuring a good rebirth. As a symbol of this they pour water into bowls placed one inside the other, and during the burial, chanting continues until the body is finally consumed.

Monks do not actually conduct a burial or funeral, but are normally present and may speak about how everything changes and nothing is permanent. They remind everyone of the Buddha's teaching about 'impermanence' that brings sorrow. The monks may be given a gift of cloth for their robes, and this is draped over the dead body but removed before burial or cremation. Buddhists look upon death as part of the natural cycle of life. They recall how the Buddha accepted death with calm and how, as he died, he heard the words: *All compounded things are impermanent; their nature is to arise and pass away. They came into being only to be destroyed: their cessation is blissful rest.*

14 ⟩ **BUDDHISM PAST AND PRESENT**

Buddhism began in North India, but soon spread to other parts. After his conversion the Buddha led an active missionary movement to spread his message. It proved popular and by the time of his death he had a large following. His message of release from life's ills won many to his way. The Buddha offered his message to everyone, irrespective of their caste, social status or religion. He cared nothing about these, and kings, and rulers and people of lower classes have all joined his movement.

When the different schools of Buddhism emerged, they continued to spread the message and to instruct and commission missionaries. After the scriptures were written and compiled these were also used to spread the message. Buddhism can be called a missionary religion without a missionary society. One Buddhist can enlighten another, just as one candle is lit from another. No-one is compelled to accept the message, but its light may spread as it shines from any enlightened person.

Buddhism flourished in India for a thousand years after the death of the Buddha, but it never achieved the status of an official religion in India. Later, schools and universities were set up to study the Buddhist philosophy, but when the Muslims began to settle in the northern provinces, Buddhism began to wane. Today its strength is in countries other than India.

SRI LANKA

Mahinda carried Buddhism to Sri Lanka in the third century BCE and converted the king of Anuradhapura. He shared his father Ashoka's enthusiasm for the faith, and ever since, Buddhism has flourished as Sri Lanka's main religion. You can see from this chart (Fig. 4.7) how Buddhism has developed in the island.

In Sri Lanka, the Pali scriptures of Buddhism were compiled and have had a profound influence. The Sangha also has been an important factor in keeping the religion active. To a great extent the Buddhist religion has moulded the social life of Sri Lanka. Here, some of the most traditional and colourful customs continue to be observed, especially those connected with the temples of Anuradhapura and Kandy. Recent political changes have caused tension and publicised the social activities of Buddhists. It remains to be seen how these will affect the old customs and practices of Buddhism.

BUDDHISM IN SRI LANKA

3rd century BCE Mission of Mahinda	conversion of King Tissa; establishing the sangha;
3rd – 4th century CE	unrest and division; rise of Maha-Vihara (in the tradition of Theravada); rise of Abhayagiri (in the tradition of Mahayana);
3rd century CE Rise of Vaitulya	mission of Sanghumita of India and support for Mahayana;
4th century CE	revival of Theravada Buddhism;
5th century CE	arrival of Buddhagosha; teaching on the Path of Purity; explanations of the Pali Scriptures;
7th – 11th century CE	revival of Mahayana Buddhism, study of the Abhidhamma;
12th century CE	the work of Anuruddha; book for monks – introduction to the Abhidhamma; the reign of Bahu; revival of the sangha, building of temples and monasteries;
14th century onwards	British influence; overthrow of kings of Kandy; care for Buddhist institutions;
19th century	new Buddhist educational establishment; establishment of Ramanya Nikaya sect of Buddhist monks); establishment of Vidyadaya and Vifyal Ankara (educational centre
20th century	Society of World Buddhists; Report of the betrayal of Buddhism; modern movements and Buddhism.

Fig. 4.7 Buddhism in Sri Lanka

BURMA

The Emperor Ashoka is thought to have sent the first missionaries to Burma about 250 BCE. Buddhism took root and became the official religion of Burma, where it is one of the strongholds of Theravada Buddhism in South East Asia. Burma has a strong monastic tradition and is a land of many beautiful temples. One special feature of Buddhism in Burma is the devotion to the Abhidhamma, which is widely studied. Monks are respected especially for their study of the religious and moral teachings of the Abhidhamma. You have already read about the Shwe Dagon, which is covered in gold and one of the greatest shrines of southern Asia. It is famous for its three images of buddhas born in the ages before the historical Buddha. The pagoda spire rises 326 feet above its platform and is a popular visiting place of pilgrims.

CHINA

In the first centry CE, travellers and merchants carried the Buddhist message to China. China was one of the most advanced countries of the time and the coming of Buddhism to China was an important step in its missionary growth. In the second century CE, the Chinese Emperor Han was converted to the faith, one important consequence of which was the translation of some Buddhist scriptures into Chinese. The Chinese showed great interest in the practical teaching, rather than the theory or abstract ideas, as this gave them an ideal for their own society.

Buddhism adapted itself to Chinese society and two important sects arose, namely, Amida and T'ien T'ai (transcendental meditation). The Amida cult appealed greatly to the Chinese, as we see from the many images of Amida in the Buddhist temples. In the seventh century CE, the Chinese began to show interest in philosophy and religious questions, and more sacred texts from India were translated. Buddhism was given great respect alongside the ancient teaching of Tao and Confucius.

During the present century, China has seen many changes and Buddhism has struggled to keep its identity. After the revolution of 1911 the monks made an effort to keep the faith alive, to reform the Sangha and to promote better education. After Mao and the communists came to power in 1949, the new order imposed another ideology on the people. The present more liberal regime has created a new climate, and the future of Buddhism in China will depend on its inner vitality and the freedom to practise it.

JAPAN

Buddhism did not reach Japan until the sixth century CE. Through the conversion of Prince Shotoku, Buddhism became the official religion of Japan. Many leading people became Buddhists and the monasteries flourished. Buddhism continued to be the official religion of Japan until 1860 when it was taken over by the older religion of Shintoism. Devotion to Amida and the *bodhisatta* are special features of Buddhism in Japan. The Pure Land Sect and Zen Buddhism are popular, but a number of other sects have emerged which reflect the culture and characteristics of the Japanese. These include Tendai (a philosophical sect), Shingon (an open sect), Pure Land (a devotional sect), Zen (meditation) and Soka Gakkai (which aims to preserve ancient values and teaching).

TIBET

In Tibet, Buddhism has developed in a unique way as a mixture of elements of Theravada and Mahayana Buddhism, but is not identified with either. Many customs, practices and observances are peculiar to Tibet, yet for many centuries Tibet has been one of the strongest Buddhist countries. One special feature is the use of sacred texts known as Tantras. These are believed to have certain magical powers and are used in devotions and celebrations. Their use in meditation involves a complex ritual, but those who recite them receive a special blessing and expect to find a clear path to *nibbana*. Monks recite them every day and teachers teach them to children.

In Tibet the monks have been political and national leaders under the Dalai Lama, the chief monk and ruler of Tibet. Like other countries in Asia today, Tibet is facing many changes. The face of Buddhism is being transformed, but even so, the monastery and its traditions remain a feature of life in spite of recent political upheavals.

BUDDHISM IN THE WEST

Buddhism has made many inroads in the west in recent times. It has a presence in many countries of Europe and the USA. In Britain its position differs from that of other non-Christian religions that have settled here. There has never been an influx of Buddhists from traditional Buddhist countries, and Buddhist communities in Britain are native. The London Buddhist Society keeps an overview of the Buddhist communities in Britain. Several new communities have developed recently, but they still follow the traditions and practices of their parent groups. The communities welcome non-Buddhists who want to learn about the Buddha's rule, to practise meditation or to share in various other activities. The communities are scattered throughout the country, but do not compete with each other. They may have individual characteristics, but basically are all devoted to a common ideal. It is important for anyone who studies Buddhism in Britain to keep this in mind, so as to have a balanced view.

Fig. 4.8 Western Buddha

APPLIED MATERIALS

BANCROFT, Anne, (1976). *The Buddhist World*. McDonald.
BECHERT, H. & GROBICH, R., (1984). *The World of Buddhism*. Thames & Hudson.
CONZE, Edward, (1980). *A Short History of Buddhism*. Allen and Unwin.
PALMER, M., (1984). *Faiths and Festivals*. Ward Lock Educational.
PATRICK, M., (1984). *Buddhists and Buddhism*. Wayland.
SNELLING, J., (1985). *Buddhist Festivals*. Wayland.

EXAMINATION QUESTIONS

QUESTION

Write a brief statement on what the Buddha taught about the starting point of the search for 'enlightenment'.

(WJEC)

OUTLINE ANSWER

The spiritual search on which Gautama engaged took him, first of all, to Hindu teachers who were unable to satisfy him. He joined some ascetics but still did not find satisfaction. He practised extreme forms of self denial but did not find what he sought. Finally, he decided to make the search 'into himself'.

He sat near a banyan tree to meditate and gave up the extreme methods he had followed. He followed what he called a 'middle path', which was neither the extreme of excessive pleasure or the extreme of excessive self denial. He practised moderation.

In this way he achieved his 'enlightenment'. The Buddha based his teaching on the acute awareness of suffering, which is central to his message. He taught a way of liberation from it which is logical and which is based on the three major characteristics of human life: suffering, impermanence and the absence of personal identity or soul.

A STUDENT'S ANSWER WITH EXAMINER'S COMMENTS

QUESTION

a) Buddhists do not have a special day each week for worship, but hold many important festivals and celebrations. Why is this?

b) Describe the Buddhist new year festival as if you were present to see and hear what happens.

c) Would you say that the Buddhist is an 'optimist' or a 'pessimist'? Give your reasons.

d) Why is it important for a Buddhist to follow the teachings of the Buddha?

(WJEC)

What about their 'special' days?

Give examples

What do these symbolise?

Why?

Do you know what optimism means in this context?

Give examples of the teaching.

How do monks help?

a) Buddhists do not have a sacred day like Sunday in Britain they think all days are the same. So they don't have to stop work. They like having festivals as they can enjoy themselves. They like having fun and dressing up and holding ceremonies. I think it is a religion of enjoyment because they don't have strict rules like some religions. They say it is proper to have a good time and celebrations and enjoyments.

b) New year is a jolly time they make a new beginning. This is in April or May I think. They put up decorations in the house and give presents. They think it was when Buddha was born so they make a fresh start. They give him presents, or they go to the temple to enjoy themselves and bring flowers. They place the flowers by the statue. They say prayers as well.

c) I think it is optimism as it gives everybody the same chance. It doesn't say you go to hell or will die when you sin. Everybody is the same and you have the same chance, it doesn't matter who you are if you do your best. So it is free for all, anyone who wants to can be a Buddha you can just do your own thing and get on alright.

d) You have to follow the teaching or else theres no point in being a Buddha. The monks help you, they will tell you what to do. The teaching is simple really you can find out for yourself and only need to do whats right and you can get there. Anyone can find the answer if he does the same as Buddha. So I think the teaching is good it tells you to do right.

Comments:

This is a fair attempt. You have done well to follow the guidance in the question and have answered each part. The main weakness is the failure to read the question with great care.

In part a) you have not mentioned *why* Buddhists hold festivals and celebrations. You must mention how important it is to commemorate events in the life of the Buddha, especially his 'enlightenment' and his missionary work.

In b) you should focus more on the actual form of the new year celebration and avoid just giving general statements. Try to imagine an actual new year festival in a Buddhist home and describe the events that take place.

In c) you should focus on i) the way the Buddhist is able to find release and inner peace; ii) how the Buddhist can arrive at *nibbana*; iii) what help the religion gives a Buddhist to reach the goal.

It will help in part d) if you refer to some points in the teaching. For example, you could refer to the Middle Path and show why this is important. The emphasis must be on the importance of the teaching – it gives direction, advice and right knowledge which helps the Buddhist throughout life.

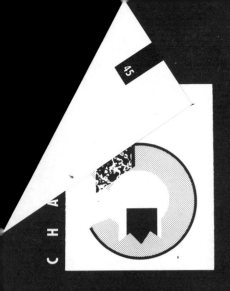

CHRISTIANITY: JESUS AND THE GOSPELS

GETTING STARTED

Christianity is the religion of the followers of Jesus Christ. It takes its name from Christ and its beliefs are practised in a variety of ways by Christians around the world. There are about 950 million followers of Christianity and the link between them is their belief in Jesus Christ. They say he is the centrepoint of Christianity.

In the GCSE you will study Christianity through learning about Jesus and the gospels, the Church, worship and celebrations, Christian communities and movements, Christian living and responses to Jesus. You should refer to your particular syllabus for details of these topics. In this chapter you will learn about Jesus and the gospels.

Fig. 5.1 Map of the Christian World

ESSENTIAL PRINCIPLES

Jesus was the son of a Jewish mother, and in accordance with the Law he was circumcised on the eighth day. He was educated in the synagogue school run by the Jewish rabbis. He learnt Hebrew, so that he could read the Bible and take part in the synagogue services, but his everyday language was Aramaic.

He was brought up in a village home in Nazareth, but he had a wide experience of life. He met people from many walks of life, including employers and vineyard owners, pious Pharisees, lawyers and judges, as well as widows and poor peasants. He spoke about them in his teaching as if he knew them personally. He also took a full part in the religious life of the Jews and in social affairs, and he had contact with political leaders.

Jesus lived in a *multi-cultural society*. Since 63 BCE, Palestine had been occupied by the Romans and before that by the Greeks. There were Greek communities in Galilee, and there was a Greek amphitheatre and hippodrome in Jerusalem and Jericho. Many people still spoke the Greek language and loved to live in the style of the Greeks.

Large numbers of his fellow Jews never accepted the Romans, who unfortunately appointed *Herod* as king. He was fascinated with the Greek way of life, but was careful not to offend the Romans. He tried to please the Jews by not allowing human images on coins or public buildings, and by allowing only priests to work on enlarging the temple. But he offended the Jews when he arrested two of their rabbis and had them executed. When Herod died in 4 BCE, Caesar Augustus appointed *Archelaus* to rule over Judaea, Samaria and Idumaea, and *Antipas* to rule over Galilee and Peraea. The third son of Herod, *Philip*, was made ruler of the territory to the north and east of the Sea of Galilee.

Palestine had three Roman governors during the last years of Augustus, namely Coponius, Marcus and Rufus. Under Caesar Tiberius there were two governors, one of whom, Valerius Gratus, made himself unpopular by removing the high priest. He was succeeded in 26 CE by *Pontius Pilate* who is best known for his part in the trial of Jesus. Pilate's headquarters were at Caesarea but he was responsible for law and order throughout the country. He had extensive powers in legal matters but allowed the supreme Jewish council (the Sanhedrin) of seventy one members to act as his advisors and also run the day-to-day affairs in the region. There were local sanhedrins who administered their own areas, and could try minor offences but not capital crimes, which had to be referred to the governor. Pilate was not popular with the Jews or Samaritans and was guilty of some outrages against them. He never sought to win over the Jewish leaders and ruled against a continuous background of intrigue and revolt. He was removed from office in disgrace in 36 CE.

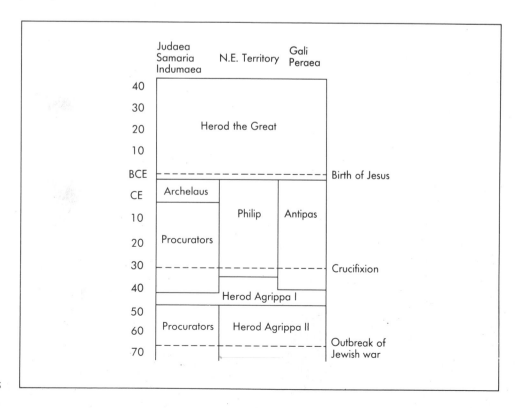

Fig. 5.2 Dynasty of the Herods

2 > RELIGIOUS
GROUPS

Jesus was a Jew and, for the Jew, race and religion could not be separated. He was born into a religious community that was dominated by the priests, who controlled the main religious institution – the temple. They were also the official guardians and interpreters of the Law (Torah), and were supported by the tithes and dues paid to the temple. The unity of the temple expressed the unity of God and religion. It was only legitimate to offer sacrifices in the temple, which was the centre of pilgrimages at the time of the festivals. The daily services of the temple were provided for by Jews throughout the country so that they felt part of the temple ritual.

However, religion in the time of Jesus was a mixture of sects, parties and movements, and you will learn about some of these when you read the gospels and the story of Jesus. Jesus was in closer contact with the leaders of popular religion than with the temple hierarchy.

SCRIBES

Jesus had many contacts with the scribes. They were lay people who performed religious duties but also followed their own trade or profession. They dressed and acted as priests and were called 'rabbi' (teacher). They were in close touch with the ordinary people and taught them the Law and how to interpret it in their daily life. Jesus complained that the rabbis often misinterpreted the Law, especially when they went out of their way to stress the tiniest points. They loved long arguments about the Law, and one of their favourite ploys when asked a difficult question was to quote a rabbi from the past. They had great regard for tradition, and the ordinary people showed them much respect. They consulted the rabbis about day to day problems, bowed to them in the streets, and gave them the chief seats in the synagogue and at parties. Most of the rabbis belonged to the Pharisee party.

PHARISEES

Although Pharisee means 'separated', the Pharisees preferred to be called 'brothers of the covenant' (*Haberim*). They were not a large party but were very active in the synagogue and among the ordinary people. The Pharisees were a Puritan party who were completely devoted to the Written and Oral Law. They interpreted the Law in a very narrow way and sometimes carried their devotion to extremes. They believed deeply that their nation had a divine destiny, and looked forward to the coming of the messiah, who would fulfil God's promise and make his chosen people great. Jesus was often opposed by the Pharisees, especially when he did not keep every detail of their traditions. They were always critical of people who did not observe every detail of the Law and they often went to extreme lengths in applying the Law to every aspect of life. They are presented in an unfavourable light in the gospels, but other writers are more favourable to their piety and enthusiasm.

SADDUCEES

The Sadducees were the establishment and aristocratic party. Their headquarters was the temple, where they upheld the traditions and authority of the priests. They were supporters of tradition but were remote from the common people. They criticised the Pharisees for being too progressive and they showed very little interest in the Oral Law. They were devoted to the Written Law in the Five Books of Moses, but they did not share the popular notions of the messiah. Nor did they share the views of the Pharisees about the destiny of their nation, or the belief in resurrection. On the whole they were conservative in outlook and were ready to compromise with the occupying power for the sake of peace. The Sadducees were bitterly opposed to Jesus and his movement, and were responsible eventually for bringing him to trial.

ZEALOTS

Nationalism was rife throughout Palestine and the Zealots were the spearhead of nationalist activities. They were openly opposed to foreign rule and were ready to use violence in pursuit of their ideals. They were extremists and commonly known as 'the people with the sword', but at the same time, they were intensely devoted to their religion. Religion and politics served the same end – freedom from all foreign influence to follow God's Law. The Zealots were ready to revolt against the Romans at any time and to attack anyone who collaborated with them. This led them to commit many acts of atrocity. One of their party, Simon the Zealot, was a disciple to Jesus.

ESSENES

The Essenes belonged to the tradition of the 'pious or virtuous ones' (*Hasidim*). They are not mentioned by name in the gospels, but their teaching is reflected in the religion of the time. They lived as 'an alternative community' near the Dead Sea and are often identified by scholars as the Qumrân community of the Dead Sea Scrolls. The Essenes were an independent sect organised on the pattern of the twelve tribes of ancient Israel, under the direction of priests. Their leader was known as the Teacher of Righteousness, and the members devoted themselves to the study of scripture and a life of piety. They were devoted to God's covenant with the Jews and looked forward to the coming of the messiah and the end of the world. They were also keen on observing the Sabbath and admitted members into their 'rule' only after a period of preparation. They spent much time in prayer, ate at a common table, and held all property in common. As far as we can tell Jesus had no direct contact with the Essenes, but some of the people he worked with probably did. Their beliefs and ideals were familiar to the religious sects with whom Jesus had dealings.

COMMENT

This brief survey of the environment in which Jesus worked shows that life in Palestine was complex. In addition, there were several groups, not mentioned above, who practised a variety of beliefs.

One thing that divided the groups was the question of the *messiah*. Three different views circulated:

i)   the Pharisees expected the messiah to be a second David, a warrior king who would liberate their people and make them great;
ii) others looked for a priestly messiah of the line of Aaron, the high priest in the time of Moses;
iii) a third group expected a prophetic messiah of whom Elijah was a forerunner.

But no matter what sort of messiah they expected, the Jews believed he would be other than an ordinary human being. The religious parties shared a common hope of the coming of *God's Kingdom*. Some looked upon their present troubles as a prelude to the coming of the Kingdom of God. Others looked forward to the Kingdom of God in the next world when the righteous who had died would be raised and share its blessings.

---

3 > THE GOSPELS

❝How to answer, What is a gospel? How to answer, Who is Jesus?❞

Each syllabus in Christianity specifies study of the *gospels* as the prime source of knowledge of Jesus and the origins of Christianity. You should look carefully at the syllabus details for your study of the gospels, but the following aspects are common to all syllabuses.

The gospels are written documents of what Jesus did and taught and achieved. Until recently it was generally assumed they were biographies of Jesus, written by contemporary authors. They were assumed to tell the story of Jesus in sequence, just like any other biography. However, the modern view is rather different. Matthew, Mark, Luke and John (the names of the four gospels) may not be the names of the real authors. Early Christians referred to them as *the* gospel that was used by one or other of the Christian communities rather than by the name of the author. They are a new kind of writing and we cannot compare them with any other written works.

What then is a gospel? The word means 'good news' or a 'good announcement', a title added many years after they were written. The writers did not intend to give personal information about Jesus, but to write about the 'good news' that they believed he brought into the world. They chose their information and organised it so that they could present Jesus in a special way, by relating his achievements. They also wrote the gospels to indicate who they believed Jesus Christ to be, so that the early Christians could use the gospels in their community activities.

These ideas are supported by the opening statement of the Gospel of Mark:

'This is the Good News about Jesus Christ, the Son of God'.

This statement reads like a confession of faith, or the reason for writing the gospel. The purpose is to present the 'good news' about Jesus, who is said to be Christ (= messiah) and the Son of God.

The gospels were written by Christians for Christians so that as well as giving information about Jesus they also make comments on the things he said and did. You may think of a gospel as *information + background* or *history + interpretation*. This means that their authors wrote them for a special (theological) purpose.

A CASE STUDY

On the evening of the same day Jesus said to his disciples, "Let us go across to the other side of the lake". So they left the crowd; the disciples got into the boat in which Jesus was already sitting, and they took him with them. Other boats were there too. Suddenly a strong wind blew up, and the waves began to spill over into the boat, so that it was about to fill with water. Jesus was in the back of the boat, sleeping with his head on a pillow. The disciples woke him up and said, "Teacher, don't you care that we are about to die?".

Jesus stood up and commanded the wind, "Be quiet!" and he said to the waves, "Be still!" The wind died down, and there was a great calm. Then Jesus said to his disciples, "Why are you frightened? Have you still no faith?"

But they were terribly afraid and said to one another, "Who is this man? Even the wind and waves obey him!"

First, pick out the details (*what you need to know*) from this narrative (Jesus asleep in the boat . . . the storm . . . Jesus' words . . .). Then, notice how the *effect* of Jesus's action is highlighted (there was a great calm). Finally, notice the *response* of the disciples (Who is this man? . . . .). From this analysis you can see that the author reports this incident in a way that gives *information + the action of Jesus + the disciples' estimate of him*. The narrative presents the 'good news' in action.

When you are asked questions about *understanding* a part of the gospels or to explain or interpret them, one technique of doing this is to ask *what* information is given, *why* is it given, and *what* comment is made on it. You will then be able to say what you think it means to Christians today.

THE SYNOPTIC GOSPELS

In the GCSE you will study the first three gospels (Matthew, Mark and Luke). They are called the *synoptic* gospels because of their common approach to the subject. Many incidents about Jesus are reported in two or more of them and it is usual to study them side by side. There are episodes that are common to all three gospels, or peculiar to one of them, but they should be seen together. This leads us to ask, "How can we account for the agreements and disagreements between the three gospels?"

BEHIND THE WRITTEN GOSPELS

Jesus instructed his disciples to teach and preach the 'good news' to others. This is exactly what they did, by relating stories about the things he said and did. They handed on information about him in a spoken form and often made their own comments on it. As time went by, there were fewer people alive who had seen and heard Jesus for themselves and Christians needed to preserve everything they could about him. Important centres of Christianity in Rome, Antioch, Alexandria, Jerusalem and Caesarea needed written gospels to help in teaching and spreading the faith, to provide evidence of Jesus' activities, and to use in worship.

It is now generally agreed that there was a lengthy period when the information about Jesus circulated from person to person in an oral form before it was eventually written down. The process may be described in this way:

Jesus teaching and healing
↓
apostles preaching
↓
Christians talking
↓
authors writing

THE PRIORITY OF MARK

Mark is assumed to be the first written account of the ministry of Jesus. Nearly the whole of his gospel is contained in Matthew and Luke. Matthew and Luke have content in common, which scholars call Q (Q = quelle = source), but they also have content peculiar to themselves.

So the synoptic problem may be expressed in this form:

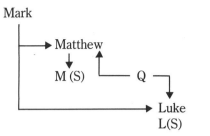

M(S) = Matthew's special material;

L(S) = Luke's special material.

As stories about Jesus grew up around important centres of Christianity, it is very likely that the gospels are associated with one or other of them. Some scholars assume it is possible to connect them with these centres in this way:

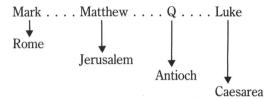

MARK

Mark's gospel was probably written in Rome about 65 CE. It is thought that Mark got some of the content of the gospel from Peter, especially those parts which give prominence to Peter (Mark 1.29–31; 8.27–30) and where the details seem to be from an eyewitness who was present at the time (Mark 4.38; 6.39).

The author uses the information about Jesus to show what kind of messiah he was, and the authority of his teaching and actions. Mark shows that something 'special' happened through the ministry of Jesus. In telling the story of Jesus he is also witnessing to God at work through Jesus (see again the first statement of the gospel). He did not write about *any man*, but about 'Jesus Christ, the Son of God'. He records the story of Jesus *and* proclaims who he was.

MATTHEW

The Gospel of Matthew was probably written ten years after Mark. The author seems intent on presenting Jesus as the messiah the Jews expected. He fulfilled the Old Testament prophecies about the messiah, so there are numerous quotations from the Old Testament (Matthew 1.13; 2.6; 6.15; 8.17; 12.18–21; 13.35; 21.4–5; 26.56; 27.9–10) which he may have found in a collection of 'proof texts' relating to the messiah.

The gospel portrays Jesus as a second Moses, who now gives God's new law just as Moses had given the old law. It presents Christianity as the New Israel or the new people of God. The Old Israel had been superseded by the New Israel, or the church. This gospel gives more prominence to the church than the others, and is the only one which actually uses the word Church (16.18; 18.17). It includes much teaching about the Kingdom of Heaven (God) as being everlasting, and although at present the kingdom is only partly seen it will be completely seen in the future. Matthew's gospel is structured in five sections, each of which ends with the words '*when Jesus finished*'. This would make it very suitable for use as a teaching manual or a lectionary of readings in worship.

LUKE

Luke's gospel was probably written about 85 CE. It is the most polished of the three, with many attractive features such as its universal outlook. Luke conceives the 'good news' as being for all people, especially the poor and outcasts and sinners. It is a gospel of joy and praise (Luke 2.9; 30. etc). It gives much space to prayer (Luke 4.42; 18.1–17), the work of the Holy Spirit (Luke 1.67 etc) and of angels (Luke 1.26 etc). It gives prominence to women (Luke 2.36 etc) and Gentiles (non-Jews) (Luke 2.30 etc). The gospel also grounds the life and ministry of Jesus firmly in history and claims to give 'authentic knowledge' of him. The gospel is orderly and recommends Christianity as a religion for all people.

JESUS IN THE SYNOPTIC GOSPELS

What portrait do these gospels give of Jesus? All three were written from different perspectives, but at no point do they contradict each other. They do not give three separate portraits of Jesus, but *one* portrait that presents him as a unique person.

They portray Jesus as a Jew who was steeped in the customs and thought of his time. He made a deep impression on his contemporaries from many walks of life, but especially upon his immediate followers. His teaching was rejected by the majority of his fellow Jews and he was eventually tried and condemned to death. However, this was not the end, for a short time afterwards he appeared again to his followers and friends.

The gospels do not give a systematic account of his life, but rather present him as a wandering teacher and healer who aroused deep passions by the things he said and did. They present him as a human being with natural human qualities *and* as someone who possessed extraordinary powers. Yet the portrait is coherent and he is shown to act in a consistent way. *The overall impression is of someone in whom human and divine qualities are mysteriously united.*

4 > JESUS OF NAZARETH

The framework of the story of Jesus in each of the synoptic gospels is as follows:

MARK	MATTHEW	LUKE
The background 1.1–13;	Genealogy and birth	Introduction 1.1–4;
Ministry in Galilee	1.1–2.23;	Birth and childhood of John
1.14–9.50;	Ministry of John 3.1–12;	the Baptist and of Jesus
Journey to Jerusalem	Ministry in Galilee	1.5–2.52;
10.1–52;	3.13–18.35;	Ministry of John 3.1–20;
The last week 11.1–15.47;	Journey to Jerusalem	The baptism and temptation
The resurrection 16.1–8;	19.1–20.34;	of Jesus 3.21–4.13;
Appearance and ascension	The last week 21.1–27.66;	Ministry in Galilee
16.9–20	The resurrection and	4.14–9.50;
	appearance 28.1–20	Journey to Jerusalem
		9.51–19.27;
		The last week 19.28–23.56;
		The resurrection, appearance
		and ascension 24.1–53.

In this section we shall pin-point some of the key events in the story of Jesus of Nazareth in the light of the above framework. He was known among his friends as *Jesus of Nazareth* or Jesus, the son of Joseph. *Christ* is a title that Christians give him, which means 'anointed' or 'messiah'. When God commissioned someone to be his agent, such as a king or priest or prophet, the Bible says the person was 'anointed', that is, endowed with special power or authority. *Christians do not speak of Christianity in the abstract but of Jesus as Christ or messiah.*

BIRTH

You should note the fact that *only* the gospels of Matthew and Luke give an account of the birth of Jesus. Mark introduces him as an adult, ready to begin his public ministry. St John begins the gospel with a hymn in praise of the Word (Logos = Christ), who existed with God from the beginning and in due time became flesh. We cannot say why St Mark omitted any reference to Jesus' birth, and must ask whether the accounts in Matthew and Luke are 'pure' history, or whether they have a symbolic significance intended to convey the message which their authors wished to transmit. Keep this question in mind as you study the birth narratives.

First read the accounts of the first Christmas in Matthew 1–2 and Luke 1–2. Both tell of Jesus' birth in Bethlehem. If you are not interested in dates it will be sufficient to know that he was born at the beginning of the Christian era (as Christians call it). If you are interested in dates then the answer is not as you might think the year one CE, but somewhere between 8 and 4 BCE. The explanation is quite simple. Our way of calculating BCE and CE was worked out by a monk named Dionysius in the sixth century CE and he got the sum wrong! Herod the Great died in 4 BCE and Jesus was born whilst he was still alive. It may surprise you that there is so little agreement between the story of the first Christmas in Matthew and Luke, so here is a break down of the two accounts:

MATTHEW	LUKE
The ancestors of Jesus traced to David and Abraham.	The birth of Jesus is announced to Mary, and his name revealed.
Joseph is engaged to Mary.	Mary's song of praise.
The angel announces to Joseph the birth of a son by the Holy Spirit.	Joseph and Mary travel to Bethlehem from Nazareth.
Joseph is told the baby's name.	Jesus is born in a stable.
Jesus is born in Bethlehem and visited by wise men led by a star.	The song of the angels and the visit of the shepherds.
Joseph is warned to take the child and his mother to safety in Egypt.	The circumcision and naming.
Herod's massacre of the children.	The return to Nazareth.
The death of Herod and the return from Egypt to Nazareth.	The ancestors of Jesus traced to Adam.

The differences between the two accounts are striking. How can we account for this? There is *bias* in both accounts which reflects the purpose of the authors in writing their gospels.

These are the important features of **Matthew's** story:

i) he traces the ancestors of Jesus to David, the ideal king of the Jews, and Abraham who Jews called 'our father';
ii) the announcement of the birth and the name Jesus is given to Joseph;
iii) there are five quotations from the Old Testament to show that everything happened as had been foretold by the prophets;
iv) Jesus was taken for safety to Egypt, a natural place of refuge for Jews.

What is the bias in Matthew's account? *He presents Jesus to Jews who had been converted to Christianity as the messiah who their prophets had predicted.*

What are the important features of **Luke's** story of the birth?

i) he traces the ancestors of Jesus to Adam, the first man;
ii) the announcement of the birth and the name Jesus is told to Mary;
iii) Mary responds with a prayer and a song (the Magnificat) that foresees the revolution that will happen as a result of the birth of Jesus;
iv) Jesus is born in a place that was kept for animals;
v) the shepherds receive a special announcement from the angels and visit the child;
vi) the family return to Nazareth.

What is the bias in Luke's account? *He presents Jesus as the universal saviour who was born in humble circumstances but whose birth was welcomed as joy and peace to the world.*

BETHLEHEM

Jesus was born in the town of Bethlehem in Judaea, during the time when Herod was king. (Matthew 2.1)

Joseph went from the town of Nazareth in Galilee to the town of Bethlehem in Judaea. (Luke 2.4)

The Old Testament prophet had predicted that the messiah was to be born in Bethlehem:

The Lord says, 'Bethlehem Ephratha, you are one of the smallest towns of Judah, but out of you I will bring a ruler for Israel, whose family line goes back to ancient times'.

Bethlehem was associated with the coming of the deliverer from ancient times. It was the birth place of David and prophecy said that the messiah would be a descendant of David. Could this knowledge have influenced Matthew and Luke to name Bethlehem as the birth place of Jesus? Matthew assumes that Joseph and Mary were already in Bethlehem, but Luke says they travelled there to register during the time when Qurinius was governor of Syria. This required Jews to go to a place where they owned property to have their names registered. Is it likely that Joseph owned property in Bethlehem when he lived in Nazareth, 150 kms away, in the north of the country? *Could it be that the birth is located in Bethlehem for the reason of connecting it with the prophecies?*

THE VIRGIN BIRTH

> This is how the birth of Jesus Christ took place . . . Mary found out she was going to have a baby by the Holy Spirit . . . Now all this happened in order to make what the Lord said through the prophet come true. (Matthew)
>
> Mary said to the angel, "I am a virgin. How, then, can this thing be?"
>
> The angel answered, "The Holy Spirit will come on you, and God's power will rest upon you. For this reason the holy child will be called the Son of God." (Luke)

Jesus was born a human being, but both Matthew and Luke describe his birth as being unnatural. His natural father had no part in his conception – he was conceived by the Holy Spirit and born of a virgin. *How do Christians explain this unusual birth*? There are broadly speaking two views:

The one view

This is the traditional view that assumes that the virgin birth is factual truth. God could only enter the world in this way – the Incarnation (that is, God appearing in a human form) could only happen through a supernatural birth. Therefore, it is believed that Mary was a virgin, Joseph was Jesus' stepfather, and the child was conceived by the Holy Spirit. The early Christian creeds refer to the Virgin Mary, and in 553 the Council of Constantinople declared her for ever a virgin.

The other view

Some Christians say that it is the meaning, *not* the manner of the birth, that is important. It is not necessary to take the stories of a virgin birth literally in order to understand *who* Jesus is and *why* he was born. They refer to i) stories of unusual births in the Old Testament in the case of Isaac and Samuel; ii) the fact that Jesus is known as the 'son of Joseph' by his friends; iii) there are no references to the virgin birth elsewhere in the New Testament.

A final note

You will *not* be asked to say which view you favour, but to show that you *know* what the issues are, that you *understand* them and are able to *evaluate* them. It is likely that Matthew and Luke added the story of the birth after they had finished their gospels. They wanted to make clear that God's plan was being initiated from the very moment that Jesus was born. They had a special (theological) purpose for including the birth stories. Jesus was born of the Holy Spirit and Christians speak of him as the 'first born' of the Spirit. They also speak of Christians being 'born of the Spirit'. They tell *how* God entered the world when Jesus was born (Matthew says he was 'Immanuel' or God with us; Luke says he is the Son of the Most High God). A new kind of being entered the world with the birth of Jesus. God was in him – and Christians believe that the birth of the 'God-man' prepared the way for them to achieve union with God through faith in him.

BAPTISM AND TEMPTATION

John the Baptist and his movement

John and Jesus were cousins and had met before Jesus began his work as a travelling preacher. John was a revivalist preacher and the leading religious activist between 26–28 CE, the time when Jesus began his work in Galilee. John had his own disciples and a following among the people of Judaea and Jerusalem. He was a wild looking character who lived in the Judaean desert where he fed on the food of the desert and dressed in the style of an old prophet. He may have been a member of the Essenes, who had a community in the Judaean wilderness, but he no longer lived within the community. Jesus declared that John was the greatest of the prophets.

John called people to repent and be baptised and receive forgiveness. The response to his preaching was electric for 'many people from the province of Judaea and the city of Jerusalem went out to hear John'.

He had considerable impact on Jewish society, and Jews thought highly of him:

> He was a good man, and exhorted the Jews to lead righteous lives, practise justice towards one another and piety towards God, and to join in baptism. In his view this was a necessary preliminary if baptism was to be acceptable to God. (Josephus)

John's baptism was popular as an alternative to the priests' monopoly of the forgiveness of sins. But his main importance for Christianity is that he prepared the way for Jesus.

John's opinion of Jesus

John recognised that Jesus had a superior role to play, and said that he was not even fit to play the part of a slave and untie Jesus' sandals. Jesus' mission was more important as he would baptise with the Holy Spirit and fire (the symbol of purification); he also proclaimed Jesus as the deliverer, or lamb of God, who would carry away the sins of the world.

Jesus is baptised

What sort of event was the baptism of Jesus? John was so overwhelmed when Jesus came and asked to be baptised that he seemed reluctant to do so. However, it is reasonable to assume that Jesus felt the need to be baptised and John therefore agreed. The baptism was a solemn happening that is described in symbolic terms . . . 'the heavens opened'; . . . 'the Spirit descended as a dove'; . . . 'a voice spoke from a cloud'.

What do these symbols mean?

- 'the heavens opening' is a Jewish symbol for seeing something that is hidden to the natural eye. It is tantamount to having a vision of God or 'seeing with a spiritual eye'; it is the symbol of intense affinity with God;

- 'the Spirit as a dove' is a symbol of peace, covenant and universal love. The dove was the harbinger of the covenant God made with Noah after the flood. The Jewish word for dove is 'jonah', which is also the name of a prophet who carried a message from God of his love for Gentiles (non-Jews);

- 'a voice from a cloud' is a symbol of God's approval and commission. In the Old Testament God is said to have spoken to Moses from a cloud.

Coming to John to be baptised showed how Jesus was willing to identify himself with the people of Judaea and Jerusalem. His baptism marked the end of an important period in his development. Mentally and physically he developed in a natural way, but at his baptism he fully realised his unique calling. The voice from the cloud declared: 'You are my own dear Son, I am pleased with you'. Hearing this gave Jesus confidence and the feeling that nothing was impossible to him.

Jesus was now equipped for his life's work and ready to initiate a new order based on repentance and forgiveness (the signs of John's baptism). *Christians see the baptism of Jesus as a further step forward in the plan which God initiated with the birth of Jesus.*

The Temptation

Immediately after his baptism, Jesus retreated to the wilderness for a time of reflection and quiet. During the forty days he spent in the wilderness he had an intense, disturbing inner experience. It was a spiritual crisis that severely tested his goodness. He was tempted to turn stones into bread, to throw himself down from the pinnacle of the temple, and to worship the devil (Satan). The temptations are described in picturesque language. *What do they mean?*

i) Jesus went into the wilderness to prepare himself for his ministry and to fast. He was tempted to break his fast and use his power to turn stones into bread. Jesus was as liable to be tempted as anyone else. He resisted and retorted: 'Scripture says, Man cannot live on bread alone'.
   Jesus shows that he was not going to be deflected from his mission. He was not dominated by physical and material needs alone. His mission is to offer spiritual food.

ii) Jesus was tempted to test God and see whether God was as good as his word. He was tempted to demand from God visible proof of his power and protection. Jesus replied: 'Do not put the Lord your God to the test'.
   He showed that he must not doubt God or demand a miracle or a spectacular display of wonders from him.

iii) Satan offered Jesus the kingdoms of the world if he fell down and worshipped him. Jesus replied: 'Worship the Lord your God and serve only him'.
   Jesus rejected the devil's bribe and refused any alliance with him. World dominion was not to be achieved by the method of worldly rulers, but only in God's way. So he alone must be worshipped.

The forty days he spent in the wilderness remind Christians of the forty years that the Israelites wandered in the desert, or the forty days Elijah spent in the wilderness. This was the beginning of many temptations of Jesus as he was hounded by temptation to turn away from his chosen path throughout his life.

After emerging unscathed from this spiritual crisis in the wilderness, Jesus began his ministry in Galilee. By now John the Baptist had been condemned and executed by Herod Antipas who had married his own brother's wife. The news of John's death affected Jesus deeply, for he took up John's message as soon as he spoke in public. In his first announcement he declared that *the Kingdom of God is near*, and called upon people to *repent and believe* the 'good news'. He announced the context for his ministry right at the beginning. *Its focal point was to be the Kingdom of God.*

INITIATING A NEW MOVEMENT

After his startling announcement, Jesus called his first disciples. Note that there is a difference in the accounts between the three gospels. The call of the disciples is of considerable interest to Christians, *firstly*, because Jesus inaugurated a movement of followers who were to share his mission, and, *secondly*, because the first disciples are held in great respect in Christianity.

A disciple is a 'pupil' or 'learner' but also a follower. The emphasis is on the call of Peter, Andrew, James and John, the first four, to leave their nets and follow Jesus. The call of Jesus was one of great authority, almost like a command from an army officer, and one which demanded complete obedience. From now on they were to 'be with him' and to share his work of preaching and his power to heal.

There are lists of the disciples in the three gospels. Twelve are named as living in intimate companionship with Jesus for the next three years, after which they became the leaders of the Church. Jesus had many other followers, but the twelve (who are also known as apostles) were his special envoys or heralds of the kingdom.

	List of Disciples	
MARK	MATTHEW	LUKE
Peter	Peter	Peter
James	Andrew	James
John	James	John
Andrew	John	Andrew
Philip	Philip	Philip
Bartholemew	Bartholemew	Bartholemew
Matthew	Thomas	Matthew
Thomas	Matthew	Thomas
James the son of Alphaeus	James the son of Alphaeus	James the son of Alphaeus
Thaddaeus	Lebbaous, Surnamed Thaddaeus	Simon Zelotes
Simon the Canaanite	Simon the Canaanite	Judas, the brother of James
Judas Iscariot	Judas Iscariot	Judas Iscariot

Fig. 5.3 A list of the disciples

JESUS AND THE KINGDOM

There are over eighty references to the Kingdom of God or Heaven (the meaning is the same) in the first three gospels. Jesus made this the core of his teaching. There were many people who were waiting for the Kingdom of God, but Jesus challenged their views. Many thought it would be an earth-shattering event, whilst others believed it was for a chosen few. *By the Kingdom of God Jesus meant the rule or reign of God.* Furthermore, it is present here and now *and yet* it will be made complete in the future. He taught mostly about the Kingdom of God in parables.

THE PARABLES

Have you ever eavesdropped on a conversation between people in the street, on the bus, or on the way home from work? If you have, then you probably remember that the conversation was about an incident, a happening, or a story. Most likely the conversation went like this, 'then she said to me and I replied . . . .' or 'I saw him driving as if he was in a great hurry . . . .' or 'I went to visit my sister . . . .'.

It's the incident or the happening or the story that matters. People are usually more ready to tell about things that happened than they are to talk about ideas.

When Jesus spoke about the Kingdom of God he usually told about an incident, a happening or a story. Much of his teaching is in stories which are called *parables*. His parables are full of illustrations of things that happen every day which made it easy for people to listen and to remember. He often began his teaching by saying:

'the Kingdom of God is like what follows after a woman uses yeast in her baking . . . . or the Kingdom of God is like what follows after a mustard seed is sown'.

The parables of Jesus are three dimensional:

- He made the listener feel part of the action. He used incidents or happenings from everyday life and drew his listeners into the action. He spoke about everyday happenings in the home, on a journey or in work, so as to make the listeners feel they were part of the action.

- He made it easy for the listeners to identify with the characters and action. He used real people from his own experience and the experience of his listeners in order to help them identify themselves with the characters. Sometimes it was a shepherd or a housewife, or a father or employer, or a traveller or farmer.

- He expected them to respond. He didn't often explain his parables as if he was giving a moral lesson. There isn't much point in telling a story if it has to be explained. Jesus left his listeners to make up their own minds about what they heard. He knew that they would be likely to remember the illustration or incident and it would stick in their minds until they made sense of it.

He told parables to teach his message or to make the point he wished to make in a way that was understood. There is always one main point in a parable and Jesus expected his listeners to make up their minds about it. *A parable is not a programme of action, but a challenge for people to make up their minds about what they heard.*

THE KINGDOM PRESENT

Many parables that Jesus told illustrate his announcement that the Kingdom of God is present here and now as 'good news'. Here are four parables that illustrate the 'kingdom present'.

The great feast (Luke 14.16–24)

This parable is introduced by someone sitting at a table and saying how good it would be to be invited to God's banquet. Jesus told a parable about a king who wished to make other people happy, so he made a feast and invited guests to enjoy it. The guests all made excuses, but the king was not insulted because his invitations were refused. Instead he offered the places to people who were never invited to anyone's party. He showed how much he cared for people who were usually ignored or despised.

Who do you think the two groups of guests represent? Who do you think the host represents? When he invited outcasts to his feast he told his servant: 'Go out to the country roads and lanes and make people come in so that my house will be full'.

What does this parable teach about the kingdom present? Note the following points . . . the feast is ready and the first guests are invited; . . . the host enlarges the invitation until the house is filled; . . . his attitude to the first guests who were invited. Finally, who do you think the servant represents?

The prodigal son (Luke 15.11–32)

Jesus told his parable to an audience made up of tax collectors, outcasts, teachers of the Law and Pharisees. The audience would find it easy to identify with one or other of the two sons. They would not find it difficult to see that the father who shared his possessions with his sons and showed that he loved them both, represented God.

In the eyes of the Law the younger (prodigal son) had rendered himself unclean and thus unfit to worship God. The elder son who stayed at home and served his father dutifully had justice on his side. The one son had squandered his inheritance, whilst the other had worked his part of his father's estate.

What does this parable teach about the kingdom present? Note the following points . . . the father showed his love for the younger son by transcending the Law about impurity; he took no account of the elder son's objection to his treatment of the prodigal son; . . . the father lavished forgiveness on the prodigal son but did not break faith with his elder brother.

The good Samaritan (Luke 10.25–37)

This is a parable with a shock element which was intended to shock the hearers into action. Jesus told it in answer to a lawyer's question, 'Who is my neighbour?' The scene is an attack on a traveller on the Jerusalem–Jericho road. It was shocking that a half-cast Samaritan should show more compassion for the victim than did the official Jewish leaders. The audience was already caught up in a situation of hatred between Jews and Samaritans. They never thought of doing good to someone who might harm them. Neither did they think of showing kindness to anyone who had given up all hope of ever being shown kindness. The Samaritan disregarded the frigid atmosphere between Jews and Samaritans to treat the victim.

What does this parable teach about the kingdom present? Note the following points . . . the two great requirements of the Law are love to God *and* love to one's neighbour; in this parable the neighbour is a person in need; . . . compassion is shown by the Samaritan without prejudice; . . . the claims of compassion transcend the claims of the Law; . . . the contrast between care and negligence; . . . the command to the lawyer.

The wicked tenants (Mark 12.1–9; Luke 20.9–19)

Jesus told this parable in Jerusalem, near the time of his death. The Jewish leaders who heard were quick to see that it was a parable against them. It is really more like an allegory, in which the vineyard represents the world and the owner God, the tenants represent those who rejected God's messengers or servants, and the son represents Jesus. The tenants are given care of the vineyard, but they reject the servants sent by the owner to collect the fruit. When the owner finally decides to send his son, they plan to kill him.

What does this parable teach about the kingdom present? Note the following points . . . the failure by the tenants to respond to the owner's call; . . . the rejection of the servants, who are the messengers of the owner; . . . the attitude towards the son, who is the central figure of the parable; . . . the judgement announced on those who heard it.

Here is a check list of the parables on the 'kingdom present' in the first three gospels:

Parable	Matthew	Mark	Luke	Parable	Matthew	Mark	Luke
New cloth and wine	9.16–17	2.21–22	5.36–39	The lost sheep	18.12–14		15.4–7
The sower	13.1–8	4.1–9	8.4–8, 11–15	The lost coin			15.8–11
The mustard seed	13.31–32	4.30–32	13.18–19	The hidden treasure			13.44
The leaven	13.33		13.20–21	The pearl of great price	13.45–46		
The seed growing secretly		4.26–29		The tower			14.28–31
The tares	13.24–30			The warring king			14.31–33
The labourers in the vineyard	20.1–16			The unworthy stewards			17.7–10
The two sons	21.28–31			The unjust steward			16.1–8
The two debtors		7.41–43		A friend at midnight			11.5–8
The wedding guests		14.7–11		The unjust judge			18.2–8
The Pharisees and the publican		18.10–14		The merciless servant	18.23–35		

When you have read any of these parables prescribed in your syllabus you should make a note of what they teach about the 'kingdom present' or the 'kingdom future'.

THE KINGDOM FUTURE

Certain parables and sayings refer to the kingdom that is yet to be completed. Jesus taught the kingdom as present *and* future. The kingdom already present will eventually be made complete. Here are three parables that teach about the kingdom to come.

The mustard seed (Mark 4.30–32; Luke 8.11–15)

It may have seemed unconvincing to some that the kingdom is already present. The parable of the mustard seed illustrates the contrast between the smallest seed on earth and the shrub which is larger than any plant. Doubts about the smallness of the seed are dispelled when it reaches its full growth. Then it provides shelter for the birds. The contrast is between small beginnings and final results. The tree is a symbol of the universal blessings of the kingdom.

What does the parable teach about the kingdom to come? Note the following points . . . the kingdom begins in insignificant ways, there are no earth-shattering events, great upheavals or campaigns; . . . the kingdom will triumph in the way God intends; . . . it will spread and all races will find a refuge in it. How does this fit the symbolism of the mustard seed, the birds and the branches?

The coins (Luke 19.12–27)

This is probably another version of the parable of the talents in Matthew 25.14–30. Jesus told the parable as he was approaching Jerusalem. A high ranking official was going to a country to be made king and afterwards return home. Before he left, he gave each of his ten servants a gold coin and told them to use it to earn what they could. The servants did not want him to reign over them, but when he returned as king he called them to account for the use they made of the gold coin. One had increased its value tenfold and another fivefold. These received a reward from the king. However, one servant hid the coin and returned it unused, so the king took away the coin and gave it to the servant who had ten coins, and said: 'I tell you that to every person who has something, even more will be given; but the person who has nothing, even the little that he has will be taken away from him'.

What does this parable teach about the kingdom to come? Note the following points . . . the king must depart in order to receive his kingdom; . . . some servants rejected the king's commission; . . . the kingdom will continue to expand; . . . the judgement of the king on the useless servant. How does this fit the attitude of the narrow-minded people who wanted to keep God's message to themselves? The departure of Jesus to receive the kingdom that was already expected? The task of his followers to promote his world wide mission? The judgement on the people who rejected him?

The wedding guests (Luke 14.7–11)

When invited to a feast the Pharisees expected to receive preferential treatment. They expected to receive the best places as a matter of right. Jesus used this illustration to show up the arrogance of such a high opinion of oneself in the presence of God. Those who thought so highly of themselves will be disappointed, for in the Kingdom of God the order of precedence will be reversed.

What does this parable teach about the kingdom to come? Note the following points . . . the expectation of those who believed they had rights over and above other people; . . . the guests who sit in the humblest places will be recompensed; . . . the host honours those who make no claim on his generosity. What does this teach about how the kingdom will be open to outcasts? Note that in the feast of the kingdom God will judge between the proud and humble?

The kingdom that is to come will come in God's own time. Jesus did not speak of the precise time of its coming, but he warned his followers to be ready to receive it. It may happen suddenly and without warning, when it is least expected. Or again, it may be preceded by great upheavals in the natural world, by famines, plagues and earthquakes. There may be wars and horrors that cannot be described. It will usher in the final age of judgement on all people. Jesus gave this teaching in picturesque language and is not to be taken literally. He used picture language to convey his meaning and to help his audience remember his teaching.

In this context Jesus referred to his return again or his 'second coming'.

In the days after the time of trouble the sun will grow dark, the moon will no longer shine, the stars will fall from heaven, and the powers in space will be driven from their courses. Then the Son of Man will appear, coming in the clouds with great power and glory. He will send the angels out to the four corners of the earth to gather God's chosen people from one end of the world to the other.

In this event God will act in a final way to make his kingdom complete. The teaching on this is found in many parts of the gospels (Mark 13; Luke 21; Matthew 24–25 etc). It is called 'apocalyptic' teaching, that is, teaching about the end of the age and the return of Jesus, which uses a variety of symbols, signs and metaphors.

6 ▷ THE TEACHING ON THE KINGDOM

Who are the people who belong to the Kingdom of God? Jesus answers this question by describing the Christian character. He provided an ideal suited to the people who enter his kingdom. He does not define the ideal, but rather describes how it can be achieved.

SEEKING THE KINGDOM

The people who enter his kingdom are those who are ready to seek after it. They are the people who respond to his teaching and answer his call. They are like people who 'ask' or 'seek' or 'knock' at a door. They then become subjects of a kingdom whose king is God. God reigns and he receives anyone who seeks sincerely to enter his kingdom. They then become the spiritual children of the king, who is also like a father. They can address God as father by using the same word (abba), as a child does in the home when speaking to his/her natural father. There is a bond of trust, intimacy and love between the subject of the kingdom and the king. Jesus describes the members of the kingdom as being 'blessed' or 'happy'. They are 'happy' at a very deep level, or live as the 'children of God'. Jesus singles out their characteristics:

- they stand before God but do not claim anything for themselves;
- they show great sympathy for human sorrow;
- they learn to control themselves;
- they seek for goodness in the same way as they seek for food and drink;
- they show mercy to everyone;
- they are utterly sincere;
- they promote peace actively at all times;
- they learn to suffer for what is right.

Jesus describes people who are 'happy' in this sense as 'the salt of the earth'. Salt is a metaphor for wisdom; wisdom consists of nurturing right attitudes and qualities; wisdom does not display itself but adds to the richness of life and spends itself for the sake of others. Jesus also describes the subjects of the kingdom as 'the light of the world'. Light is essential for life and there is no substitute for light. The kingdom is just like light – it is essential to direct and guide its members.

THE ETHICS OF THE KINGDOM

Jesus did not compose an ethical theory or a moral code. Instead he gave pictures or told stories about the moral way his subjects must behave. *The central core of his moral teaching is love* as the ideal which directs the way his followers behave. Instead of defining it he said:

> Love your enemies; do good to those who hate you; bless those who curse you; pray for those who ill treat you . . .
> Do to others what you want them to do to you.

He gave a deeper meaning to the law about murder, divorce and making promises. The law condemned *murder*, but Jesus condemned the hatred that leads to murder. Anyone who holds a grudge, or is angry is guilty of committing murder in the heart. Evil thoughts make a person guilty in the sight of God and sour human relationships.

Take the case of *adultery*. In Jewish law this meant breaking someone else's marriage and was punishable by death. Jesus condemns the lust that leads to adultery, and does not separate the act from the intention or motive. To entertain thoughts of adultery means being guilty of the act. Scholars call this the 'inner ethic' of Christianity. He taught the same principle about *making vows*. The Jews taught that swearing an oath by mentioning a sacred name or place made it binding. Jesus declared that *every* vow or promise is binding. It is not proper to keep one promise and break another. He extended this teaching to the way his followers should *treat other people* They should do to others whatever they wish others to do to them. He illustrated this by describing how his followers should treat those who are hungry; or thirsty; or sick; or strangers; or prisoners; of other races; or children. (Read Matthew 25; Mark 10; Luke 10.)

He followed the same principle when giving his *social message*. He did not teach a social theory but a social message based on service. Service to other people in society is the basis of social necessity. He said he came not to be served, but to serve. Unselfish service promotes good order in society and can transform it. This ideal of outgoing service involves the use of personal assets for the good of others. He taught this through the parable of the gold coins (Luke 19.11–27). Notice how the parable teaches that God has invested his gifts in his servants; . . . these are not to be hoarded; . . . the gifts are to be invested in service to others; . . . those who do so receive the reward of the kingdom.

Consider the case of the young man who questioned Jesus about eternal life (Mark 10.17–24). It means the same as entering the Kingdom of God. Jesus saw at once that the man was addicted to his *wealth* as his chief asset. Jesus answered the question by telling the young man to sell his possessions and give the proceeds to the poor. The young man went away sad, because he could not part with his love of material wealth. Jesus distinguishes between wealth that is accidental and that which is essential. He said 'A man's life does not consist in the abundance of things that he possesses'. This is *accidental* wealth. On the other hand, those who accept his teaching have *essential* wealth or treasure in heaven. Wealth is not an end in itself and can be a barrier to entry into the kingdom. Anyone who makes wealth such a barrier must be prepared to let it go.

Keeping society in good order also involves *political action*. The Pharisees and Herodians asked Jesus about his political attitude. Should they or shouldn't they pay taxes to Caesar? To do so was tantamount to accepting the Roman occupation without protest, something which few Jews were prepared to do. To refuse to pay the tax was subversion and punishable. What did Jesus say in reply? He astonished his questioners by saying: 'Render to Caesar the things that are Caesar's, and to God the things that are God's'.

Did he assert the divine right of Caesar, or did he evade the question? He reminded the Pharisees and Herodians that they carried Caesar's money and enjoyed the services of the civil government. Must they not therefore perform their civic duty and keep the laws of the state? Jesus did not make a party political point, but showed it was right to observe the laws of the state. He himself did so at his trial. At the same time, service to the state is not the same as service to God. Duty to Caesar is one thing and duty to God another. His followers must perform all necessary service in the spirit of the 'good news' and so promote good social order.

PRAYER

Jesus gave his disciples a model prayer which is *the* prayer of the citizens of the kingdom:

> Our Father, who art in heaven,
> hallowed be thy name;
> thy kingdom come; thy will be done;
> on earth as it is in heaven.
> Give us this day our daily bread,
> And forgive us our trespasses,
> as we forgive those who trespass against us.
> And lead us not into temptation,
> but deliver us from evil.

Christians call this the 'Pater Noster' (the Our Father). It addresses God in a special sense as Father and is a community prayer. You should note the *structure* of the prayer. It is for the time when God's name will be holy and his will made manifest on earth. It is a prayer for the necessity of daily bread and for forgiveness. It is a prayer not to be tested (tempted) beyond the limit.

Jesus intended prayer as a regular commitment on the part of his disciples. He himself prayed regularly and at every major turning point in his career. He taught about the spirit of prayer in the parable of the Pharisee and publican (Luke 18.9–14) and how the kingdom will come in response to prayer in the parable of the persistent widow (Luke 18.1–8).

THE WORKS OF THE KINGDOM

The gospels make no mystery of Jesus performing *miracles*. His miracles are features of his view of the kingdom of God. *They are signs of the Kingdom in action.* Jesus made this clear in his message to John the Baptist:

> Go back and tell John what you have seen and heard: the blind see, the lame can walk, those who suffer from dreaded skin disease are made clean, the deaf can hear, the dead are raised to life, and the Good News is preached to the poor.

Jesus believed that he lived in the presence of God and that God was working through him. The natural world is God's creation and he is able to express his will through the operation of natural laws. The physical world is not bound by a system of closed laws, but is the *sphere* of God's activity. Therefore the mighty (dynamic) works of Jesus (the way the gospels describe his miracles) are 'signs' of God's power at work.

It will help you to understand the term 'miracle' if you consider these three points:

First, God created the laws of nature (so Christians believe) and they do not change. Jesus worked *with* the laws of nature and not against them.

Second, Jesus sought to understand the causes of illness and treated these. This may have been anxiety, worry, or guilt.

Third, Jesus performed miracles on the basis of faith in his power to heal. He was not a faith healer but rather he demonstrated how God's power and love are at work when people have faith in him.

Christianity gives much attention to the *meaning* of the miracles of Jesus. They are part of his total ministry and proof of the 'kingdom present'. They point Christians to his unique powers. Each success is a 'sign' of God at work through him in a way that was unparalleled. He spoke of the 'finger of God' at work through his miracles. There were many miracle workers and faith healers active in the time of Jesus. He did not wish to be known as a faith healer and the sheer scale of his miracles is without equal. However, his purpose was to demonstrate that: *It is rather by means of God's power that I drive out demons*, and this power proves that the Kingdom of God has already come to you.

His mighty works complement his teaching. You should explore how he responded to the needs of people who needed his help there and then. Consider how his miracles express his own human concern as well as his divine powers. Where there was no faith he did not perform any mighty works. Christianity finds the meaning of his miracles in the following way of understanding them:

i) they are his response to genuine faith and human need;
ii) they demonstrate that all things are possible to God;
iii) they perform a special part of his ministry as redeemer;
iv) they are part of the Kingdom of God in action.

Jesus knew from the commencement that he would perform miracles. He read the manifesto he intended to follow in the synagogue in Nazareth. He said that this was now being fulfilled. Take note of the reference to miracles:

> The Spirit of the Lord is upon me, because he has chosen me to bring good news to the poor.
> He has sent me to proclaim liberty to the captives; the recovery of sight to the blind; to set free the oppressed and announce that the time has come when the Lord will save his people.

In his message to John the Baptist, Jesus mentioned five of his mighty works which show that the 'good news' is preached. We may illustrate this from these five miracles.

'The lame walk' (Mark 2.1–12; Luke 5.18–26)

Jesus is in Capernaum, the centre of his work in Galilee, probably in the house of Peter which he made his headquarters. So popular was he with the crowds that they filled the house and when four men carried a lame man on a stretcher they were unable to get near him. So they climbed on to the flat roof and lowered their friend directly in front of Jesus. He saw their faith and said to the paralysed man, 'your sins are forgiven'. Note how Jesus acts to forgive the man's sin. At once, the scribes protested, as only God could forgive sins. They accused Jesus of acting beyond his powers. However, Jesus replied to the opposition by saying: 'the Son of Man has authority on earth to forgive sins'. Then he demonstrated his power by healing the lame man, who then was told to walk away.

How does the miracle demonstrate the kingdom present? Note the following points . . . Jesus made the man completely whole, he healed him spiritually as well as physically; . . . he manifested the power of God at work in him; . . . he offered the man forgiveness; he did not ask what the sins were, but forgave them. *How does the offer of forgiveness to the paralysed man link up with the forgiveness of the parables of Jesus?*

'The blind can see' (Mark 10.46–52; Luke 18.35–43)

Just as Jesus and his disciples are leaving Jericho, Bartimaeus, a blind beggar, cried out, 'Son of David. Jesus. Have pity on me'. The crowd tried to restrain him but he would not be silenced. Jesus stopped and told the crowd to call Bartimaeus, who jumped for joy and came to Jesus. He asked Jesus to give him sight. Jesus replied, 'Go, your faith has made you well'.

Bartimaeus knew the family tree of Jesus! He called Jesus son of David. Had some rumour of this spread as far as Jericho? He also called Jesus 'teacher'. Was he just being polite, or had he heard (and maybe believed) in Jesus as a special teacher?

How does the miracle demonstrate the kingdom present? Note the following points . . . Jesus does not reject the appeal of the beggar, but calls him to him; . . . Jesus links his healing with the beggar's faith in him; . . . the beggar joins the pilgrimage procession as one of Jesus' followers.

'Lepers are cleansed' (Mark 1.40–45; Luke 5.12–16)

In the society of Jesus lepers were written off as being beyond hope. They were only able to keep alive by living on scraps that were thrown to them. They did not mix with other people because of the fear of catching the dread disease. Jesus was filled with pity when a leper said to him 'If you want to, you can make me clean'. Jesus answered, 'I do want to, be clean'. Then he told the leper to follow the normal procedure and get a certificate from a priest (who was also the medical officer of health) so that he could return to his family and live a normal life again. Being 'cleansed' he was able to join in the worship of the synagogue once more.

How does the miracle demonstrate the kingdom present? Note the following points . . . the leper broke the law in approaching Jesus, but Jesus showed that compassion comes before observing the law; . . . the leper was excluded from the community but Jesus touched him as a sign of welcoming him back to society; . . . the leper was thought to be far away from the Kingdom of God, but Jesus dealt with him as though he belonged to the kingdom already.

'The deaf hear' (Mark 7.31–37)

As in the case of the paralysed man, some friends brought a deaf mute to Jesus and asked him to heal him. Jesus took the man away from the people and then put his fingers in the man's ears, spat and touched the man's tongue, saying to the man in Aramaic 'Ephphatha' (which means 'open up'). Jesus made physical contact with the deaf mute as if power flowed from him to heal him. Spittle was thought to have healing qualities and Jesus reinforced his words, '*Open up*', with the action of touching the man's ears and tongue.

How does the miracle demonstrate the kingdom present? Note the following points . . . by touching the man's ears and tongue Jesus expresses the life power he possessed; . . . Jesus took the man to one side so as to avoid exhibitionism; . . . he recognised the man's need of healing and shared his compassion and power with him.

'The dead are raised' (Luke 7.11–17)

This miracle is only reported in Luke's gospel and once again it shows the pity of Jesus. When he was in Nain a funeral procession arrived at the gate of a widow's only son, probably the bread winner. Jesus acted without anyone prompting him and told the widow not to cry. He then walked over and touched the coffin, and said, 'Young man! Get up I tell you!' At that time, death was looked upon as the work of the devil but Jesus acts in the manner of the Old Testament prophets Elijah and Elisha in showing his power over death. Is this related to his own resurrection? There is only one other incident in the synoptic gospels of Jesus restoring someone to life who had died (Mark 5.35–42; Luke 8.49–53).

How does this miracle demonstrate the kingdom present? Note the following points . . . Jesus manifests his compassion at every level of human need; . . . he drew forth faith on the part of the people present, they said, 'A great prophet has appeared among us'; . . . Jesus showed his work as redeemer from the grip of death, and the people replied, 'God has come to save his people'.

A final note on the miracles

You will come across one group of miracles that Jesus did not mention when he sent his report to John the Baptist. This is the 'miracles of nature' (Jesus stilling the storm, walking on the water, feeding the multitude). Some scholars regard these as legends similar to those which are found in other religions. You will learn that they have special features and that these stories may be included by the gospel authors to convey their ideas of Jesus, that is, to show Jesus as someone who made God real. Christians today often interpret them in the same way. The miracles, they say, show that Jesus makes the power of God real in the natural, as well as the human world.

When you study the miracles of your particular syllabus it will help you to see how they can be divided into these four classes, as in this check list:

1 Exorcisms
(casting out evil spirits)

A man with an evil spirit

Demons in many people

People troubled by evil spirits

A man with demons

A boy with an evil spirit

The dumb spirit

2 Restorations
(restoring people to physical health)

Simon's mother-in-law

Sick friends

The leper

The paralysed man

The withered hand

The centurion's servant

A crippled woman

A sick man

Ten lepers

A blind beggar

The high priest's servant

3 Power over death

The widow of Nain

Jairus's daughter

4 Nature miracles

Stilling the storm

The catch of fish

Walking on the water

Feeding the multitude

7 ▷ JOURNEY TO JERUSALEM

From the time he began his ministry in Galilee, Jesus was never free from conflict. (Read Mark 2.1–3.6 for information about the conflicts in which Jesus was engaged.) Here is a list: conflict about the right to forgive sin; conflict about eating with publicans and sinners; conflict about fasting; conflict about the Sabbath; conflict about healing on the Sabbath. In each conflict story Jesus made a significant pronouncement. You will find what these pronouncements are from Mark 2.10; 17; 20; 28. The dice seemed loaded against him from the beginning:

> So the Pharisees left the synagogue and met at once with some members of Herod's party, and they made plans to kill Jesus (Mark 3.6).

The religious and political parties found plenty of evidence against Jesus. He had broken the sacred law and incited others to do the same; he made claims for himself that only God could make; he spoke against God; he made friends of outcasts and people of the lowest kind; he claimed that God would justify everything he did.

Just before he began his journey to Jerusalem he told his disciples that he must suffer and die. He had broken the sacred law of the Jews, and he knew that the Romans allowed the religious leaders to put to death anyone who flouted their law. This was by throwing the guilty person over a precipice and stoning him. The Romans only acted in cases of crimes against the state. Jesus was under no illusion about what was to happen to him, but he still decided to make the fatal journey to Jerusalem.

ARRIVAL IN JERUSALEM (MARK 11.1–11; LUKE 19.28–40)

Jesus arrived in Jerusalem at the time of the Jewish passover. Every pilgrim entered the city on foot, but Jesus did not. He went to some trouble to secure a donkey, so as to be seen riding into the city. As he entered in procession the people cheered and waved branches of palm trees, as if they were greeting a king. As he passed by they chanted *Hosanna* (save now) and sang 'God bless him who comes in the name of the Lord'.

There are some interesting features about the entry into Jerusalem for you to note: i) Jesus rode into Jerusalem on a humble beast; a warrior messiah would ride a horse, the donkey was a symbol of humility; ii) Jesus entered the city in peace, not as a conquering hero; iii) the chorus of greeting echoed the chorus of the angels at the birth of Jesus.

How do Christians interpret the entry into Jerusalem? Christians refer to this as the 'triumphal entry'. Jesus must have thought about his entry, for he planned to ride on a donkey. Did he intend the people to receive him as messiah? The thought must have been in the minds of the people and they must have asked some searching questions about the stranger riding on the donkey. Perhaps they thought that he was a mighty prophet, but not the messiah. Waving palm branches as the procession went by is what happened when the temple was rededicated after the time of Antiochus, who had desecrated the holy place. They were symbols of triumph and gladness. Many followers of Jesus expected him to be proclaimed as messiah in Jerusalem and bring to an end the present rule. Therefore they greeted him with the signs of triumph and joy.

| 8 | THE LAST WEEK |

The importance that the gospel writers attach to the last week of the life of Jesus may be seen from the amount of space they give to it. Mark devotes about one third of his gospel to it; Matthew and Luke, about one fourth. The story of the last week was probably written earlier than any other parts of the gospels, but the 'form' of the story is not very obvious. It is not easy to reconstruct the sequence of happenings from the different gospels, but you will find this attempt helpful:

1 Three notable events	the anointing at Bethany;
	the triumphal entry;
	the cleansing of the temple.
2 The day of questions	the question about authority;
	the question about paying taxes;
	the question about resurrection;
	the question about the first command.
3 Teaching near the temple	the discourse on the last things or the final events.
4 The last supper	the celebration of the passover in the upper room.
5 The trials of Jesus	the retreat to the garden;
	the arrest and trial before the sanhedrin;
	the civil trial before Pilate.
6 Crucifixion	the crucifixion according to the Roman pattern.
7 Resurrection	the empty tomb and the resurrection appearances.

CLEANSING THE TEMPLE (MARK 11.15–18; LUKE 19.45–48)

According to Mark this took place on the Monday of the last week. The temple was the first place that pilgrims visited on arrival in Jerusalem. During the passover it was

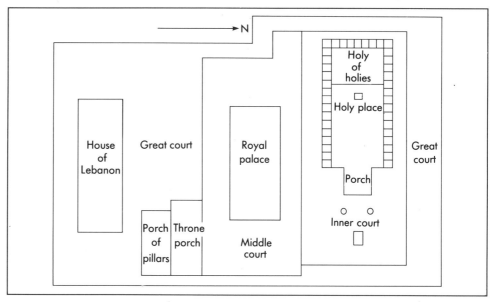

Fig. 5.4 A plan of the temple

thronging with people, who gathered to exchange money into temple coinage and to buy materials for sacrifice. Jesus reacted to this use of the temple and showed his physical courage and his mastery of the situation. The trade was legal and provided a service to pilgrims, but Jesus acted as he did because it debased religion and desecrated a holy place. This activity took place in the Court of the Gentiles, which was the only place in the temple where non-Jews were allowed to go. Jesus also objected to this very narrow outlook and attitude. He declared that the temple is a place of prayer for people of *all* nations. Jesus performed a most courageous action by overturning the tables of the money changers and driving out the merchants. *It is a symbolic action intended to show the authorities that the messiah they expected had come to his temple.*

THE LAST SUPPER (MARK 14.12–26; Luke 22.7–14, 21–23)

Jesus arranged the place where he and his disciples were to celebrate the passover meal. Passover was held on the 15th Nisan (the Jewish month corresponding to March/April), to commemorate the delivery of the ancient Jews from the captivity in Egypt in the days of Moses. The celebrations lasted a whole week, but the focus was the passover meal or *seder*.

Sometimes scholars question whether the last supper *was* a seder meal. This is on account of the different timing of the events in the four gospels. However, there are clues that it *was* a seder meal – there was wine on the table, indicating a celebration, and Jesus used words which were usually spoken by the head of a Jewish family at the seder. The account in the gospels is rich in symbols. Interest centres in the *meaning* of the meal and the new elements which Jesus introduced. He identified the *bread* and *wine* of the seder with his *body* and *blood*. During the meal the Jews ate lamb, to remind them of the passover lamb that was sacrificed in the wilderness during the journey from Egypt. (See Exodus 12.) Many Christians believe that *Jesus saw himself as the sacrificial lamb who was to give his life for others*. Hence the symbol of the bread and wine.

During the meal, Jesus also told of his imminent departure. This was the 'last supper' he and his disciples would eat together. The memory of the meal impressed itself on the minds of the disciples. Christians today commemorate it in the *eucharist* (mass or Holy Communion). When they do, they understand it in a special way:

- they remember the common meal which Jesus and his disciples shared with gladness and how he said that the bread represented his body and the wine his blood;
- the symbol of the bread as the body of Christ is in the 'breaking';
- the symbol of the cup of wine and the blessing (the *kiddush*) is of the time when Christians will share in the banquet of God's kingdom;
- he promised there will be renewal of their fellowship in the Kingdom of God.

GETHSEMANE (MARK 14.32–51; LUKE 22.39–53)

After the seder, Jesus and his disciples sang a hymn, after which he took Peter, James and John into the garden of Gethsemane or on to the Mount of Olives, as Luke calls it. Here Jesus passed through an inner crisis and extreme emotional stress. Did Jesus know the fate that awaited him? His sweat was as blood, a very rare condition triggered by intense inner agony. He prayed that the cup (the symbol of suffering) might be taken from him. He felt weak in body, but there was no turning back. His commitment to God's will was as absolute as it was when he refused the temptation in the wilderness. The moment of his ultimate self sacrifice had arrived and he committed his life into God's hands. He placed complete reliance on God. An angel came to strengthen him (as in the wilderness at the beginning of his ministry). His obedience to God was complete; he stood his ground when Judas led his captors to arrest him.

The arresting party was armed and Luke says that one of them was injured in the scuffle. Jesus still showed his compassion in the moment of supreme personal crisis and healed the young man. Mark tells that a young man fled from the scene naked (probably wearing only an undergarment); he may have been someone who told later what happened. Jesus' own disciples fled in terror.

THE TRIALS (MARK 14.53–15.15; LUKE 22.54–23.5)

The arrest seems as if it was well planned, although why Judas betrayed Jesus is not clear. Luke says that Satan entered into him, since he was the treasurer of the disciples and greed may have been the motive. He may have expected Jesus to save himself and show his power as the messiah. Or he may have expected Jesus to act and bring in his kingdom there and then.

Jesus was led to the Jewish court presided over by *Caiaphas,* who held office as high priest between 18 and 35 CE. Jesus was on trial for his life before the religious leaders he had often spoken against, or who had always opposed him. It was a night trial, a very hasty arrangement. It is not very likely that the whole sanhedrin (seventy one members) were present, and the interrogation was probably conducted by the Sadducees, who were determined to satisfy their self interest. *Peter* followed at a distance and mingled with the crowd in the courtyard of Caiaphas' palace. When he was identified by one of the servants his nerve failed him and he denied that he ever knew Jesus. When he realised what he had done, he broke down and wept. Luke reports that Jesus 'looked on Peter', but did not rebuke him for his failure of nerve. *Was Jesus'* look one of *pity,* of *disappointment* or of *indignation*? We are not told. What do you think?

The Jewish trial seems a shambles. Jesus was bullied and mocked by the guards before the trial began and the court had to pin a charge on him that merited the death sentence. So they asked the crucial question – *'Are you the messiah?'* It was an offence for any Jew to claim that he was the messiah and to admit it meant facing the death penalty. Mark reports that witnesses were called but they couldn't agree, so their evidence was ignored. The high priest clinched the matter by asking if Jesus admitted that he was the Son of the Blessed (God). To do this was blasphemy, but Jesus could not deny it. So Jesus was pronounced guilty and taken to the Roman court for sentence.

It is not certain whether *Pilate* held his court in Herod's palace or in Fortress Antonia. It was his duty to see that justice was done, whatever contempt he may have felt for the Jews. *What was his attitude to Jesus?* Pilate did not act without some feeling for Jesus, and he did not capitulate easily to the demands of the mob. Jesus was a Galilean peasant and he wondered why he had been brought before the court. So the Jews had to be cunning in the way they brought the charges against him; they knew that Pilate would have no patience with their religious charges. Luke reports that Pilate tried to stall by sending Jesus to Herod, but Herod treated the whole matter lightly and seemed to look upon it as an entertainment. Through it all Jesus kept silent.

Once the Jews had made a political charge against Jesus, Pilate was bound to take it seriously. The Jews accused Jesus of high treason by making himself a king, refusing to pay taxes to Rome and inciting people to rebel against the Roman occupation. Even so, Pilate seemed reluctant to act in an extreme way and made three declarations that would have saved Jesus. He suggested the minor punishment of being flogged and then set free. This incensed the crowd, who called for the death sentence. Pilate gave them a choice of Jesus or Barabbas, who ironically had committed a political crime. The crowd cried out for Barabbas, not Jesus. Pilate hesitated. After all *was* Jesus a rebel? *Did* he lead a revolt against Rome? Eventually he yielded and condemned Jesus to be crucified, a peculiar Roman form of execution reserved for non-Roman citizens and criminals of the lower classes.

THE CRUCIFIXION (MARK 15.16–40; LUKE 23.26–43)

When you read the accounts of the death of Jesus you should notice the special features of each of the accounts. Ask how far do these differences reflect the special interests of the writers?

When Jesus was handed over by Pilate to be crucified, he was mocked as a bogus king and dressed in purple and a crown of thorns. He was made to carry the cross beam of the cross, as every convict did. On the way, *Simon of Cyrene* was commanded from the crowd to take the cross beam and carry it to the place of the crucifixion. This was Golgotha or Calvary, which was known as the place of a skull, probably because of the shape of the hill. There is an old tradition that Adam's skull was buried here. The cross beam was fixed to an upright pole driven into the ground and the victim stripped and placed on the cross, whilst being supported by a block. His clothes were the spoils of the executioners. The account tells that the Roman soldiers gambled for them. The method of crucifixion varied but it was a barbaric form of execution administered by the Romans to slaves and rebels against the state.

A title stating the crime was attached to the criminal's neck. However, you should note that no two gospels agree about the exact wording of the title. They all assume that the title made him a messianic pretender. It was written in Hebrew, Greek and Latin, the three languages most familiar to the people concerned.

Fig. 5.5 Methods of crucifixion

Jesus' cries from the cross are variously interpreted by Christians. The *tearing of the temple veil* is the symbol of the access that Christians have to God on account of the death of Jesus. It corresponds to the rending of the skies when he was baptised. The sour wine given him to drink was probably the *posca* which Roman soldiers drank. The darkness that covered the earth may have been an eclipse or a black sirocco wind. There were women nearby who saw the crucifixion. The centurion in charge paid Jesus the tribute of being a son of God, that is, someone extraordinary like the mythical heroes of Rome.

The account of the crucifixion is very restrained and unemotional. For Christians, it is the *meaning* of the death of Jesus that is important. *How do they interpret this?* Here are some of the ways in which they explain it:

1 Jesus offered his life as a *substitute* for the sins of the world; he paid the debt which sinners owe God on their behalf.
2 He died so that he might be proclaimed as the messiah; he had to offer his life and suffer in this way to show that he was *the saviour*.
3 He died on *behalf of his followers* and for the sake of those who had been his companions.
4 He died in order to *placate God* on behalf of the people who had incurred God's anger.
5 His death is the means of reconciling or bringing people together; it was an 'atonement'.
6 His death is a *prelude* to his glory; through offering his life as a sacrifice he achieved 'greatness'; his suffering as a victim is a prelude to his reign as a king.

Today, not all Christians find these images helpful. They prefer to explain the death of Jesus as a way of *bringing God and believers together and uniting them in one fellowship*. Jesus' death was an essential part of God's purpose for him. It is part of the kingdom in action. He died to show how compassionate God is in offering forgiveness. So Christians speak of *the death of Jesus as salvation* and of *Jesus as saviour*.

THE BURIAL (MARK 15.42–47; LUKE 23.50–56)

Why did Joseph of Arimathea arrive and offer a tomb for Jesus when none of his friends came to the rescue? The women who witnessed the crucifixion also saw where he was buried. Had Jesus or his family made arrangements for this beforehand? Joseph asked Pilate for the body of Jesus, and since the Jewish Sabbath was at hand there was little time to lose. The body was taken from the cross, wrapped in a shroud and buried in a tomb in a rock. Normally a Jew would be buried in his best clothes but Jesus' clothes had been taken from him. A shroud used to wrap around a body of someone buried in the manner of Jesus, with blood stains and a facial imprint, is preserved in the Cathedral at Turin. However, in 1988 scientific proof emerged to show that the cloth of the shroud was made in about the 13th century. The traditional site of the burial is the Church of the Holy Sepulchre in Jerusalem, which at the time was outside the city walls; another theory is that Jesus was buried in the garden tomb.

THE RESURRECTION

A few days after the burial the tomb was empty, and the body had mysteriously disappeared. Many Christians find the explanation difficult. Why is this? *What is the evidence?*

The empty tomb

The gospel writers report the story of the first Easter morning in this way:

MARK	MATTHEW	LUKE
Three women brought spices to anoint the body;	Two women looked for the tomb;	Three women took spices to the tomb;
They wondered who would roll away the stone;	There was an earthquake;	They entered the tomb;
The stone was already rolled away;	An angel rolled away the stone;	They could not find the body;
They entered the tomb and were alarmed;	The angel told the women that Jesus had been raised.	Two men in shining white stood beside them;
A young man in white told them that Jesus had been raised.		The men announced that Jesus had been raised.

You will see that the gospels agree in saying i) that women visited the tomb; ii) that they found it empty; iii) that they heard an announcement that Jesus has been raised.

What happened to account for this? Some say that this is the central mystery of the Christian faith. Various explanations have been offered, but you may consider the following:

  i) Joseph removed the body secretly or the Romans decided to rebury it;
  ii) Jews removed the body in case the place might become a centre of pilgrimage for his followers;
  iii) the women went to the wrong tomb and were under deep emotional strain and were confused about what they saw and heard;
  iv) Jesus did not finally die on the cross and his body was resuscitated.

Many Christians do not believe that these explanations account for what really happened. They say that Christianity teaches that Jesus is mysteriously alive and that he was raised from the tomb. *What is the basis of this belief?* The gospel writers refer to the *appearances* of Jesus in Jerusalem and Galilee to his disciples and others, although accounts of other appearances occur in the Gospel of John, in the Acts of the Apostles and in 1 Corinthians 15. The appearances recorded in the first three gospels are:

MARK	MATTHEW	LUKE
To Mary Magdalene	To two women	To two travellers to Emmaus
To two disciples	To eleven disciples	To his disciples
To eleven disciples		

You will notice that these appearances were made at different times and in a number of places. At first, the disciples did not recognise Jesus but once they knew who he was, they confessed that they had 'seen the Lord'.

What made the disciples so sure that it was Jesus? The one common feature is the Christian belief that Jesus had been raised from the grave. The disciples did not deny this once they had seen him; the belief caught on among the first Christians; it spread among people of different countries. *Why was this?*

After his resurrection the disciples call Jesus 'Lord'. It is as if they had seen a more exalted being. Only God could exalt him and each of the gospels report that 'Jesus was raised', that is, it was an act of God. He exalted Jesus at the end to show that he approved of him, as he declared at his baptism. *They believe that the resurrection is the ultimate sign of God's action in Christ.* At the end God vindicated everything he did.

You will find that Christians sometimes refer to the resurrection as an 'event', while others prefer to speak of it as an 'experience'. Some speak about the appearances as 'happenings'; others speak of them as 'explanations' of the belief that Jesus is mysteriously alive. *Basically, all Christians believe that the resurrection is an act of God which gives authority for believing in the living Christ.*

9 > WHO IS JESUS?

Christians regard Jesus as the centrepoint of Christianity. The gospel writers knew that the question, *Who is Jesus?* is important for Christians. Jesus also asked his disciples, *Who do people think I am? Or What are they saying about me?* Read the story of Jesus and his disciples at Caesarea Philippi (Mark 8.27–30). At the same time he asked his disciples who *they* thought he is. You should remember that the gospels don't tell us whether or not Jesus agreed with what people were saying about him. Instead, they tell us who they *thought* he was. The gospels declare their own view of Jesus, and include a number of titles of Jesus that *identify* who he is.

Messiah

This is the title given most often to Jesus. The gospels present him as someone who was chosen for a special task, and 'anointed' by God with special powers to accomplish it. Messiah was used so often that it became a common name for Jesus. Christians at first referred to him as 'the Christ' (messiah) and then simply as Jesus Christ.

Son of God

This is a title of intimacy which occurs at some strategic points in the story of Jesus, such as his baptism and transfiguration (Mark 1;9). It expresses the intimate relationship between Jesus and God. Jesus only uses it of himself rather overtly when speaking about the 'end things' (Mark 13.32), and during his trial before the high priest (Mark 14.61). God commends Jesus as his son, that is, someone who shares his nature. Son of God implies that Jesus' life expresses his 'oneness' with God. He conveys the spirit and will of God in his life and actions.

Son of Man

Jesus often uses this title of himself, not meaning that he is simply a human being, but that he (the Son of Man) has power to forgive sins, is Lord of the Sabbath, must suffer and die. At the same time, Jesus identifies himself with other people as the messiah who must suffer. As Son of Man he acts as a servant who gives his life a ransom for many. He will also return as judge and in the glory of his father to share a place of honour in his kingdom (Mark 8.38; 13.26; 14.64).

Lord

This was sometimes a title of courtesy, but also a title of dignity and authority. In this case it is a synonym for God, and conveys the divinity of Jesus, as he used it of himself (Mark 2.28; 11.3). It is interesting to note that a Syro-Phoenician (non-Jew) also called Jesus 'lord', but in this case it may mean no more than 'sir'.

Son of David

The messiah was commonly expected to be a descendant of King David, so Son of David became a traditional title for the expected messiah. He was expected to be a royal person, who would restore the fortunes of the Jewish nation. Bartimaeus addressed Jesus as the Son of David, probably meaning that he was a majestic person.

You will see from this list of titles that the gospel writers present Jesus in an exalted way. They thought that Jesus merited these titles; what is less certain is whether he used them himself. The first Christians were anxious to present Jesus in this way to prove that he was the messiah, and so to win people's allegiance to him. He himself preached about the Kingdom of God and only rarely used any special titles of himself.

10 > RESPONSES AND ESTIMATES

From the time he began his ministry, people began to respond to the teaching and claims which Jesus made. Broadly speaking there are two kinds of response that you will meet in the course of your studies: i) the response of believers; and ii) the response of opponents.

Those who believed, like the first disciples, responded to him by showing faith and commitment to his mission. This initial response was won from others during the course of his ministry. Their estimate of him is reported in the gospels and Jesus never lacked a following.

At the same time, he had to face opposition and unbelief. Sometimes this took the form of abuse or bitter jealousy. In other instances it was stubborn unbelief or murderous rage. Jesus had certain attitudes and ideals that won some to follow him and others to reject him outright. *The gospel writers present him as they saw fit.* They made their testimony through their writings; any unbiased reader will agree that from these writings there emerges a picture of an impressive and unique person who opens up a new way of approach to the mystery and meaning of life.

APPLIED MATERIALS

ALLEN, J. C., (1978). *The Way of the Christian*. Hulton Educational.
DALE, A. T., (1979). *Portrait of Jesus*. O.U.P.
DODD, C. H., (1971). *The Founder of Christianity*. Collins.
GREEN, M., (1981). *What is Christianity?* Lion.
MORGAN, D., (1987). *Jesus in the Synoptic Gospels.* Mowbray.

EXAMINATION QUESTIONS

QUESTION

Set out briefly some relevant points from the teaching of Jesus which describes the Kingdom of God as already present.   (WJEC)

OUTLINE ANSWER

In order to answer this question you must show that you understand the meaning of the Kingdom of God. That is, this is 'God's reign' or 'God's rule'. It means that God reigns wherever the kingdom is present.

You should refer to the announcement which Jesus made about the kingdom having arrived. This means that because he is present so is the rule of God. He shows how the kingdom works by his own presence and his works. He also implies that the kingdom is not a visible kingdom but it is the rule of God in human life.

He taught that the kingdom is present by teaching parables about it. You need to select examples that illustrate this and show why these are relevant. In each case you should highlight the point of the teaching so that it refers to the 'kingdom present'.

Finally you should conclude your answer with a summing up of your discussion.

A STUDENT'S ANSWER WITH EXAMINER'S COMMENTS

QUESTION

a) i) From what social classes did Jesus call his disciples?
    ii) Why do you think he did not call some of the Pharisees and priests instead?   *(6)*
b) i) What do you think their friends may have said when the first disciples followed Jesus?
    ii) What do you think people today would say if someone gave up his work in order to follow Jesus?   *(4)*
c) How did the teaching of Jesus differ from the teaching of the Jewish teachers of his time?   *(4)*
d) Describe the groups of people Jesus called 'happy' or 'blessed' in the beatitudes.   *(6)*
                                                                                                                        (WJEC)

a) i) He called them from the working class mainly such as fishermen and also from other classes such as Matthew the tax collecter. Matthew would have been classed as a sinner because of his job.

ii) He did not call any of the Pharisees or priests mainly because they wouldn't have listened to him and they would have put him into jail before he had time to spread his word. And also they were so self righteous that they thought that there was nothing more to learn about God.

b) i) The friends probably would have laughed at the disciples and told them that they were mad dropping everything just to follow some mad man who claimed that he was the Son of man.

ii) Today the attitude of people would vary more because some people would have to above attitude while others would admire the person who did just that and was willing to give up everything for what they believed in. Many people do give up a lot to follow Jesus now, as monks, nuns, and people who go to poor places to help the poor.

c) Jesus taught that God loved and forgave you. that he would forgive your sins, and that you should be humble towards him and love your neighbour even if he is your enemy you should still love him. The Jewish teachers of the time though taught that if you did anything wrong God would punish you and you would go to hell. Jesus taught that that if you sinned and repented you would be forgiven and go to heaven. The Jewish teachers taught that you should keep all the Jewish laws such as not doing anything on the Sabbeth, be ritually clean and generally very cerimonious about everything. They also taught that the messiah would come and overthrow the Romans by bringing in armies and there would be great battles.

d) The groups he called the happy and blessed were the poor and sinners and also people who, had seen the light and realised who god really was and that he was the Son of God. They were the people who thought it more important to be rich in the heart than to be wealthy in terms of money.

Comments

This answer is only satisfactory in parts. There are gaps in your knowledge of the subject. You must make fuller use of the content of your syllabus. In part a) you must mention the other groups from whom the disciples came, e.g. Zealots etc. You must also refer to the religious views of the Pharisees and priests as reasons for Jesus not calling them, e.g. he was not an official religious leader, they could not accept him as the messiah and God's Son.

In part b) you should think positively about why the disciples were ready to follow him – he made certain claims, he offered a new message, he spoke about God's kingdom etc. People today may follow the example of Jesus by service, by doing good works or by joining with other Christians.

In c) you make some useful points but you must arrange them more systematically. If you can, try to support your points by giving examples or evidence. As well as saying what the Jews taught, you need to show how the teaching of Jesus is different.

Part d) is the weakest as you have not studied the 'beatitudes' which tell about the people who Jesus called 'happy'. You have only offered a very garbled response. Remember that you must show your knowledge in a clear way – but to do this you must *learn* the information.

CHAPTER 6

CHRISTIANITY: GROWTH AND PRACTICES

GETTING STARTED

The syllabus items we shall consider in this chapter are the growth of Christianity and its practices. You should of course consult your own syllabus for details of these topics.

The story of Christianity after the ascension of Jesus is wrapped up with the story of the Christian Church. His followers remained together after his departure until the first great forward movement of the Day of Pentecost. Whilst they were together in Jerusalem, the Holy Spirit descended on the disciples in a dramatic experience, as if a mighty wind was blowing and a strange power was possessing them. Afterwards, *Peter* stood up and addressed the pilgrims who had come from many parts of the world to celebrate the Feast of Pentecost.

This cosmopolitan gathering foreshadowed the world wide spread of Christianity. When Peter had declared the things that Jesus had done and achieved, the impact was electric and three thousand people were baptised into the new faith.

ESSENTIAL PRINCIPLES

The converts formed an active and intimate community which was the nucleus of the Christian Church. It had neither a formal organisation, nor a visible badge or emblem. It was a community of young Christians who joined together to learn from the apostles about Jesus; to share fellowship meals together; to pray; to share their possessions; and to praise God. They soon referred to themselves as an *ecclesia*, a Greek word which means 'assembly' or 'community'. Jesus had used the word when he told Peter that he would build his Church (ecclesia) (Matthew 16.19). Christians still speak of the Church as a community of believers.

IMAGES OF THE CHURCH

When Christians describe this community or the Church they often use images. Three images are used today, as they were in the time of the early Christians. These are:

The Church is the body of Christ

If you think of the human body as an organism made up of different parts that work together in harmony, then you can see *why* Christians describe the Church as a body. It consists of many members, who belong together to form one body (the Church), and all work in harmony because they are united with Christ.

The Church is a family or household of faith

Just as the human family belongs together, has common interests, and every member is part of the family and carries the family name, so members of the Church belong together, share the same faith, and call themselves Christians.

The Church is the people of God

A 'people' is a corporate unit, but everyone who belongs to a 'people' has the same origin and destiny, and their own identity and characteristics. In the Old Testament, Israel was called the 'people of God', while in the New Testament, the Early Church is called the 'new people of God'. You should read 1 Corinthians 12.14; Ephesians 4.12; Colossians 1.11; Galatians 6.10 to learn more about these images.

THE FIRST CHRISTIANS

The first Christians met in private houses and open places. Some of them were women, who were called the 'co-workers' of the apostles. The day-to-day affairs of the Church were in the hands of the apostles, *Peter* being the most prominent. From the Day of Pentecost he was the leader of the young church and was active as a preacher and healer. He defended the new faith with great courage and was imprisoned by the Jewish authorities for his activities (Acts 4.1–31).

   The young church took an important step towards being a universal community at the *Council of Jerusalem*. The Council was called to settle a dispute about whether Gentiles (non-Jews) must first become Jews before becoming true Christians. *James* presided, but Peter gave the main address. Peter said that God did not make any difference between Jews and Gentiles, because everyone was saved by the grace of the Lord Jesus. *Paul* and *Barnabas* also spoke on behalf of the Gentiles. The council then decided to send letters to the churches, admitting the Gentiles. Peter spent his last years in Rome; tradition says that he died during Nero's persecution in 64 CE.

THE COMMON LIFE

One feature of the community was that its members:

   would sell their property and possessions, and distribute the money among all, according to what each one needed.

It was a 'communistic' community, in which everyone had equal shares. They had a common fund, in the same way that Jesus and his disciples had their community fund, with Judas Iscariot as the treasurer. The community did not own property but shared its goods to help each member. Barnabas sold his land and gave the proceeds to the community (Acts 4.36–37). They didn't all live off the common fund, but anyone in want was cared for, so that 'there was no one in the group who was in need'.

The widows were especially cared for, but this caused problems, especially in the Church in Jerusalem where there were Greek- and Jewish-speaking members. The Greek-speaking widows were a special charge on the common fund and were given charity or food daily, but according to the Greek Christians, they were being neglected. Immediately the apostles stepped in to settle the matter and chose seven men to look after the interests of these widows. They became known as *deacons* (although the name is not mentioned) (Acts 6.1–7).

PERSECUTION

The early Christians were under fire from the beginning. Peter and the other apostles were marked men, but the first to die as a martyr was *Stephen*. He was one of the deacons appointed to administer charity to the widows, but was also a preacher and healer. Some Jews who were once slaves came from Cyrene and Alexandria and accused Stephen of speaking against the law of Moses. Stephen made a spirited defence before the high priest and the Jewish Council. This infuriated them, and they rushed at him, hounded him out of the city and stoned him to death (Acts 6.8–7.60). In the fourth century the Church began to celebrate Stephen's martyrdom, and in the next century his body is said to have been discovered by *Gamaliel*, in a vision to Lucian not far from Jerusalem. Today the Church observes St Stephen's day on 26 December.

2 ▷ **SAUL OF TARSUS**

Someone who approved the death of Stephen was *Saul of Tarsus*. He was well known enough to be mentioned by name, and at the time was causing havoc for the young church, going from house to house, dragging off men and women, and having them put in jail. He received permission from the high priest in Jerusalem to go to Damascus, to round up Christians and bring them bound to Jerusalem.

From now on, Saul of Tarsus is at the centre of the story of the early Church. He was a religious genius before he became a Christian. He was a Jew, a strict observer of the Law, and a Pharisee. He had inherited Roman citizenship through being born in Tarsus about 10 CE. He studied in Jerusalem under a famous teacher called *Gamaliel*, and was present when Stephen was condemned to die. But on the way to Damascus he was converted to Christianity. A bright light shone around him and he was thrown to the ground. He heard Jesus calling to him, commanding him to stop persecuting the Church. Saul was struck blind and entered Damascus sightless (Acts 9).

Paul (as he became known) had never met Jesus, but Jesus' appearance to him on the Damascus road is one of the most dramatic post resurrection appearances. Paul was converted to Christianity and became the foremost champion of the Christians. In Damascus he was cured of his blindness by *Ananias* and received by the Church. Why the Christians received someone who had been their sworn enemy so readily is not mentioned, but straightaway Paul began to preach that *'Jesus is the Son of God'*. Paul dominated the story of the church for the rest of his lifetime. Some Christians say he is the greatest Christian of all times. He rendered three outstanding services to the church as a missionary, a church builder, and a writer.

Figs. 6.1–6.3 Paul's missionary journeys

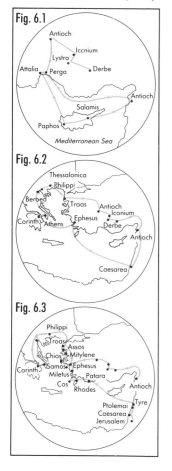

PAUL THE MISSIONARY

After escaping from the Jews of Damascus, Paul went to Jerusalem to meet the church leaders, and then to Tarsus. *Barnabas* persuaded Paul to return with him to Antioch and two years later in about 45 CE he and Paul set out on their first missionary journey (See Fig. 6.1). Check the route of the journey on this map and read the account in Acts 13–14. Make your own notes on the expansion of Christianity during this journey.

After the Council of Jerusalem Paul set off on another missionary journey, this time on his own (see Fig. 6.2). He visited Macedonia, Athens, Corinth, and returned via Miletus, Caesarea and Jerusalem to Antioch. Again, trace the route on this map and read the account of the journey in Acts 15–18. Make your own notes on the main events during this journey.

Paul began his third missionary journey in about 53 CE (see Fig. 6.3). It began with a visit to Galatia and Phrygia, then on to Ephesus where he stayed for more than two years. He was back in Jerusalem by 58 CE. Trace the route on the map and read the account in Acts 18.24–20. Make notes on the chief happenings.

Paul probably travelled fifteen thousand kms on these journeys. In the Book of Acts, Luke only gives an outline of Paul's work and a lot happened that we don't know about. But we have enough to sketch a picture of Paul's immense service to the Christian Church. He himself wrote an account of his experiences during his travels:

> 'Five times I was given the thirty nine lashes by the Jews; three times I was whipped by the Romans; and once I was stoned. I have been in three shipwrecks, and once I spent twenty four hours in the water. In my many travels I have been in danger from floods and from robbers, in danger from fellow Jews and Gentiles; there have been dangers in the cities, dangers in the wilds, dangers on the high seas, and dangers from false friends. There has been work and toil; often I have gone without sleep; I have been hungry and thirsty; I have often been without food, shelter or clothing'.
>
> (2 Corinthians 11.24–27)

Paul wrote this about eight or ten years before he died. There was still another shipwreck to come (on the voyage to Rome) as well as two periods in prison at Caesarea and Rome. It is generally assumed that Paul died during Nero's persecution.

PAUL THE CHURCH BUILDER

Although Paul never actually erected or set up a church building, he was a church builder in two other senses. *Firstly*, he helped to found new churches, that is, communities of Christians. *Secondly*, he helped to build up their life by instructing and encouraging them.

The Church grew rapidly during Paul's lifetime. As a founding missionary he visited and revisted local churches, to work out his plan for the whole church. Those people who joined Christian communities often came from pagan backgrounds and didn't always find it easy to live up to the high standards set by their faith. Paul insisted that their life together must be worthy of Christ, as wrong behaviour would rock the Church. The Church had to be the guardian of the faith and be united in love and obedience. His vision was of a universal church which extended to every part of the expanding Roman Empire.

Paul's work as a church builder was effective; converts came from all classes; he visited important cities, but also less significant places; he visited culturally backward areas; Jews and Gentiles joined the Church. Paul ensured that the essential content of the Christian faith was presented to churches, so as to protect them from mis-interpreting or misrepresenting their faith. There was some diversity in the organisation of the Church, but Paul worked to maintain its spiritual unity. By the time he died there were churches in all the main centres of the empire and the process had begun of organising the churches in a more unified way (see Fig. 6.4).

PAUL THE LETTER WRITER

It is not difficult to visualise Paul writing a letter and sending it by courier to one of the churches of Asia Minor or Europe. He wrote his letters in different places – the home of a friend, or from prison. Some letters were written in response to a request from one of the

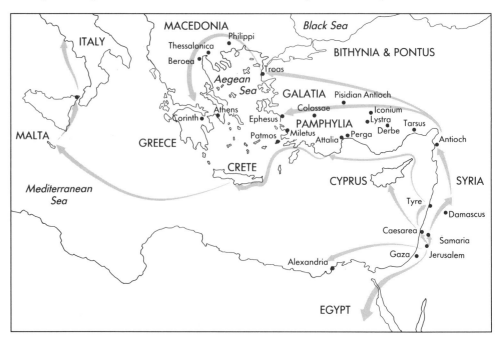

Fig. 6.4 The spread of Pauline churches

churches for guidance on a problem, to settle a dispute or to explain and present some aspect or other of the Christian faith. An occasional letter was in reply to news he had received from a church. Most of them were written to churches, but a few were to individuals, such as the letter to Philemon or Titus and Timothy, although some scholars question whether he was the author of these last letters.

It is important to remember that these are letters *not* books or essays or treatises. They are letters to friends and churches that Paul knew and had visited. They give a good picture of Paul the man. The style is fairly common – Paul introduces himself and sends greetings to the church, then he deals with the main subject of his letter – usually to present and explain the faith, and show how it can be put into practice. Finally, his letters end with greetings to his friends. Here is an illustration of the style of one of Paul's letters. The Christians at Philippi had sent him a gift and his letter is sent to acknowledge the church's generosity.

> From Paul and Timothy, servants of Christ Jesus – to all God's people in Philippi who are in union with Christ Jesus, including the church leaders and helpers:
> 'I thank my God for you every time I think of you; and every time I pray for you, I pray with joy because of the way in which you have helped me in the work of the gospel from the very first day until now. And so I am sure that God, who began his good work in you, will carry it on until it is finished on the Day of Christ Jesus. You are always in my heart'.

3 ▷ DIVISION AND UNITY

Today, Christianity is a world wide religion. It has spread through using many different methods and new ways and means of winning new converts. In the early period it used the *labours of specially gifted people*, such as missionaries, evangelists and teachers. *Ordinary Christians* shared their faith and spoke about it as they went about their daily tasks. The church also used *special methods* such as organised missions and campaigns to spread its message.

New experiments are being undertaken by Christians continually to spread their faith, as they believe that its prime task is to offer Christianity to everyone. You may consider *why* the Church is prepared to use all available aids, which include modern technology and communications in order to communicate its faith. Here are some of the key events in the growth of Christianity:

The apostles' mission . . . St Paul and the early apostles
Early Christian authors . . . from Ignatius to Augustine (110–430)
Conversion of Constantine . . . Edict of Milan 313
Ecumenical Councils . . . Nicaea 325–Nicaea 787
Mission of Gregory . . . Augustine sent to convert English
East-West division . . . 1054
Protestant Reformation . . . Martin Luther 1483–1546
Jesuit missions . . . India, Japan
Conversion of the New World . . . 1456–1514
Missions to China . . . 1513
Missions to Africa . . . 1840s
Vatican Councils . . . 1869–70; 1962–65
Ecumenical Movement . . . 1911
World Council of Churches . . . 1948

You will learn about these key events if you study a particular period of Christianity. This will be specified by your syllabus. Take note, however, of the special emphasis that Christianity places upon spreading its faith. From the beginning it has acted upon the command of Jesus: 'Go, then, to all peoples everywhere and make them my disciples'. Some churches believe this is the Church's main purpose in the world.

THE EASTERN AND WESTERN CHURCH

The Church in Rome assumed prominence because it was situated in the capital of the empire. It was headed by a *bishop* who became the figure-head of Christianity, and to whom other church leaders looked for leadership. The Church in Rome grew rapidly and by the third century there were some forty thousand Christians in Rome. It became a wealthy church and amassed property and estates. After *Constantine* issued the Edict of

Milan and restored property to the churches, Rome became more influential in the Christian world. The leaders of the five main churches of the empire – Rome, Alexandria, Antioch, Jerusalem and Constantinople, were known as *patriarchs*. But they did not all agree on matters of faith, and the government of the Church. So the first ecumenical (world wide) council of the Church was called at Nicaea in 325. The council was presided over by the Bishop *Athanasius*, and although it did not settle the differences, it did produce a creed (the Nicene creed) that is still in use.

The Church in the west used Latin as the official language, while that in the east used Greek. This caused difficulties in interpreting some parts of the creed. Other major difficulties concerned the authority of the bishop of Rome and the forms of worship. So a series of councils were called to try to settle these matters, at Nicaea, Constantinople and Ephesus and Chalcedon. Matters came to a head when the patriarch of Constantinople and the leaders of the church in the east condemned the way the church in the west was interpreting the person or status of Jesus Christ. The crux of the difficulty concerned the 'filioque' clause of the Nicene Creed which means literally 'and the son'. The Western Church maintained that 'the Spirit proceeds from the Father (God) *and* the Son (Christ), and demanded to keep the 'filioque' clause. The Eastern Church maintained that 'the Spirit proceeds from the Father'. The issue divided the Church in 1054, and Christianity was split between the eastern and western divide.

THE EASTERN ORTHODOX CHURCH

Today the Eastern Orthodox Church has about 75 million members and 300 bishops. Its strength is in Russia, Bulgaria, Hungary, Rumania, Czechoslovakia, Yugoslavia, Cyprus, Turkey and Greece. In Britain the Eastern Orthodox Church is small (it has about 4,000 members), but active. Its members are mainly people from eastern European countries who have settled in this country. It now has an archbishop and four auxiliary bishops. Co-operation between the Eastern Orthodox Church and other churches is amiable and the rich ritual of that church often adds colour to ecumenical worship.

Teaching

The faith of the Eastern Orthodox Church is rooted in scripture and in 'the tradition'. 'The tradition' refers to the decisions of the Ecumenical Councils of the Church. The teaching may be set out in this form:

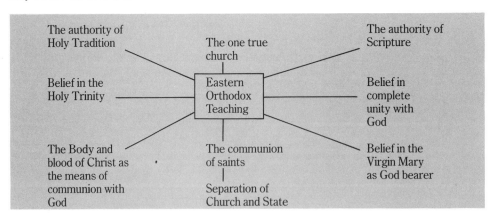

THE ROMAN CATHOLIC CHURCH

This is the great church of the west and today its numbers exceed 540 million all over the world. It's head is the pope, who is said by the church to be the successor of Peter. The name Peter – who was told by Jesus: 'you are a rock, and on this rock foundation I will build my church' – actually means 'rock', but non-Roman Catholic Christians interpret this to mean the 'rock' of Peter's faith. In 1870 the Vatican Council pronounced the pope to be 'infallible', that is, the guardian of the church's faith with authority to interpret it to the faithful.

Roman Catholics were granted civil rights in this country in 1829 and in 1850 the Roman Catholic hierarchy was restored when the head of the Catholic church in England became the Archbishop of Westminster. At the end of the 19th century there were 1,500 Roman Catholic churches in Britain; today, the number of members is around 4,250,000.

The main teaching of the Roman Catholic Church can be set out as follows:

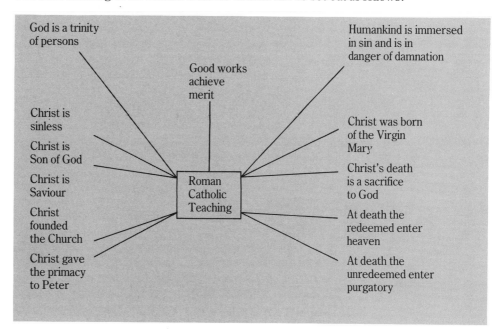

---

4 ⟩ REFORMATION

During the Middle Ages the Roman Catholic Church was supreme in Europe. However, by the end of the Middle Ages great changes were taking place in science and the arts. New continents were being discovered through the voyages of Vasco da Gama and Christopher Columbus, which gave European people a larger view of the world. There was a revival of learning and new developments in literature and art which is known as the 'renaissance'. One of the leaders of the new learning was *Erasmus* of Rotterdam who produced a version of the Greek New Testament that paved the way for the reformation of the Church.

At the time there was unease within the Church, and some felt the need for reform 'from within'. They wanted to reform the spiritual life of the Church and lead it away from some of its worldly ways. But the decisive step towards reformation was taken by *Martin Luther*.

Luther entered a monastery of the Augustinian Order as a monk, where he began to study the New Testament and the origins of Christianity. He surmised that the church was not following the teaching of the Bible and the Early Church in the way he believed it should. He came to a different understanding of Christianity from that of the Roman Church, and also believed that there were many church practices, such as selling pardons or indulgences, that went against the teaching of the New Testament. His idea was not to attack the Church, but to reform it.

One way to do this was to challenge the church authorities to debate the issues in public. So in 1519 Luther posted ninety five theses or propositions, which he wished to debate, on the door of the Cathedral Church of Wittenburg. The propositions did not please the church authorities, but they couldn't ignore them. Luther was called upon to debate his views before a number of church councils but his views were rejected. He refused to withdraw them or give them up and declared that he was bound to stand by them. His main teaching was that a person is saved by *faith in Christ*, and not by performing good works. 'Faith alone' in Christ's grace can save. This flew in the face of the official teaching of the church and Luther was excommunicated, or in other words, turned out.

Although excommunication was the ultimate punishment the Church could impose on any one, it did not deter Luther from preaching his views. Many people were ready to listen and follow Luther, and he won over political leaders and princes to his cause. As the reformation gathered momentum it spread to many parts of Germany; Protestant churches sprang up and the reformation spread to Switzerland, the Netherlands, England and Scotland. The break with the Roman Catholic Church was complete. Not all those who broke away followed Luther's teaching slavishly, and the reformation took its own course in different countries. Yet it sprang from Luther's protest and the impact of his teaching. These are its main features:

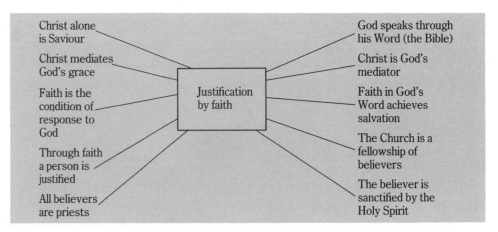

5 ▷ **COUNTER-REFORMATION**

The Roman Catholic Church reacted to the Protestant Reformation in a positive way. The counter-reformation was led by *Ignatius Loyola*, a Spanish nobleman, who aimed to reform the spiritual life of the Church. He founded a movement known as the Society of Jesus or *Jesuits* which was based on strict spiritual discipline and personal devotion to Jesus Christ. He made prayer and self discipline essential practices for all Jesuits. They were to be 'sanctified' and 'cleansed' by Christ. One special emphasis of the Jesuit movement was to spread the Christian faith. They sent missionaries to South America, the Mississippi valley in North America, and to Asia. The Jesuits became a powerful missionary movement which introduced Roman Catholic teaching to many parts of the world.

6 ▷ **FREE CHURCHES**

The Protestant Reformation reached England when King Henry VIII was on the throne. A delicate situation arose over the king's desire to divorce Catherine and marry Anne Boleyn. When the pope refused permission, Henry took things into his own hands and pronounced himself head of the English Church. Religious and political leaders rallied to the king's support. *Thomas Cranmer* prepared a prayer book for the English Church which included materials in line with the teaching of the continental reformers and the Early Church. The reform of the English Church continued under Edward, but when Mary came to the throne she sought to lead the Church back to Rome. However, by now the reformation had taken root in England and when Elizabeth I came to the throne she established herself as the head of the Church, as well as the state. She imposed a policy of uniformity on the Church which kept its affairs under the control of the state.

The more radical church people believed that this did not go far enough to reform the Church. They wanted a 'pure' Church and so they were called 'Puritans'. They rejected the right of the state to interfere in church affairs and claimed that the Church must be free to organise its own worship. The authority of the Church was in the *church* and not in the *government*. Parliament upheld the Established Church and there was a struggle, led by the Puritans, for the freedom to worship according to conscience. The struggle continued until the 17th century and many people suffered as a consequence. However, in the 17th century some 'independent' or 'free' churches were formed and the Free Church tradition in Britain was set on its way. These churches are sometimes called 'nonconformist' because they do not 'conform' to the state in matters of religion. The Free Churches are known by a variety of names which reflect differences between them on matters of church government and on baptism. The three main groupings of the Free Churches are:

Baptists	**Congregational**	**Presbyterian**
Belief in believers' baptism only.	Church and state separate.	Church governed by Christ and a hierarchy of church courts.
Church governed by the Holy Spirit.	Each congregation governed by Christ's Spirit.	
	Where Christ is, there is the church.	

From the English Presbyterian Church arose the:

Unitarians	**Quakers**
Belief in the spirit of free enquiry in religion.	The Holy Spirit is the sole inspirer of faith.
	Free operation of the Spirit without any church structure.

In the 18th century there arose the **Methodist Church** whose main beliefs include:

God's salvation is Christ offered to everyone.	Christ both sanctifies and justifies.	The church is a society of believers by God's grace.

The heyday of the Free Churches in Britain was the 19th century. They were centres of religious fervour and popular culture, and were particularly strong in the new centres of population. They produced many national and political leaders. During the 20th century the influence of the Free Churches has declined, while at the same time there has been a drawing together of all churches in closer co-operation. The major beliefs of the Free Churches may be set out in this way:

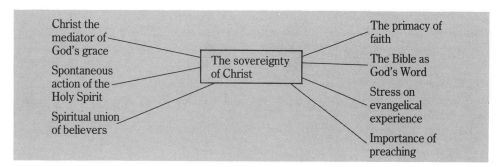

Christ the mediator of God's grace

Spontaneous action of the Holy Spirit

Spiritual union of believers

The sovereignty of Christ

The primacy of faith

The Bible as God's Word

Stress on evangelical experience

Importance of preaching

7 > WORLD CHURCH

In the 20th century there has been a notable movement to unite the churches. The word 'ecumenical' (world wide) is used to describe the movement that seeks to bring churches closer together, or to unite. The *World Council of Churches* was formed at Amsterdam in 1948, when one hundred and forty six separate Protestant Churches from all over the world formed a World Council and made a declaration:

> Here at Amsterdam we have committed ourselves afresh to him (Christ), and have covenanted with one another in constituting the World Council of Churches. We intend to stay together.

Many other Protestant Churches have since joined the World Council, whose head-quarters are in Switzerland. The Council works through five main divisions: Faith and Order; dialogue with people of living faiths; world mission and evangelism; theological education; church and society. The Eastern Orthodox and Roman Catholic Churches do not belong to the World Council of Churches, but observers attend the council meetings and there is co-operation on matters of common concern.

In Britain the *British Council of Churches* is formed by the Church of England and the Free Churches. It is a forum which deals with many aspects of church life where co-operation between them is possible. Churches which do not belong officially to the British Council send observers or consultants to their meetings. In many places there are 'ecumenical' experiments, which involve a number of different churches worshipping together and taking part in joint enterprises, including social and charitable work.

The movement towards re-uniting the churches this century has resulted in many churches forming a United Church. A notable example of this is the *Church of South India*, which was formed in 1947 between the Presbyterian and Congregational Churches, the Methodist Church and the Anglican South Indian dioceses. In 1970, the *Church of North India* was formed between Anglicans, Baptists, Congregationalists, Methodists and Presbyterians. In Britain in 1972 the *United Reformed Church* was formed as a result of a union between the Presbyterian Church of England and the Congregational Church. This was the first across-boundary union of churches in this country since the Reformation. A growing number of churches in Britain and throughout the world are seeking how they can draw closer together.

8 > WORSHIP AND CELEBRATIONS

WORSHIP

If you ask Christians why they 'go to church' on Sunday, they will probably reply 'to worship God'. They may attend any one of a number of churches and take part in different forms of worship, but there will always be some parts of worship that are common to all churches.

Case study on worship (1)

In the small village in the north of Scotland on a Sunday morning the bell calls the faithful to worship. Everyone going to church (kirk) carries a Bible. At ten o'clock the bell stops and the church organ is played. A short procession takes place, led by a church elder carrying an open Bible. He places the Bible on the communion table. The minister enters and invites the people to worship God. They join in singing hymns, prayers are said by the minister, but not from a prayer book. There are two readings from the Bible, a sermon and the benediction. The congregation stands as the minister leaves.

Case study on worship (2)

In an English town on Sunday evening the church bell calls the worshippers to evensong in the parish church. This is a style of worship which combines ancient and modern elements. First the choir and clergy process from the back of the church as a processional hymn is sung; the act of preparation and prayers for forgiveness; singing the psalm for the day; lesson from the Old Testament; the Magnificat; lesson from the New Testament; the Nunc Dimittis; prayers of intercession; the sermon; hymn; benediction; recession.

Questions

What do these two forms of worship have in common?
How do they reflect the variety of worship?
Why does evensong combine ancient and modern aspects?
What part does the congregation have in the worship?

SACRAMENTS

The two sacraments that are most widely administered by the Church are baptism and the eucharist (mass, Lord's supper, holy communion).

BAPTISM

Baptism is administered in two forms – infant and believers' baptism. In either case, it is an act of initiation and a visible sign of the union of the baptised with Christ and the Church.

Infant baptism

It is not certain when the Church began to baptise infants. A leading churchman named *Origen* who lived in the 2nd century said it had been practised from the beginning. The Early Church did conduct 'household' baptisms and these may have included children (Acts 16.15; 33; 1 Corinthians 1.16). Nowadays, the usual time for infant baptism is when the child is two or three months old.

Case study on infant baptism (1)

In the Eastern Orthodox Church the child is brought to be baptised on the eighth day. The ceremony begins with chanting of:

> Glory to God in the highest
> and peace on earth
> to men of goodwill.

The Lord's prayer is chanted and the priest moves forward, lays his hands on the child and offers a baptismal prayer. A hymn is sung and a procession moves towards the baptistry. The priest, deacon and servers join the procession and the gospel, a cross, lights and a censor are carried. At the baptistry the priest says:

> Be thou signed with the oil of unction,
> in the name of the Father, and of the Son,
> and of the Holy Spirit. Amen.

Further prayers are said and a chant is sung. The priest now blesses the child and then anoints it all over with oil. The child is held facing the east and is dipped by the priest three times into the font. The child is named and confirmed at one and the same time.

Case study on infant baptism (2)

The infant is brought by its parents and godparents to the English parish church. They take their place at the font near the entrance. The congregation is present and they sing a baptismal hymn. The priest introduces the service and reads from the gospel how Jesus welcomed children and blessed them. He then offers prayers for the child and its parents. Afterwards he takes the child, blesses it and addresses the parents and godparents on their responsibilities to bring up the child in the teaching of the church. They are asked to make a public promise to do so. The priest then baptises the child by placing water on the forehead in the sign of a cross and says . . . I baptise (then the child's name) in the name of the Father, the Son and the Holy Spirit. The child is handed back to the parents and the priest pronounces the benediction. When the child is of age the promises or vows made on its behalf will be confirmed in the church's act of confirmation.

Believers' baptism

The first Christians were baptised by immersion on confession of faith in Christ. In the early centuries baptism took place during the Easter vigil to symbolise how the believer passed from death and darkness to new life and light. This was a symbol of dying with Christ and being raised with him. Today, the believer undergoes a period of preparation for baptism, which normally takes place in a baptistry in church. A congregation is present and the ceremony includes a baptismal hymn and readings from the Bible. These usually are either about the journey of the Israelites through the desert on the way to the promised land, of Jonah being released from the belly of the great fish, or an account of baptism from the New Testament. Passing through the waters is also a symbol of release from sin and embarking on the new life of purity. A public declaration of faith in Christ is made by the believer, who is now admitted to full membership of the church.

HOLY COMMUNION

Christians have always celebrated the last supper of Jesus and his disciples. When they do they use bread and wine to symbolise his body and blood, but they give different meaning to the symbols. All believe that the authority for the communion (or the mass or eucharist of breaking bread) comes directly from Christ. It is summed up by Paul in his letter to the Christians in Corinth:

> For I received from the Lord the teaching that I passed on to you: that the Lord Jesus, on the night he was betrayed, took a piece of bread, gave thanks to God, broke it, and said, 'This is my body, which is for you. Do this in memory of me'. In the same way, after the supper he took the cup and said, 'this cup is God's new covenant sealed with my blood. Whenever you drink it, do so in memory of me'.

Case study on the Roman Catholic Mass

The congregation is assembled for the Sunday morning mass. The altar is prepared and the mass commences with a hymn sung by the congregation, then all repeat the words, 'In the name of the Father, and of the Son, and of the Holy Spirit', and make the sign of the cross. Then they sing the Gloria (Glory to God on high) and the priest offers a prayer for forgiveness. The priest, wearing special vestments (clothes) which denote that he is not acting on his own behalf, but on behalf of the church, takes his place at the altar where the candles are lit to symbolise Christ the light of the world. On the altar there is a plate for the bread and a chalice (cup) for the wine. Incense is burning as a symbol of God's presence.

The priest reads the gospel and the congregation recites the Nicene Creed. Further prayers are said and the Hail Mary, a special prayer to the Virgin Mary. This part of the mass ends with the Sanctus (Holy, holy, holy, Lord).

Now the priest consecrates the bread and wine and reads the words which Christ spoke at the last supper, when he broke the bread and blessed the wine. More prayers are said and the congregation recites the 'Our Father' (the Lord's prayer). The priest offers the congregation the 'Peace of the Lord', and they respond by making the sign of peace and greeting their neighbours.

The priest takes the bread and breaks it, whilst the congregation sings, 'Lamb of God, who takes away the sins of the world, have mercy upon us'. Now the congregation moves in orderly procession to the communion rail where they kneel to receive the bread (wafer), which is held by the priest over the chalice as it is given. The priest bids each eat the bread, which is the body of Christ. After everyone has eaten the bread, 'in accordance with the command of Christ', the priest drinks the wine from the chalice.

The mass ends with the priest saying prayers and the blessing.

Case study on the Holy Communion (Lord's Supper) in a Free Church

The communion table is covered with a white cloth and trays of bread and individual cups of wine. The minister gives an invitation to those present to share in the Holy Communion.

The minister offers the peace of the Lord Jesus Christ and the congregation share this with their neighbours. The offerings of the people are collected and brought to the table and dedicated. A hymn may also be sung.

The minister reads the words of the institution as given by St Paul. Then the bread is distributed by servers to the congregation who serve each other as a sign of the priesthood of all believers. Usually, all eat the bread together in remembrance of Christ. Afterwards the wine is distributed and all drink together in remembrance of Christ.

The minister offers prayers of thanksgiving, and there may be a final hymn before the blessing.

A case study on the eucharist in an Eastern Orthodox Church

The congregation is assembled and they stand in the centre of the church. The clergy take their place behind the screen. The deacon forms a link between clergy and people.

The reader sings the epistle in the body of the church, and the book of the gospel is carried into the midst of the people. The gospel is now sung by the deacon. All take part in the offertory. During this there is a solemn procession when the bread and wine are carried.

A prayer is said for the descent of the Holy Spirit. Then the curtain across the central doors of the screen is drawn during the breaking of bread and the communion of the clergy. The communion of the people now follows as the priests stand before the holy doors and are assisted by the deacon.

You will see from the three case studies that the Holy Communion is observed differently in different churches. It is the *meaning* given to the sacrament that is most significant. These are some of the points of difference between the Roman Catholic and Protestant Churches:

- the sacrament is a *sign* of grace (Protestant) but it *confers* grace (Roman Catholic);
- the bread and wine are *symbols* of Christ's body and blood (Protestant) but they *contain* the body and blood of Christ (Roman Catholic);
- the sacrament is an act of *remembrance* (Protestant) but is a true and proper *sacrifice* offered to God (Roman Catholic);
- the sacrament is an act of *communion* (Protestant) but is a *propitiation* (= to atone or make favourable) for the living and dead (Roman Catholic);
- the sacrament does not require a *permanent order of priests* (Protestant) but requires a permanent order of priests instituted by Christ with power to consecrate the sacrifice of the mass (Roman Catholic).

PRAYER AND PRAISE

Prayer

Prayer is a feature of worship in all churches. There are no set rules and the practice of prayer may differ from one church to another. Usually the prayers are led by the priest, or minister, or whoever conducts the worship. The congregation respond by saying 'Amen'. Certain prayers may be said by the whole congregation and there may be time for silent prayer. Many churches have official prayer books or set forms of prayer, whereas in others the prayers are spontaneous. In the Church of England, for example, a service book is used which contains set prayers, but in a Pentecostal Church and many Free Churches the prayers are spontaneous. In the Roman Catholic Church the worshipper may use a rosary as an aid to prayer. The rosary consists of five sets of beads, with each set separated so that the worshipper can repeat the Hail Mary:

Hail Mary, full of grace,
The Lord is with you.
Blessed are you among women
and blessed is the fruit of your womb, Jesus.
Holy Mary, Mother of God,
Pray for us sinners now and at the hour of
our death. Amen.

Christian prayer is a form of communion with God and most prayers end with 'through Jesus Christ our Lord'. Prayer is usually *adoration* – its focus is 'God is great'; or *thanksgiving* – it delights in God's goodness and providence; or *petition* – asking for forgiveness; or *intercession* – asking on behalf of others. Christians are taught to pray regularly and believe that prayer is one way in which they respond to God. It is acting on their faith that Jesus is mysteriously present and that they can converse with God as a personal being. Prayer is their means of seeking to experience God for themselves. They do not include prayer in their worship as just a useful practice, but as a way of communing with God and meeting their own needs.

Praise

Praise is interwoven into Christian worship. At first, the singing of psalms had a unique place in the Church's worship, but slowly, other hymns than psalms found their way into worship, and in the course of time their numbers grew quite considerably. For the first thousand years Latin hymns abounded and hymn singing became a regular feature of church worship. A famous churchman named *Ambrose*, who lived in the fourth century, gave direction to the music and hymnology of the Roman Catholic Church. Christians still use the *Te Deum* which he composed. In the time of the Protestant Reformation many innovations took place, including singing religious songs in the language of the people, and carols. Luther composed many congregational hymns which helped to spread the reformation across Europe. In the 18th century many famous hymn writers such as *Isaac Watts, Philip Dodderidge, Charles Wesley*, and other evangelical leaders added to the store of Christian hymns. In the 19th century *Newman* and *Keble* contributed notable hymns. In recent times, new hymns have been composed for church worship in a modern idiom and set to modern music. Here is an example:

> I want to go out,
> I want to go home,
> I want to be single,
> I want to belong,
> I want to grow up,
> I want to stay young,
> I want to do both and all at once and anything else that takes my fancy whether it hurts or helps to pass the time of day:
> show me the way!
>
> (David Goodall)

THE PLACE OF WORSHIP

Christians meet for worship in a church. Church is the name used of a community of worshippers, but also for the *place* of worship. In the latter sense, a church is a consecrated building and every part is meant to focus attention on the purpose of worship. A church building is not just a structure, and the different styles of church building reflect the different styles of worship. From visiting a church and noting its form and its furnishing, it is possible to form a picture of the kind of worship that takes place in it.

"" The variety of Christian worship. ""

Inside an Anglican Church

The central part of the church is the *nave* where the congregation sits. It is often compared to a ship (navis = ship) from the time when the clergy were described as the mariners and the people as passengers on the sea journey of life.

The *chancel* is divided between the *sanctuary* at the furthest end, and the *choir*, which is raised above the floor level of the nave.

The *altar* stands at the east end towards the sanctuary. It may be simple or ornate and covered with embroidered drapings. A *cross* and candles stand on the altar. It is the focus of the church building. It is set apart to create a feeling of mystery and awe. The altar is divided from the choir and sanctuary by the altar rails.

The *pulpit* is placed in the nave and may be made of wood and octagonal in shape and carved with tracery and figures from Christian history. The pulpit became a feature of most churches in the 15th century.

The *lectern* stands opposite the pulpit. A lectern may be carved in the shape of an eagle and made in brass or wood. The spread of the wings symbolises the spread of God's Word.

The *font* stands near the west door and is shaped like a basin on a pedestal. It has a cover of wood which was originally intended to keep superstitious people from taking the holy water, which was thought to have healing properties.

On the walls, there may be paintings, which in earlier times were placed there to teach the story of Christianity. Stained glass windows also had this purpose, but today they may be more decorative and symbolic.

Inside an Eastern Orthodox Church

The shape of an Eastern Orthodox Church is that of a Greek cross with a massive dome over the centre.

The church is divided between the '*hieron*', the place where the liturgy is celebrated, and the 'naos', the place where the congregation assembles.

Between the two parts there is a solid *screen* (ikonostasis) which is covered with pictures and has three doors. The centre door is the 'Royal or Holy Door', the north door is the 'Servers' door and the south door is the 'Deacons' Door'.

There are no seats, but on the walls and pillars there are *ikons* and places for the candles that are burnt during the worship.

The *altar* is on the east side and behind this is the bishop's throne. On the altar there is a large painted picture of Christ. The altar is covered with a white cloth and the holy book of the gospels is set on it.

Inside a Free Church

The furnishings of a Free Church are usually less ornate. There is a central *pulpit* and under this the *communion table*. The pulpit may be covered with a fall with the letters IHS (the first letters of the Greek name for Jesus) or INRI (an abbreviation of the Latin for Jesus of Nazareth, King of the Jews). The pulpit may be carved with symbols or figures from the Bible, telling the story of Christianity. The symbols of Christianity are drawn mostly from the world of nature (the fish, eagle, water, wine, bread, oil, stars, wind) and these may be found on some of the furnishings. On the communion table there may be a cross. The most common is the Latin cross, but a Calvary cross (with three steps to symbolise faith, hope and love) or a Celtic cross (with a circle at the juncture of the upright and cross beams) may be used.

CELEBRATIONS

The church's year revolves around events in the life of Jesus. Other festivals and celebrations may be kept, such as harvest, or the founding of a local church, or to remember a notable Christian from the past. *Sunday* is observed as a holy day. The Early Church assembled on Sunday to remember the resurrection of Jesus, and it continues to be a day of assembly for worship. Some Christians refer to it as the 'Lord's Day' and believe it should be kept completely as a day of worship and rest. These Christians oppose all kinds of organised work on Sunday.

> How the universal Church celebrates the Christian year.

Advent

Advent begins the church's year when Christians prepare to celebrate the advent (drawing near or coming) of the child Jesus, and remember his promise that he will come again in glory to judge the world.

Advent begins on the fourth Sunday before Christmas day and in many churches an Advent candle is lit. On each of the following Sundays until Christmas another candle is lit, as a symbol to light the way to the child Jesus. Children may be given an Advent calendar to mark off the days to Christmas. In church services during Advent suitable hymns are sung and there are appropriate readings from the Bible which tell about the coming of the messiah. Sermons are also preached on the theme of Christ's coming. This side of Advent is joyful but there is also a solemn aspect as Christians examine their own lives in preparation for the return of Christ. He said that he would return without warning, like a 'thief in the night', when he is not expected. Christians believe they must be ready to receive him and some may spend time in fasting during Advent as a sign that they are prepared for his coming.

Christmas

The Roman festival of the sun fell on 25 December and was a time of great revelry and joyous celebrations. Christmas is the most popular Christian festival, but not all Christmas customs are of Christian origin. The Christian symbols of Christmas are often intermingled with others. Shops display scenes of the birth of Jesus alongside scenes of merrymaking and non-Christian celebrations.

The Church celebrates Christmas by decorating the church with symbols of the story of the birth of Jesus – the crib and the holy family; the star and the angels; the shepherds and the wise men. Special Christmas services are held on Christmas eve (the Christmas vigil) and on Christmas day. Christmas carols are sung (a carol is a song, dance or folk song that tells the story of the birth of Jesus) and a nativity play may be performed. The lessons and sermon focus on the birth of Jesus and its meaning.

Christians believe that the birth of Jesus heralded good will to the world and they celebrate this by exchanging greetings and gifts. Families gather together and children receive presents from *Saint Nicholas* (Santa Claus). Homes are decorated with lights and trimmings and evergreens. There is also a Christmas tree, decorated with lights and gifts. A conscious effort is made to generate a spirit of happiness and peace.

Lent

Lent is a very old name for the lengthening of the days of spring after winter. It is a period of fasting for Christians that starts on Ash Wednesday and continues for forty days and six Sundays before Easter day. Ash Wednesday is so called because of the old custom of placing a piece of ash on the forehead in the form of a cross and wearing sackcloth as a sign of penitence.

On the previous day, Shrove Tuesday (shrove = shriven), fats and cream may be cleared from the house and all revelry and sports come to an end for the period of Lent. At one time Shrove Tuesday was a day for confessing sins to a priest, i.e. 'shriven' for one's sins. Then on Ash Wednesday, a special prayer may be offered for protection from further sins. As a sign of this the priest may sprinkle water on the ash before it is placed on the forehead as a sign of protection. The prayer is:

Lord, protect us in our struggle against evil.
As we begin the discipline of Lent,
Make this day holy by our self denial.

Holy Week

Christians call the seven days before Easter *Holy Week*, when they follow the progress of Jesus during his last week in Jerusalem. They regard these days as the most significant events in Christianity and they seek to relive them by following the progress of Jesus from his entry into the city until his burial. The narrative of the events may be read in church services and Christians observe them as a time of solemn remembrance.

Palm Sunday

The Church celebrates the entry of Jesus into Jerusalem in different ways. In some churches, there are processions with branches of palms and special services are held when the story of Jesus' entry into the city is read, and hymns in praise of his triumph are sung. The branches may be in the form of small crosses and are blessed by the priest.

Maundy Thursday

Maundy means 'command' and today the Church observes it in different ways. Some Christians recall the command of Jesus to wash each other's feet and they hold a symbolic feet-washing service. They also recall the command of Jesus to his disciples that they should love one another and so they give gifts of charity. In the Church of England the queen distributes 'maundy money' to needy people in a cathedral church, as an act of love. In the evening of Maundy Thursday many churches hold services of Holy Communion to commemorate the last supper before Jesus entered the Garden of Gethsemane.

Good Friday

This is the Church's most solemn day. It is sometimes called 'Black Friday'. Special services are held to commemorate the crucifixion of Jesus, and which may last for three hours – the time that Jesus was on the cross. The story of the crucifixion is read and explained and Jesus' love and sacrifice are extolled. The services on Good Friday are unadorned, that is, all decorations are removed, and in the Roman Catholic Church there is a service of 'venerating the cross' when the priest and people bow and kiss the cross. An ancient custom is that of eating hot cross buns on Good Friday; these are spiced buns marked with a cross, which originally signified the end of the fast of Lent.

Easter

Easter centres on the death and resurrection of Jesus. Easter is a form of an Anglo Saxon word (Eostre) for the goddess of spring. It is the most joyful of the church's celebrations.

In the second century it was customary to hold an Easter vigil on the night that Christ 'passed over' from death to life and to prepare to receive the new life of the resurrection.

The church is usually decorated with spring flowers for the services on Easter day. In the Roman Catholic Church a paschal candle is lit and carried into the darkened church to symbolise the new light of Christ's resurrection. The worshippers light their candles from this, until the whole church is a blaze of light. The Easter paschal candle may be marked with the wounds of Christ and the first and last letters of the Greek alphabet (alpha and omega) which are used of Christ. The clergy wear their brightest vestments on this day. On Easter day the church bells are rung for the first time since before Good Friday and the service begins with a hymn of resurrection. The readings tell the story of the resurrection and the sermon is on the theme of the 'new life' of Christ. Worshippers may join in the ancient response: *The Lord is risen! He is risen indeed!*

In the Eastern Orthodox Church, Easter is the 'feast of feasts'. The celebration begins with the dawn of Easter day. Clergy and people come in a procession to the church, just as the women went to Jesus' tomb in the morning. They process around the church three times and then pause at the door until it is opened. The closed door is a symbol of the sealed tomb. The people wait for the priest's blessing and announcement: *Christ is risen from the dead: By death he has trampled down death: And to those who are in the grave he has given new life*. The people repeat the words and then a bell is rung. The door swings open and the procession moves into the church, with everyone carrying a lighted candle. During the service the worshippers greet each other joyfully: *Christ is risen!* And the reply comes: *Risen indeed!*

Pentecost (Whitsun)

Fifty days after Easter the Church celebrates Pentecost and the coming of the Holy Spirit to the disciples in Jerusalem. This initiated a period of intense fervour among the disciples and three thousand were baptised into the Christian community or Church. Today, the church celebrates this event as the 'birth' of the Church. New Christians used to be baptised on this day and it became known as Whit Sunday (Whit = white), since they dressed in white as a sign of purity. Many churches hold processions of witness on this Sunday or services with appropriate hymns on the theme of the Holy Spirit. Where the clergy wear vestments the colour is red, to symbolise the flames of fire in which the Holy Spirit descended to the disciples.

9 > PILGRIMAGE

Pilgrimage is not compulsory in Christianity but Christians often use its imagery to describe the journey of life. The first Christians were called 'people of the Way' and ever since, Christians have thought of themselves as pilgrims on a journey. Many Christian hymns use this image, but probably the most famous example is John Bunyan's *Pilgrim's Progress*. To many Christians pilgrimage is like an inner journey, or the *pilgrimage of the soul*, which leads them to God.

Even so, from early times Christians have made journeys to places associated with the story of Jesus and the saints of the Church. At the time of the major festivals pilgrims visit *Bethlehem*, where Jesus was born and *Jerusalem*, where he died. They visit the Church of the Nativity and the grotto in Bethlehem, or join pilgrims along the route Jesus followed on his way to Golgotha. They pause at each of the 'stations' of the cross and recall the story of Jesus on his journey. On Easter day there are processions to the Church of the Holy Sepulchre or some may visit the garden tomb.

Pilgrimages were popular in the Middle Ages, not only to sacred sites in the Holy Land (Palestine), but also to places in Europe associated with the apostles and saints. *Rome* was one such place; the Church of St Peter's is said to contain the tomb of Peter and maybe that of Paul as well. *Santiago de Campostela* in Spain became a famous place of pilgrimage in the ninth century, as it was thought that James the apostle was buried there. In England, *Canterbury* became a place of pilgrimage after the murder of *Thomas a' Becket* before the high altar in the cathedral in the twelfth century. Three years later he was canonised as a saint and his tomb is one of the main centres of pilgrimage in the west. The tomb of *St Cuthbert* in *Durham*, *Lindisfarne* off Northumberland where *St Aidan* made his head-quarters, and *Walsingham* in Norfolk are some examples of sacred places for Christians in England. In Scotland, Ireland and Wales, places associated with the Celtic saints have been centres of pilgrimage for many centuries, notably *Iona* in Scotland, where *St Columba* landed in 597, *Downpatrick* in Ireland, the site of the tomb of *Patrick*, and *St David's* in Wales, the site of the tomb of *St David*, the patron saint.

Pilgrimage is an act of piety and a search for spiritual blessing. Some Christians make pilgrimage in the hope of receiving some spiritual blessing or healing. *Lourdes* in France is a popular centre of pilgrimage for people in search of healing. Here, a young girl named *Bernadette* said she saw a vision of the Virgin Mary many times. Once, the Virgin pointed to the ground and a spring of water gushed forth. This is believed by many to have been a miracle and that the waters have special healing powers. Pilgrims visit the spot in droves, in the hope of tasting the waters and being cured. Even if they do not find physical healing they say they find inner peace from visiting the place.

10 > LIFE STYLE

BIRTH AND CHRISTENING

Christians do not observe any special birth rites, but the naming of an infant is marked by a religious ceremony. This is known as 'christening' and it takes place when the child is baptised. In churches which do not conduct infant baptism there is often a service of blessing the child. At the naming (Christening) ceremony the priest or minister names the child and blesses it. In a service of infant baptism the parents and godparents make vows on behalf of the child.

CONFIRMATION

Confirmation is the completion of the act of infant baptism. The person is 'confirmed' in the faith of the church and is strengthened (confirmed) to live the Christian life. A candidate for confirmation is prepared by the priest or vicar and then is confirmed by the bishop. The bishop lays his hands on the head of the person as a sign of receiving the Holy Spirit. The person makes a public declaration of Christian faith and is given the bishop's blessing. So he or she becomes a full communicant member of the church, and is now eligible to take part in all church activities.

In the Eastern Orthodox Church, confirmation and baptism are one single act. In the Free Churches a baptised person is prepared to be received into full membership on request, or may be received by believer's baptism.

MARRIAGE

Marriage is a sacrament, that is, the union of two people in the sight of God. In the Church of England the Banns must be read in church on each of three Sundays before the wedding, so that anyone who may have an objection can make it. The form of marriage follows basically the same pattern in all churches. The groom and guests arrive to await the bride. There is no compulsory form of dress but the bride often wears white and is led to the front of the church by her father or some other person who 'gives her away'. The service may begin with a marriage hymn and the priest or minister reminds the congregation of the meaning of marriage. The groom and bride make promises to each other to love, cherish, honour and keep true to each other as long as they live. The priest or minister blesses the ring(s) and these are placed on the third finger of the left hand. As this is done, the bride and groom say: *With this ring I thee wed*. Then the priest pronounces them husband and wife and says: *Whom God has joined together let no man put asunder*. Prayers are said for the newly weds and there may be readings from the Bible and a sermon. Another hymn may be sung and the benediction is pronounced.

In the Eastern Orthodox Church the marriage ceremony is called 'crowning'. The bride and bridegroom speak the words: 'The servant of God A is crowned unto the handmaid of God B. In the name of the Father, and of the Son, and of the Holy Spirit'.

DEATH AND BURIAL

The funeral rites of Christianity are fairly simple. Death is a time of natural grief but not of despair. Christianity teaches a view of life beyond death; the soul lives on with God to enjoy eternal life with him. The deceased person is prepared for burial by being washed and dressed in a shroud and placed in a coffin. A service may be held in the home, as well as in church. In church a eulogy may be spoken on the deceased and suitable readings from the Bible and hymns sung. The Christian view of death may be explained for the comfort of mourners. Burial may be by cremation or in a grave. The priest speaks the words of committal and commits the soul to God. There are further prayers and a benediction.

11 > THE CHURCH'S BIBLE

The syllabus items under this topic are i) the status of scripture; ii) the New Testament; iii) translations.

THE STATUS OF SCRIPTURE

Christianity has one Bible, but if you look at the table of contents you will find it is divided into two major parts – the Old Testament and the New Testament. The Old Testament is what Christians call the Bible of Jesus, but if we think this is a book solely for Christians then we shall be in trouble. The Old Testament is the book of another of the world's great religions, Judaism, and it would be unwise to think that Christians have a greater right to it or understand it better than Jews.

The role of the Bible in Christianity.

Yet the Old Testament is part of the Christian Bible . . . so *what is it?* It is certainly not a single book but a library of books, rich in variety, written by different authors at different times and for different purposes. The books span over a thousand years of religious teaching. The key question is, *How do Christians regard the Old Testament?*

Broadly speaking, the Old Testament is an authentic account of God's activity among his chosen people, Israel. Christians believe that this activity continues in the New Testament. *They do not have two Bibles in one but a Bible which is a unity.* The Old Testament is like the first act of a single drama whose theme is God's action, for and among his people. Christianity sees the unity between the Old Testament and the New Testament in *what* God reveals of himself, *how* he acts, and *why* he acts in this way. Christians use the Old Testament as their sacred scripture for these reasons. The library of the Old Testament is divided into three sections: The *Law* (Torah): the *Prophets*; and the *Writings*. Christians use all three in their worship and personal devotion.

The Law (Torah) consists of five books – Genesis, Exodus, Leviticus, Numbers and Deuteronomy. But you should not think of them as collections of laws or of rules, like a school rule book. Torah means 'instruction' and 'teaching' and 'guidance'. The five books read very much like a story which runs from the beginning of the world to the death of Moses. Christians read these stories because they tell *what* God did when he made the world and called Israel to be his special people, *how* he acted among them, and *why* he led them from Egypt to the land of promise. Christians read the books of the Law on account of what they tell of God. You will see why this is so if you read any part of the Torah, such as this part which tells about God's command and the people's response:

> In time to come your children will ask you, 'Why did the Lord our God command us to obey all these laws?' Then tell them, 'We were slaves of the king of Egypt, and the Lord rescued us by his great power. With our own eyes we saw him work miracles . . . He freed us from Egypt to bring us here and give us this land, as he had promised our ancestors he would'.

The second part of the Old Testament library is the *Prophets*. You must remember that a prophet in the Bible is not like someone who prophesies by gazing into a crystal ball or who predicts the date of an event or happening. The prophet was someone who spoke for God, or declared God's message for the people of the time. The message was usually announced by the prophet declaring, *'This is what God says'*. The message was not always popular, or what the people wanted to hear. But the prophets gave the people a message of hope, as well as of judgement. Christians believe that God spoke through the prophets and revealed what his will is. So they use the books of the Prophets in their worship, especially when they tell about how God will act to save his people, as you can see from this passage:

> Shout for joy, you people of Jerusalem!
> Look, your king is coming to you!
> He comes triumphant and victorious,
> but humble and riding on a donkey –
> on a colt, the foal of a donkey.
>
> The Lord says,
> I will remove the war chariots from Israel
> and take the horses from Jerusalem;
> the bows used in battles shall be destroyed.
> Your king will make peace among the nations;
> he will rule from sea to sea,
> from the river Euphrates to the end of the earth.

The third class of books in the Old Testament is the *Writings*. They are a miscellaneous collection, but some of them are widely used by Christians. One of the books of the Writings which is probably used more widely by Christians than any other part is the Book of Psalms. The psalms are used regularly in Christian worship and are popular because they spring out of many different experiences and human situations. They are suitable for use in all forms of church celebrations, as they reflect the wide variety of religious experience. If you read any of the psalms you will discover how they can be adapted by worshippers for all forms of worship.

If you can imagine seeing the first act of a drama, having met all the characters and having seen what the plot is, you will want to continue the drama to find out what the end is. You will want to know what happens at the climax. Christians think of the Old Testament in the same way. It leaves them with an unfinished plot; it looks forward to the next act; it leaves them waiting in hope. A final chapter is needed. This is how they understand the New Testament and how the two testaments belong together. Jesus did not speak about a new God, but the God of Abraham, Isaac and Jacob who continued to act in his own life. The New Testament makes no sense, so Christians say, without the Old Testament.

THE NEW TESTAMENT

The New Testament is also a collection of individual books which are written by different writers and for different purposes. They can be grouped into four classes – *gospels, letters, history* and *apocalypse*. The exact date of their writing is a matter of debate among scholars, but they were all probably written within a hundred years from 50 CE.

The *gospels* are placed at the beginning as the most important books of the New Testament. They record and amplify the 'good news' about Jesus Christ. The Acts of the Apostles is the first *history book* of Christianity which tells how Christianity spread from Palestine to the lands around the Mediterranean from the Day of Pentecost until the imprisonment of Paul at about 60 CE. Most of the *letters* were written by St Paul, to commend or explain the Christian faith and encourage the young church. They were probably written earlier than the four gospels. There are letters by other writers such as Peter, James and Jude in the New Testament. The Book of Revelation stands on its own as an *apocalyptic* work. It was written to encourage Christians who were facing persecution. Apocalyptic literature uses strange symbols and images to describe God's control of events and what will happen at the end of the world.

The gospels as we know them were not the only ones that were written in the early centuries. Neither are the letters or epistles of the New Testament the only ones to have been written. When the Church came to compile its scriptures it had to decide which books to include and which ones to omit. It took a long time before the final decision was made in 365, but it has never been altered afterwards. The Christians who compiled the New Testament thought that these twenty seven books were inspired in the same way as the Bible (the Old Testament) of Jesus. They gave the books equal status and so there came into being *the* Bible (Bible = book). *Christians believe that they form an organic whole, that the sixty six different books of the Bible are a record of God's action which culminated in the work and achievement of Jesus Christ.*

The Church received the Bible as a 'holy' book or God's book. It was written on scrolls by human hands and handed down by human methods. At the same time Christians say, *All scripture is inspired by God*. Some Christians assume that this means that God inspired writers to write what he told them, without thought of its meaning. Such people have a fixed view of the Bible as the Word of God. They say it is verbally inspired. However, in the 18th century many scholars began to question the verbal accuracy of the Bible and began to study *when* and *where* and *why* the different books were written. They searched ancient manuscripts for information about the earliest forms of the text of the Bible. They discovered the great variety of the Bible, and how varied its content is, that it consists of myths and legends, stories and parables, prose and poetry, history and letters. So they began to question the 'verbal' inspiration of the Bible. They did not *deny* that the Bible is inspired; it is God's message which is alone conveyed through the message of the Bible; but this is recognised by understanding its meaning and what it must have meant to the people who wrote it. These Christians claim that they must interpret its meaning in the light of new knowledge from the past, just as God inspires them to do. This makes the message of the Bible more relevant to Christians today.

TRANSLATING THE BIBLE

Long after Christianity had reached Britain the Bible was only heard in Latin. This was the Vulgate translation of St Jerome in the fourth century. The Old Testament was written in Hebrew and the New Testament in Greek. The Old Testament had been translated into Greek before the times of Jesus (this translation is called the Septuagint) and the New

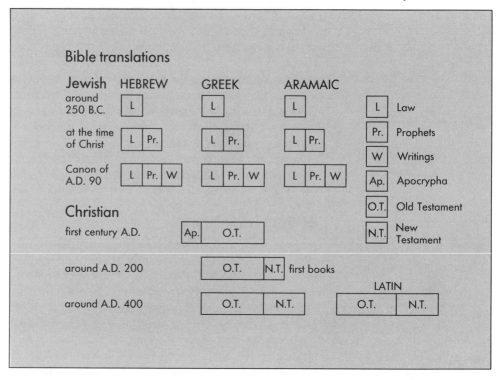

Fig. 6.5 Translations of the Bible

Testament had been translated into other languages. The translation used by the Church in the west was in Latin, until (as far as English is concerned) the Authorised Version was produced in 1611.

Before this, small parts of the Bible had been translated into English from as early as the seventh century, but in 1604 a conference at Hampton Court considered translating the whole Bible into English. King James appointed a committee of fifty to do this work and by 1611 it was complete. It has been the most widely used translation in English.

Over the centuries many translations of the Bible have been made and today there is a wide choice. The Bible has been translated into more languages than any other book and new versions are being made regularly. As far as English is concerned, many new translations have appeared recently which have made use of new discoveries of ancient texts. They have also aimed to convey the meaning of the Bible in contemporary language. Some of the new translations have been the work of individual Christians but others have been sponsored by groups of churches.

12 COMMUNITIES   IONA

Iona, which lies off the west coast of Scotland, houses Britain's best known Christian community. Its members began building the community in 1910, when work commenced on restoring the ancient abbey. Iona has been a holy place for centuries; here *St Columba* landed and made his headquarters. There were monks and missionaries on Iona for six hundred years. It is known as the 'isle of saints' and is a centre of pilgrimage.

The modern community dates from 1938, when the lead was taken by *George McLeod*, who with eight helpers decided to rebuild the ancient monastery on Iona and to establish a community of corporate and personal devotion. The community's motto is '*to learn, in a true community life, how the church should live and work in the world today*'. The community has a simple rule: prayer and Bible study; the responsible use of money; and worship. The community is not residential, but its members are made up of ministers and lay people. The members come together for a period during the summer and are held together by the promise, '*By the power of God and in company with other seekers, I dedicate myself anew to closer discipleship in response to his free gift to me in life*'. There are associate members all over the world. The abbey was rebuilt by the 1960s and is now the focus of the community. The members who meet during the summer share in community activities of many kinds, especially in thinking about the renewal of the Church and its mission in an industrial society. They discuss about caring for the poor and destitute. There is time for prayer, worship and Bible reading. The community welcomes young people to spend time on Iona, to discuss and learn about world problems and Christianity's response to them. Members of the community come from all walks of life and

> Christians sometimes form separate communities.

all levels of society. After spending time at Iona they return to their own employment to put into practice the ideals of the community. In 1951 the Church of Scotland officially recognised the Iona community and its work of relating Christianity and politics. The community numbers about 150 members and has links with other groups throughout the world who share the same ideals.

TAIZE

Taize stands on a hill in Burgundy in France. The small village is surrounded by meadows, vineyards and woods, and is where the Taize community was founded in 1944 by *Brother Roger Shutz*. At the time, Europe was fighting the Hitler war and Brother Roger wanted to do everything he could to help refugees escape from France to Switzerland. He formed the small band of helpers into a community, but he intended it to be open to everyone, especially people who were in distress or who needed special help. The seven who worked with him made a vow that they would work and serve together.

From the start Brother Roger hoped that the community would be a focus of unity for all Christians. By now this dream has come true. In 1962 a new chapel was built at Taize by some German young people, with a crypt that is open to members of the Eastern Orthodox, Roman Catholic and Protestant churches. The community has grown in numbers and is made up of people from many nations. They work to earn their living and then return to the community as their home. The community vow is: celibacy; community of goods; and the authority of the prior.

There are now fraternities of the Taize community in many parts of the world. Whilst the members of the community follow their usual occupation during the day time, and wear ordinary clothes, in chapel they wear a white habit. Worship is the heart of the community life and is held three times daily, in the morning, at noon and in the evening. Silence is considered to be important and time is spent in quiet meditation. The Taize community is open to people who wish to spend time in study or who wish to meet for prayer and devotion, or simply for relaxation. Not far away from the church there is a conference centre which has as its aim *'to communicate a broad-minded spirit of adventure, a thirst for clear insight into the social problems of today, as well as to give factual information, devoid of prejudice'*.

In 1970 Brother Roger announced his intention of forming a Council of Youth. This came into being in 1974, when 40,000 young people came together. Brother Roger urged everyone: *Open yourself to understand each person fully, every woman and man made of the same stuff as you and who, like you, searches, struggles creates and prays.* Brother Roger has geared the community towards Christian unity and to express the Christian message in modern terms. The community aims to live as a witness to peace and unity through faith in Christ. It is a community of joy and is always open to change.

CORRYMEELA

This community was founded in 1965 by a Presbyterian minister, *Ray Davey* in County Antrim, Ireland. They took over a house with a small group of young people, aiming to form a community that would help to heal the social, political and religious divisions in Northern Ireland. Ray Davey had previously been a prisoner of war as well as chaplain to students, and realized the need to create a centre that would serve the cause of unity between all peoples. The Corrymeela community offers opportunities for people to come together from all parts of society to share their experiences. They aim to foster good relationships and to spend time together in a relaxed atmosphere. The basic belief is that in this way people will grow to understand each other and this will produce a change in attitude. The community is open to men and women, lay people as well as clergy. There is no test of membership and persons without religious views or beliefs are also welcome. Conferences and gatherings for different ages are organised and 'family weeks' are held to encourage whole families to spend time together. A special feature is the international camps for young people and the support which the community gives to groups all over the world. It has also introduced a 'Mixed Marriage Association' to support marriages of mixed religion, and established links with other organisations such as the Coventry House of Reconciliation. The name Corrymeela means 'Hill of Harmony' and the community takes its ideal from this name.

APPLIED MATERIALS

BROADBERRY, R. St. L., (1973). *Thinking about Christianity*. Lutterworth.
BROWN, A. (ed.), (1984). *Festivals in World Religions*. Longman.
Christian Denomination Series. Pergamon.
DOWLEY, T., (1981). *History of Christianity*. Lion.
GREEN, V. J., (1978). *Festivals and Saints Days*. Blandford.
SMART, N., (1979). *The Phenomenon of Christianity*. Collins.
YAMAUCHI, E., (1981). *The World of the First Christians*. Lion.
The Message of the Bible. (1988). Lion.
BROCKETT, L. J. M. (ed.), *The Ecumenical Movement*. CEM.

EXAMINATION QUESTIONS

QUESTION

The Church in the Modern World: Its Life and Practice
a)   i) Give two names for the special festival in the Christian year which comes fifty days
         after Easter Sunday.   *(2)*
      ii) What is a pulpit? When is it used?   *(2)*
      iii) For what purpose is a font used?   *(1)*
      iv) Give two names for the service in which Christians carry out the command of
          Jesus 'Do this in memory of Me'.   *(2)*
      v) In any two Christian denominations, give the official title for the people who
         normally conduct the Sunday service.   *(2)*
      vi) What word do we use for a gathering of Christian people?   *(1)*

b)   i) Explain the importance for Christians of the coming of the Holy Spirit at Pentecost.
                                                                                    (8)

      ii) Why might a Christian celebrate the death and resurrection of Jesus Christ?
          Suggest ways in which this celebration might help the Christian in daily life.   *(10)*
                                                                              (NISEC)

OUTLINE ANSWER

In questions carrying marks for understanding (U) and evaluation (E) examiners look for
the skills of understanding and evaluation in relation to any of the knowledge (K) points
mentioned.

The Church in the Modern World: this section is marked out of 30.
a)   i) Pentecost and Whitsun (2)
      ii) A piece of church furniture (1) used by preacher or reader (1)
      iii) Baptism – receptacle for baptismal water (1)
      iv) Any two of:
          Communion service/Mass/Eucharistic celebration (2)
          Breaking of bread, Lord's Supper etc.
      v) Any two of: pastor, vicar, rector, curate, minister, priest or any valid alternative
         (2)
      vi) Greek ecclesia – a gathering of people. Any valid alternative (1)

b)   i) 3 marks (K)   a further 5 (U)
         Examiners should look for understanding in relation to knowledge: e.g. detail of
         events in Upper Room (3)
         Examiners should look for understanding: (5)
         e.g. the world not abandoned – promise of the Spirit
               Birth and mission of the church
               The Spirit present in all the members of the church
               or
               The gifts of the Spirit

ii) *Over-all meaning of the Easter event 5 (U)*
   e.g. That the Father loved the world so much that he sent his son to redeem us.
         That Jesus came to save us; the 'necessity' of the Passion.
         Jesus the perfect redeemer – sinless.
         Effects and consequences of the death of Jesus.
         The centrality of the resurrection to the faith.
         The resurrection – sign of the Father's ratification of Christ's work and death.
         – pledge of the resurrection of our bodies.
   These latter will not be listed explicitly in the answer but will be implied in the candidates' evaluation efforts.

Personal faith response 5 (E)
   e.g. a) The experience that Christ is alive in Christian's own life. How this affects one's view of the world and its values.
        b) In suffering, difficulties and disappointment, faith in the saving death of Jesus on the Cross gives courage and hope.
        c) Guilt and sin need not turn to despair or self-hatred because Jesus prayed,
            'Father, forgive them'.
        d) Despite doubts and many unanswered questions, joy in the knowledge that one 'belongs'.
        e) A realization of the need for personal prayer:
            – to the Father who loves us and sent us his Son
            – to the Son who died to save us.

A STUDENT'S ANSWER WITH EXAMINER'S COMMENTS

QUESTION Write about an incident from the missionary journeys of Paul which shows i) his method of spreading Christianity; and ii) how God gave him encouragement.

(WJEC)

> When Paul went to Corinth, he met up with Aquila and Priscilla, both worshippers of God, and he went to their house, for they were of the same trade as him: – tentmakers. Aquila and Priscilla were both faithful to the Lord and instructed Apollos about the baptism of Jesus.
>
> Every day, Paul went to the synagogue, arguing and preaching about the kingdom of God. When Silus and Timothy arrived from Macedonia, the Jews opposed and reviled him. Paul was angry and he shook out his garments and said 'Your blood be upon your heads. I am innocent. From now on I will go and preach to the Gentiles.' He was annoyed that the Jews opposed him, and, because he knew that God accepted the Gentiles, since Peter's vision at Joppa, he decided to go and preach to the Gentiles instead.

66 Perhaps more detail here 99

66 Why did he need to argue? What did he preach? 99

66 A good point 99

66 Perhaps a
little more detail on
the vision and how it
reassured Paul 99

66 Good detail and
description 99

66 No conclusion! 99

So he went to the house of Titus Justus, a worshipper of god who lived next door to the synagogue, with Crispus, the ruler of the synagogue.

Paul must have been feeling very discouraged at this time, so one night, the Lord came to him in a vision and said 'Do not be quiet and do not be afraid for I am with you. You will come to no harm for I have many people in this city'. This reassured Paul.

However, about this time, the Jews made a united attack on Paul, and they took him before the council and said 'This man is persuading us to worship God contrary to the law'. At this time, Gallio was the proconsul of Achaia, and he said to the Jews, 'If it were a matter of vicious crime or an evil wrong doing I should have reason to bear with you, O Jews. But since it is a matter of questions about words and the law, see to it yourselves. I refuse to be a judge of such things'. Gallio was a judge of criminal offences and remained imparshal, because he did not want to get involved. The Jews were furious that he would not punish Paul, and they violently beat up Sothesnes, the leader of the council, but Gallio refused to take any notice.

Comments

The incident chosen is very apt; you might have said a little more about Aquila and Priscilla and their work for the young church. Why was it necessary for Paul to argue in the synagogue? What did he preach about the Kingdom of God?

You describe very well how Paul was encouraged. You might show how you understand this vision and why it reassured Paul.

You should write a short conclusion to bring together the main theme of your answer. A good effort.

HINDUISM

GETTING STARTED

The word 'Hindu' comes from the word 'Sinhu' which is the name for the river Indus in North West India. It came to be used for India and Hinduism, the faith and way of life of most of the people of India. It has more than 450 million followers and is one of the most colourful and varied religions in the world today. It is more like a family of religions than a single religion. It does not have a historical founder and Hindus often refer to it as 'the eternal religion' (*sanatana dharma*) as it is based on eternal principles. It does not have an official creed or central shrine or set rules or ritual. It is a social organisation as well as a system of beliefs.

ESSENTIAL PRINCIPLES

You will find it helpful to enter the complex world of Hinduism by reading this account of life inside an Indian village:

VASNA INSIDE AN INDIAN VILLAGE
વાસણા : ભારતીય ગામની ભીતર
મધ્ય ગુજરાતના ગામનું પરંપરાગત જીવનનું પ્રદર્શન

RELIGION

The villagers in Vasna are almost all Hindus with only a few Muslim neighbours. The main tenets of the Hindu faith are adhered to but, as elsewhere in India, people choose which particular deities shall be important in their daily lives.

Many villagers have a special affection and respect for the propitious elephant God, Ganesh. Weavers hope he will prevent rats from eating their yarn, for the rat is traditionally the vehicle of Ganesh.

Visible signs of religious life in the village include gaudy devotional prints, often attached to calendars advertising commercial companies, which people pin up indoors; wall-niches or domestic shrines in which the figure of a deity may be placed and offerings made by members of the household; and several larger, outdoor temples, usually whitewashed, patronised by members of particular castes or subcastes.

Hinduism is combined with belief in, and active worship of local folk deities and spirits. These include *mata*, god- desses held responsible for various kinds of illness and other influences on human life. One goddess traditionally associated with smallpox is now blamed for various other diseases; an anxious parent may offer a piece of stone carved in the shape of a head and marked with vermilion.

Some villagers are especially devout and deeply interested in religious philosophy; sometimes they receive formal instruction from a guru or religious teacher. Such men are usually sceptical of folk beliefs which they regard as superstitious diversions from the path of true religion. A few men have reputations for spirit possession and they are sometimes consulted in times of personal crisis or uncertainty.

Village religion is thus a personal and varied set of beliefs and practices; it is local but not parochial. Whole groups of villagers may undertake religious pilgrimages to a favoured temple or guru, and friends may gather from neighbouring villages for an evening of devotional music and intense philosophical discussion.

 Life in a Hindu village.

Underline in the above the following points from this description of life in Vasna:

the affection for the elephant god Ganesh;
the deity in the domestic shrine;
the active worship of local folk deities;
the villagers' interest in religious philosophy;
religion is a personal and varied set of beliefs and practices;
villagers undertake pilgrimages.

Now answer this question:

Life in a modern Hindu village shows how varied Hinduism is. State the evidence for this statement.

Much Hindu worship takes place in the home. In the village of Vasna the homes have 'wall niches or domestic shrines in which the figure of a deity may be placed and offerings made by members of the household'. The family is the basic unit of Hindu society and the custodian of its traditions. The Hindu family is an extended family which gives its members a feeling of solidarity and identity. Here, children learn about the traditions of the village and to observe the caste customs. They are brought up to observe the Five Daily Duties: yoga and meditation; worship and reverence to the deity; respect for elders and ancestors; hospitality to the needy and holy men; kindness to all living creatures.

The picture or image in the family shrine room is of the favourite family god who may be Krishna, who is known for his love and kindness, or another god or gods. Worship is offered to one god only, which may begin by lighting a lamp with a wick dipped in 'ghee' (clarified butter) and placed in a container. Incense sticks are lit and names of God repeated and the daily prayer (*Gayatri Mantra*) said. The prayer is:

'Let us meditate on the glorious light of the creator.
May he guide our minds and inspire us with understanding.'

There may be a reading from one of the sacred books of Hinduism and there may be a mystical design to help concentrate the mind on God and the self. During the meditation the worshipper may sit upright on the floor with legs crossed; breathing deeply helps to relax the body and concentrate the mind. The sacred name for the deity (AUM or OM) may be chanted. Every member of the family may join in the devotions and place a gift of food or flowers near the shrine to be blessed. A flame may be waved before the deity and passed from one to the other as a symbol of the blessing. The worship may include singing devotional songs to give it a joyful tone.

WORSHIP IN THE TEMPLE

India is a land of temples and you saw that in Vasna there are several large temples, usually whitewashed, patronised by particular castes or subcastes. Here is a design of a Hindu temple:

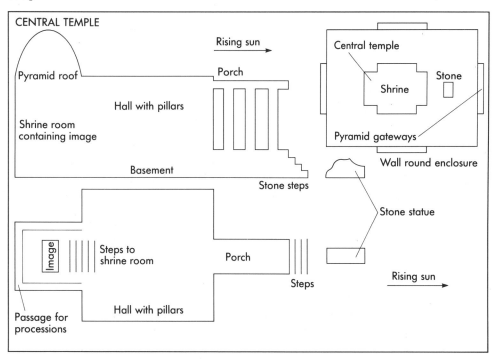

Fig. 7.1 Hindu temple

The temple is the home of the god and is dedicated to him. The inner sanctuary houses his image and Hindus worship the god of their choice, maybe because of a local connection, a special character, or favour received. There is a canopy or pyramid over the shrine as a symbol of honour, and on the walls there may be pictures of other religious leaders such as Jesus, Nanak or Muhammad. Hindus are tolerant to other religions.

Many Hindus never worship in a temple and there is nothing that corresponds to congregational worship in the west. Hindus sit on the floor facing the shrine. Families may sit together, or men and women may sit on different sides. The priest and his assistants conduct the worship and the image is dressed in royal robes and garlanded with flowers ready to be welcomed as an honoured guest. During the worship music is played and sacred texts chanted. Near the shrine a portable altar holds the sacred flame and liquid butter is poured onto the flame as sacred texts are chanted. Prayers are said and priest and worshippers dip a finger of the right hand in water and touch the ears and eyes and other parts of the body as a sign of cleansing. The priest waves the sacred flame clockwise and passes it to each worshipper in turn as a sign of blessing. Everyone joins in chanting sacred songs, bells are rung and there may be handclapping to the accompaniment of music. In larger temples there may be dancing.

At the end of the worship, any food left over from the sacrifice is shared by the priest on behalf of the deity. This is usually fruit and sugar, the symbols of goodness and kindness, and some may be taken away to share with others so that they have a part in the blessing.

Points to note about worship in Hinduism: Hindus identify with the deity through worshipping the god of their choice; worship is offering the whole life to God (I offer unto the Lord all of the actions which I perform through my body, senses, mind and intellect); worship is directed to God and *not* to the image.

66 The variety of Hindu *puja*, celebrations and pilgrimages. 99

The festivals of Hinduism are numerous and colourful. They centre around one or other of the Hindu deities, but they also overlap in their form and customs. Broadly speaking they can be divided into three groups:

i) 'calendar' festivals which follow a lunar cycle – the traditional Hindu calendar is of twelve lunar months and 354 days. Two lunar months give a season: spring (March–May), summer (May–July), rainy season (July–September), autumn (September–November), winter (November–January), the good season (January–March);

ii) 'occasional' festivals which celebrate the birthday of a notable person, for instance, in January the birthday of Vivecananda, and in February Sri Ramakrishna;

iii) 'seasonal' or 'agricultural' such as the autumn festival Durga Puja or the spring festival Holi.

Four festivals are widely celebrated and it is important to know *how* and *why* they are celebrated.

DIWALI

This is the Hindu festival of light which takes place over five days in October/November and marks the Hindu new year. The word 'diwali' means a cluster of lights, and clay lamps containing oil are lit in the home and may be floated in leaf cups along the river. Light symbolises the victory of goodness and virtue. The goddess of success and good fortune, Lakshmi, visits the home where the light burns, to bless it with happiness. Gifts are exchanged and prayers are said to Lakshmi for the year ahead. Hindus hope to begin the new year free from evil so wrongs are forgiven and debts are paid.

One reason for observing this festival is that it reminds Hindus of the victory of Vishnu over the demon Bali. Bali aimed to control gods and humans, so Vishnu, disguised as a dwarf, attended his sacrifice. Bali showed Vishnu kindness by offering him whatever gift he asked. Vishnu asked for as much land as he could cover in three strides. Bali agreed, but in three strides Vishnu covered the whole earth, thereby winning a victory over evil and darkness.

HOLI

This is an outdoor spring festival which lasts for five days. It is a popular, hilarious and riotous festival with processions, music, dancing and singing. Images of the god Krishna and his consort Radha are carried through the streets, where people throw coloured papers and sprinkle water to add to the revelry. Children dress in gaily coloured clothes and play practical jokes. Any past ill-feelings are forgotten and visits are made to friends. One popular myth connected with Holi is that of Krishna passing himself off as a cowherd and playing with the milkmaids. Krishna was pursued by King Kamasa until at last Krishna slew the wicked king and took over his kingdom. Holi celebrates Krishna's victory and the return of spring.

DUSSEHRA

This festival is held in October and is the climax of the Hindu religious year. It celebrates the goodness and protection of the gods. It generates goodwill and friendship, old disagreements and differences are forgotten in a spirit of peace and goodwill. During the festival pictures of Rama are displayed prominently and his victory over the greed of Ravana is acclaimed.

Rama was despised by his stepmother, who plotted to deprive him of his kingdom and gain the throne for her son. She managed to get Rama banished to the forest. The demon king Ravana captured Rama's wife, Sita, and carried her off to Sri Lanka. Rama searched for his wife until he came face to face with Ravana and defeated him in single combat. Rama returned with Sita to the forest and later to his father's kingdom where the people received him with great joy. After the death of his father he reigned for ten thousand years.

SARASVATI

This is a movable festival which may be held at any time. Sarasvati is the goddess of learning, knowledge and wisdom, and her festival is popular with children and adults alike. Money is collected for the *puja* fund and schools are decorated for the celebrations. Artists and musicians show off their skills as they give the goddess a place of honour. On the festival day the priest chants a hymn and places a clay pitcher on a bed of unthreshed rice (paddy) in front of the statue of Sarasvati, which is painted and decorated with coloured garments. A collection of books, a reed pen and ink pots, an oil lamp in the shape of a boat are placed nearby. The priest offers prayers and rings a cow bell, and a worshipper rings a conch bell three times. The priest chants the words: *'O Sarasvati, come to life'*. The statue is raised high and the worshippers stand in awe before her wisdom and knowledge.

In Hindu art, Sarasvati is represented as a lady of culture, refined, eloquent, the patroness of music and literature. Sometimes she is portrayed standing on a white lotus, calm and serene, or sitting on a bird or animal. Her four arms represent mind, intellect, conscience and self. Sometimes she is shown playing a musical instrument or displaying her other skills. In Hindu mythology, Sarasvati is said to be born out of the mouth of Krishna through the combined action of Brahma, Vishnu and Shiva. When Brahma created the world she helped Krishna by giving the 'sound' with which he brought the Vedas into being. The sound may have been music or speech, hence Sarasvati is the goddess of the arts and learning.

4 ▷ PILGRIMAGE

In the account of the village of Vasna you will recall that *'Whole groups of villagers may undertake religious pilgrimages to a favoured temple or guru'*. Pilgrimage is a special form of worship, but it is not compulsory. It is not mentioned in the Vedas but the Upanishads say it is a means of attaining merit and spiritual gain. Pilgrimage (*yatra*) is an act of devotion; a personal search for some gain; a popular outing with friends; discharging duties to ancestors; to find release from the cycle of rebirth.

Benares (Varanasi) on the banks of the Ganges is the most sacred pilgrimage site, where pilgrims come to perform ritual acts, to worship in the temple of the goddess Annapurna, to feed on the spirits of ancestors and to bathe in the sacred river. The pilgrim hopes to attain spiritual merit and the opportunity of a better life in the future. To die in sight of the Ganges, or with part of the body immersed in its waters, is believed to attain release from the cycle of reincarnation. The stairs built into the river are usually crowded with pilgrims offering gifts, shaving their hair, or bathing.

5 ▷ MAJOR BELIEFS

In the account of Vasna you will have read that *'Hinduism is combined with belief in, and active worship of, local folk deities and spirits'*. You will note that many deities and spirits are referred to. Over the centuries Hindu views of God have multiplied and been revised. Many of the early gods or godlings (gram devata), and also myths about them, are mentioned in the Vedas. They are given names but it is not always easy to say whether or not they have a separate existence or are manifestations of one deity. A Hindu wise man was once asked who the gods were and he replied:

'They call It Indra, Varuna, Agni
And also Heavenly, Beautiful Garutman;
The Real is One, though sages call it variously.'

The early gods were associated with the five elements, earth, water, light, wind and fire. They performed personal functions, but there were also gods of good and evil, disease and sickness, success and failure. The gods were worshipped at the domestic hearth, but we must not assume that more than one was worshipped – rather that Hindus understand 'deity' in different ways.

BRAHMA

From the plurality of gods there developed belief in a single creator god. He was known as Prajapati (Lord of Beings) and then as Brahma. By the 9th century BCE, belief in an Ultimate Reality emerged which manifested in a triad of gods – Brahma, Vishnu and Shiva. In mythology Brahma is depicted as a royal person, with four heads and riding on a goose while reading the Vedas. There are still some temples dedicated to Brahma but he is less popular today than Vishnu and Shiva.

VISHNU

Vishnu shared the creation of the world with Brahma and acts to preserve the world as a benevolent being. Many temples in North India are dedicated to Vishnu. His symbol is the salagram – an ammorite stone with spiral markings. Many Vishnaivites keep a salagram in

Fig.7.2
a) Brahma, b) Vishnu, c) Shiva.

their homes. In art he is portrayed with four arms sitting on a throne and wearing a crown, a holy jewel, a tuft of curly hair on his chest, clutching a conch, a discus, a mace and a lotus. His consort is the goddess of success (Lakshmi) and his best known *avatars* (incarnations) are Rama and Krishna. He appears to save and revive:

> 'Wherever there is a decline of virtue and ascendency of evil, I manifest myself in a body.'

SHIVA

Worshippers of Shiva (Shaivaites) call him the 'great God' (Mahadeva). His symbol is the lingam, a phallus symbolised by a cone-shaped collar. It represents the powers of creation and reproduction. His consort is Durga, a mother goddess known for her boundless energy and vitality. Shiva is portrayed with three eyes, four hands, matted hair, a garland of skulls and serpent around his chest. He has a terrifying side to his nature as the destroyer, yet his son, the elephant god Ganesh, brings good fortune.

Vishna and Shiva are manifestations of one God and are not worshipped separately. They do not compete for worshippers, neither is one superior to the other. They are aspects of the Supreme God. Hindus say:

> 'What is but one the wise call by many names.'

BRAHMAN

You must not confuse this with Brahma. Brahman is the word for Ultimate Reality or the Absolute. It has no form or gender and may be addressed as He, She or IT. Brahman is the power that is present everywhere and in everything. It is near and yet far, it is transcendent and imminent, resides in everyone but is identified with no-one, sees all things:

> 'He who inhabits all beings, yet is without all beings,
> whom no being knows, whose body all beings are, and who controls all, being from within.
> He is yourself, the Inner Controller, the Immortal.'

BRAHMAN AND ATMAN

There is a spark of God in everyone, which Hindus call *atman* or the breath of life or the inner vitality. Atman is the soul which is not controlled by the body or affected by evil and is eternal. Atman and Brahman unite to become ultimately one. The one is fused with the other, just as salt dissolves in water. When this happens the soul or inner self merges with the Absolute. This is what Reality is, and Hindus say, 'You are that' (*Tat tvam asi*).

REINCARNATION

Everyone is born into a state of transmigration (*samsara*) and enters the cycle or wheel of existence. Everyone is subject to the cosmic law of *karma* which determines a person's destiny. Every action is good or evil and is rewarded by good or bad rebirth. Every action produces an effect either in this present or in a future existence. Individuals must strive to achieve a good *karma* as their deeds give value to life. One of the prime conditions for achieving a good *karma* is by following the path of *yoga* or the yogis.

YOGA

Yoga literally means 'yoke' and is a method of achieving self control through meditation. By controlling the body and mind through concentration on God, life becomes so pure that it achieves union with God. This union experiences the presence of God which gives 'insight' and freedom from desire and evil. To help the individual to achieve a good *karma* there are four stages of *yoga*: *knowledge*, which is achieved through knowing the Ultimate; *work*, which includes meritorious actions including prayer, worship and good deeds; *devotion*, which develops an attitude of love and devotion to God; *meditation*, which is the intense concentration on God and the self. Hindus may receive help to achieve a good *karma* from holy men, who offer instruction and point the way to liberation. These men are known by many names but the most familiar are: priests, the guardians of tradition and ritual; gurus, who are spiritual guides; sannyasi, ascetics who live a holy life and are itinerant teachers.

LIBERATION

The ultimate goal of life is to achieve liberation (*moksha*) which is entry into eternal peace. The soul that achieves perfection enters into the eternal realm and becomes fused with it. This is described in a conversation between Chitra and Uddalaca:

> 'The soul that passes through the heavenly door arrives at the world of the gods . . . It casts away the works of good and evil . . . the soul arrives at the palace that is invincible, the abode that is beyond improvement, the throne that is supremely luminous. Here sits the Supreme Being and asks, Who art thou? He replies, What thou art, I am. Who am I? The Real? What is the Real? It embraces the universe. Thou art the universe.'

6 ⟩ HINDU SACRED WRITINGS

❝❝ The types of Hindu sacred writings, their authority and use. ❞❞

SCRIPTURES THAT ARE 'HEARD'

Hindus have an extensive range of sacred writings. It is important to know *how* they use them and *what* their importance is to Hinduism. Their most obvious use is in worship in the home and the temple, in private devotions and in the festivals and on all important occasions. Hindus teach them to their children, and scenes from them may be dramatised in the temple. Hindus believe that the sacred writings provide a practical guide for living and the authority for answering ultimate questions. The scriptures were handed down by word of mouth for a long time before they were put into writing. Many changes and additions were made during this time before they were written in Sanskrit, the classical language of India, which is still used by scholars and Indian members of parliament, who take the oath in Sanskrit. There are two classes of sacred writings:

i) those that were 'heard' (*sruti*), that is, received by ancient seers and sages through revelations or were divinely inspired;
ii) those that were 'remembered' (*smriti*) as memorised traditions of people and events.

SCRIPTURES THAT WERE 'HEARD'

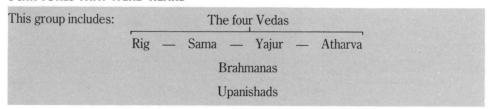

This group includes:	The four Vedas		
	Rig — Sama — Yajur — Atharva		
	Brahmanas		
	Upanishads		

The four Vedas

The Vedas (= knowledge) are the earliest scriptures, and a collection of hymns, prayers, ancient customs and traditions of the early gods and their exploits, sacrifice, ritual and worship. There is much content in common between the four. They were completed by about 800 BCE. They are still used by Hindus in their devotions, but we must be cautious in thinking about them as 'revealed', since this assumes the existence of a 'revealer'. At a more profound level the Vedas wrestle with age-long problems about the origin of life and the nature of divinity. They often give glimpses of later development in Hindu thought.

Brahmanas

These are commentaries on the Vedas which explain many of the practices, symbols and ritual. These are often complex and were given by priests who received special powers from the gods. A collection of Brahmanas existed about 300 BCE, and a further collection Aranyakas (forest treatises), for the use of those who achieve the fourth stage in life, was added.

Upanishads

The Upanishads contain the main stream of Hindu teaching, the philosophic and religious questions which were referred to in the account of the village of Vasna. There are 108 Upanishads in all, which were compiled between 500–200 BCE. They cover a variety of subjects and questions about God, the soul and human life. One method used by the Upanishads (the word means 'session with or near a teacher') is dialogue and question and answer. Use is made of repetition in order to induce concentration. By repeating the sacred name OM or AUM the mind focuses on God. They also introduce new formulae, symbols, images and comparisons to enliven their teaching. For the study of Hindu philosophy and teaching about reward and punishment, evil and suffering, God and salvation, the Upanishads are the main source.

SCRIPTURES THAT ARE 'REMEMBERED'

This group includes scriptures that were compiled between 200 BCE and 200 CE:

Mahabharata
Bhagavad Gita   Ramayana
Laws of Manu
Puranas

Mahabharata

This is the world's longest poem, written in a popular style as the Great Story of the War of the Bharatas. The stories were popular in India for many years before they were written down as they were recited or danced by travelling entertainers. The stories captured the popular imagination and became part of the folk culture of India. Their moral teaching was very easily remembered and artists and poets were inspired by them.

The Bhagavad Gita

This is Hinduism's best loved scripture. It is widely used in worship and celebrations and is popular among non-religious Indians as well as practising Hindus. The Bhagavad Gita (Song of the Lord) is a dialogue betwen Arjuna and Krishna. It extols the virtues of service, goodness, righteousness, unselfishness and devotion. Those who surrender to Krishna receive the reward of grace and compassion. Love is free of caste and gender, and love for Krishna achieves inner peace, serenity and security. Love is unaffected by changes or contradictions of life in a material world and is never at the mercy of warring passions. The Bhagavad Gita was first translated into English in 1785 and is quoted more than any other Hindu writing. Gandhi, a modern Hindu saint, said:

> 'When disappointment stares me in the face and all alone I see not one ray of light, I go back to the Bhagavad Gita. I find a verse there and I immediately begin to smile in the midst of overwhelming tragedies, and if they have left no visible, no indelible scar on me, I owe it all to the Bhagavad Gita.'

Ramayana

This is a long work of about 24,000 couplets, by an unknown author. It comes from the 2nd century BCE and is still popular among Hindus. It tells the story of Rama as an avatar of Vishnu and Sita. Rama is extolled as an ideal ruler and the story portrays his courage, godliness and perseverance. Hindu villagers who are unable to read are taught these virtues through hearing the story of Rama.

Laws of Manu

This collection of sacred laws was compiled in the 2nd century CE and prescribes rules for personal and social behaviour. Manu or Purusha is the father of humankind who received his laws from the gods. These cover many aspects of life, religious rites, civil duties, and laws governing the four Hindu classes.

Puranas

These are ancient myths about gods, wise men (rishis) and rulers. The major and minor Puranas are the last of the scriptures to be 'remembered'. Completed around the 12th century CE, Hinduism has since extended its literature considerably, but only the works referred to have a place among scriptures 'heard' and 'remembered' (*sruti* and *smriti*).

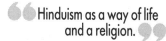

The inner beliefs of Hinduism regulate the life style and things that are permitted or forbidden. As you saw from the account of Vasna, these include personal habits, hygiene, disease, purity, fasting and devotion. The natural and supernatural intertwine in all the rites of passage or in every *samskara*.

BIRTH AND NAMING

> ❝Hinduism as a way of life and a religion. ❞

When a child is conceived the parents pray for the future life and the mother is protected from evil spirits and impurity. At birth sacred formulae are uttered in the child's ear, who is given gold, dipped in honey, to suck. After giving birth the mother is isolated until she has performed the ritual acts of purification, and the symbolic mark (*tumeric*) is made on the child's forehead. The naming ceremony takes place on the twelfth day in the presence of relatives. The name is not disclosed earlier, in case evil spirits carry the child away before it receives ritual protection. Scarlet threads are tied to the child as a sign of protection and a piece of gold is given to it for good luck. The child is named in the presence of the Brahmin priest, who records it on behalf of the family.

INITIATION

A Hindu boy is admitted to one of the Hindu classes when the sacred thread (*Upanyan*) ceremony is performed. It differs from place to place, but is performed before marriage. It confers on the boy the status of adulthood and marks the beginning of the student stage of life. It gives him the right to perform worship (*puja*), to sacrifice, and confers the duty of keeping the rules of purity. It is seen as a kind of 'spiritual birth', and the boy is now 'twice-born' (*dvija*).

The sacred thread (*yagopavit*) is a symbol of consecration and is placed over the left shoulder to the right knee. During this, mantras are recited by the priest. The thread is renewed every year and is never cast off. In earlier times it was customary to give the boy a present of a cow, but it is the spiritual meaning that dominates:

> 'This thread is most purified and will lead you to the knowledge of the Absolute. The natural source of the thread is the Lord himself, and is bestowed again and again for eternity. It gives long life and favours thoughts of God. This youth, decked with new and beautiful clothes and the sacred thread, will always dedicate himself for the service of mankind.'

MARRIAGE

A Hindu marriage can be elaborate and last over many days, but nowadays, there is a tendency to limit it to one day only. In the past it was unusual for the bride and groom to see each other before the wedding. The bride's veil was not removed until she was given away by her parents.

A marriage may take place in a home or a temple. The bride's father pays homage to the groom and her mother performs the consecration ceremony with the other women. The priest reads the family tree of the couple and they are linked by tying the bride's sari to the groom's scarf. They make a fire offering, whilst the priest chants mantras and prayers. The couple walk around the sacred fire seven times as the groom recites:

> 'This I am, that art thou; that art thou, this I am; I the heavens, thou the earth. Come let us marry, let us beget offspring. Loving, bright, genial, may we live a hundred autumns.'

Gifts are exchanged and the couple are toasted. For the day of their marriage they are looked upon almost as gods. Monogamy is the law and marriage is expected to last for life. The bride may make a sign of the permanence of the union by standing on a grinding stone as the bridegroom says: *'Be firm as a rock'*.

DEATH AND BURIAL

A funeral is very much a family affair and as the body is prepared for its last journey to the place of cremation, dirges are played on drums. The eldest son whispers the letters AUM or OM to attune the deceased with God and he leads the funeral procession carrying a ceremonial lamp. He also lights the funeral pyre, whereupon the soul is released to assume a spiritual body. As the body is cremated, these words may be spoken:

> 'May your eyesight return to the sun, your breath to the winds; may your waters mingle with the ocean and your earthly part become one with the earth.'

After the cremation there is a period of mourning, during which offerings of food may be made to assist the soul of the departed on its journey. After twelve days the purification rites are performed, so as to remove all signs of pollution. On the anniversary of the death a memorial ceremony (*shradda*) may be held and offering made for the deceased. Priests and family may then eat a meal together.

8 > SOCIAL ORGANISATION

There are two main markers of the traditional Hindu social system, namely, caste (*jati*) and class (*varna*). You need to exercise great caution when you study the concepts of caste/class in Hindu society. Bear in mind that the situation is changing in India and the barriers between castes are breaking down, especially in towns and cities. Here is a brief account.

CASTE

Caste is a social group into which a Hindu is born. There are numerous castes, each with its own laws of purity, eating, marriage, social mixing, and which do not relate to other castes. The caste defines a person's social position and their religious and social duties and responsibilities. Over the centuries a hierarchy of castes has evolved which places strict regulations or restrictions on their members. It is more difficult in the modern world to retain a rigid caste system. Since 1951 it is contrary to the Indian constitution, and to isolate any caste as 'untouchable' is against the law. It is no longer legal to speak about 'lower' and 'higher' castes. Older traditions are disappearing, and there is more social mixing, but even so, there are still many remnants of the caste system in the villages.

CLASS

In the 7th century BCE hereditary rulers governed many communities in India. From these rulers there emerged four social groups, each with their own characteristics. A power struggle developed between the priests and the rulers (*rajahs*), when the priests became dominant. The four classes are:

1 The Brahmin priests, the teachers and spiritual leaders.
2 The warriors (*kshatriyas*), who wear the sacred thread and maintain law and good government.
3 Merchants (*vaishyas*), who are responsible for trade and commerce, agriculture and industry.
4 Labourers (*shudras*), who are socially deprived.

The myth of the origin of the four comes from the Vedas which describe how each class evolved from Perusha, the first human being: the *Brahmins* from his mouth; the *kshatriyas* from his arms, the *vaishyas* from his thighs, and the *shudras* from his feet. By itself, class does not constitute a full caste and is less important.

THE FOUR STAGES OF LIFE

Just as there are phases in the cycle of the year so there are phases or stages which everyone passes through in life. These lead to the attainment of the goal of life and perfect knowledge and action. They are:

1 The *student stage*, which is spent in celibacy and receiving instruction and learning the Vedas at the hands of a teacher.
2 The *householder stage*, which is the stage of marriage, rearing a family, and serving the family and the community in accordance with the rules of the Vedas and Brahmanas.
3 The *forest stage*, which is the time of 'middle age', when the person is free of family responsibilities and able to spend time in reflection and meditation in accordance with the teaching of the 'forest treatises'.

4 The *'wander' stage*, when a person is free from worldly ties and desires and able to enjoy complete release from material attachments. The wanderer no longer needs the aids of ritual or sacrifice but is simply guided by wisdom.

The beginnings of Hinduism cannot be traced with certainty. In the middle of the second millennium BCE the Aryans invaded North India and settled along the Indus valley. They established communities and built the earliest Indian urban civilization. Two of these Aryan cities, Mohenjodaro and Harappa, have been excavated this century and show how sophisticated the life of the invaders was. They brought their own customs and religion, which included fertility rites and sacrifice. The Aryans developed a class system and by 900 BCE the priestly class dominated. Their poets sang about their gods and the principle that gives unity to the idea of divinity.

Hinduism has passed through innumerable phases and has always been amenable to new ideas. It may be compared to a mighty river on a journey to the sea, but which takes in many streams on the way. Teachers and philosophers have added to its diversity and interpreted Hinduism in a variety of ways. You will see that this is the case from considering these Hindu teachers and philosophers.

SHANKARA

Shankara is a Hindu Brahmin who lived from 788–820 CE. He was devoted to the Hindu sacred writings and interpreted them from a particular point of view. This is called 'monism'. He believed that the reality behind the world and the human soul is really one, and that they can be fused. There is no need therefore to worship or offer devotion to God. Salvation can be achieved through intuition that leads to deeper knowledge. Whoever realises this knowledge is free from reincarnation.

RAMANUJA

Ramanuja lived in the 11th century and modified the teaching of Shankara. He too was a Brahmin, but stressed that whilst the reality behind all things is one, everyone has a soul and it is right to worship God and not think only of being absorbed in him. He was a worshipper of Vishnu and believed in the way of devotion which achieves unity between body and soul.

MADHVA

Madhva also belonged to the Vedanta School (a school of orthodox Hindu philosophy; *vedanta* = the end of the Vedas). He lived in the 13th century and was devoted to Vishnu. He believed that the human soul is distinct from God, yet is dependent on him. He was a fervent advocate of devotion (*bhakti*) as a means of experiencing God's grace and help.

More recent movements and individual Hindus have continued to interpret and add to the diversity of Hinduism. Here are some examples:

BRAHMA-SAMAJ

This is a movement founded by Ram Mohan Roy (1772–1833) and is also known as the 'Spiritual Association'. It arose to defend and foster belief in the One Self Sufficient God and to advance the theistic teaching of Hinduism. Mohan Roy was set on freeing Hinduism from foreign influences and advocated the return to pure Hinduism which he conceived to be 'monotheistic' (belief in one God). He did not disapprove of members of other monotheistic faiths such as Christianity and Islam sharing in the worship of the One God. Many Hindus saw the reforms of Brahma-Samaj as going against the spirit and practices of Hinduism handed down from the past.

RAMAKRISHNA

Ramakrishna preached a message of tolerance in religion. He was born in Bengal in 1834 and aimed to break down the barriers between religions. He was an ardent devotee of the mother goddess of Hinduism but believed that God is the reality that is present in every religion. He passed through a number of mystical experiences which convinced him that the creeds of religion are only different ways to the same goal. They all lead to God and so must be tolerated with sympathy. At his death in 1886 his followers formed a small community which developed into the Ramakrishna Order.

TAGORE

Rabindranath Tagore is one of India's great poets who was attracted by the Brahma-Samaj movement. He welcomed and advocated the emphasis on One God who alone is worshipped. He advocated a movement away from the ritual forms of worship and set traditions so as to allow greater freedom. He also called for a break with the practices of self denial and withdrawal as being too restrictive. Everyone must be free to worship God in their own way and not be bound by the rigid patterns of the temple or set forms. He received the Nobel Prize in 1913.

AUROBINDO

Sri Aurobindo (1872–1950) was a Brahmin and mystic who was devoted to *yoga*. He taught that all people can live in harmony with God by practising *bhakti* (devotion). He claimed to have heard God speaking to him and calling him to leave many of the traditional beliefs and practices of Hinduism. He gave up belief in any incarnation of God, in *karma* and *moksha* (liberation). He tried to interpret his teaching in a way that modern, scientific people can understand.

GANDHI

Mahatma Gandhi (1869–1948) is the outstanding Hindu saint of recent times. He was widely loved and called Mahatma (great soul). He spent some years in England studying and afterwards practised as a lawyer in South Africa. There he began to champion the cause of the dark-skinned natives against the white people. He rejected violence of every kind and relied upon truth and love (*ahimsa* = respect for life) as the most effective weapons against violence. When he returned to India he took up the cause of the natives, who were being oppressed by the British. He challenged British rule and worked for the independence of India. He rallied thousands to his cause and they acclaimed him as though he were an *avatar* of God come to deliver them. He urged his followers to show love (*ahimsa*) to the British and show that they loved justice and human dignity. He led the lowest classes, or children of God (*harijans*), into the temple that was forbidden to them, in order to show them that they had rights to freedom and dignity as human beings.

In 1947 India won independence from British rule through the non-violent advocacy of Gandhi. He often fasted for long periods and was imprisoned, but still rejected all forms of violence, as it only breeds more violence. But on 30 January 1948 Gandhi became the victim of violence when he was assassinated. As he fell, he uttered the words 'God, God'. He believed that he made his stand for truth and *ahimsa* for the whole world.

10 ▷ HINDUISM IN BRITAIN

Hinduism has achieved a new identity in Britain during the past twenty-five years, through the influx of immigrants. There are many well established Hindu communities with their own temples. The majority have come here from India, but others have come from East Africa. They reflect the diversity that is characteristic of Hinduism in their eating habits, modes of dress and patterns of belief. They do not all speak the same language but are prepared to mix for worship and other religious purposes. The traditional extended family is common and marriage outside Hinduism is very rare.

The main Hindu population is found in London and other major cities. They tend to be clannish and those who hail from the same background tend to cling together. The home is the bastion of Hindu practices in Britain. The shrine room is tended by the women and the image or picture of the favourite deity is the focus of family worship. The major festivals such as Diwali and Holi are celebrated, although without all the colourful ritual of an Indian celebration. The rites of passage are observed and the temple may have an extended function as a school for teaching children the language of their native group and for social purposes. The link between the local temples in Britain is the National Council of Hindu Temples.

A number of associated movements have emerged over the years, including the Krishna Consciousness Movement and the Swaminarayans, a Hindu religious movement. Holy men take an active role in such movements, which serve to maintain contact between Hindus and to give instruction in the faith. Special attention is given to developing in young people a sense of commitment to the faith. At present it is estimated that there are about 300,000 Hindus in Britain. They face the challenge of maintaining their identity in a different culture, and inevitably, with the passing of time, it is likely that new variations in practices and organisation will take place. These will test the resilience of Hinduism to survive and adapt to a changing environment.

APPLIED MATERIALS

Knowing and teaching about Hinduism. (1984). Scottish Working Party on Religions of the World in Education.
BAHREE, P. (1984). *Hinduism.* Batsford.
BENNETT, O. (1986). *Diwali.* Macmillan.
DAVIES, R. (1980). *Holy Books.* Longman.
KANITAR, V.P. (1985). *Hinduism.*
KILLINGLEY, D. (ed.) (1984). *A Handbook of Hinduism for Teachers.* Grevatt and Grevatt.
MITCHELL, A.G. (1982). *Hindu Gods and Goddesses.* HMSO.

EXAMINATION QUESTIONS

QUESTION

Read the following passage and answer the questions which follow.

'Krishna, when these mine own folk I see
Standing before me, spoiling for the fight,
My limbs give way . . .
Should I strike down in battle mine own folk
   No good therein I see . . .
They are our venerable teachers, fathers, sons
They too our grandsires, uncles,
Fathers-in-law, grandsons,
Brothers-in-law, kinsmen all.'

(Extract from the translation of the *Bhagavad Gita*)

a) The above words were spoken by Arjuna. Where was he, what was the occasion, and to whom was he speaking?   *(5 marks)*
b) What reply did he receive? Explain.   *(5 marks)*
c) Explain the importance of the following in Hindu religion:
   i) the Vedas;
   ii) the Mahabharata   *(10 marks)*

OUTLINE ANSWER

a) Full marks will be given for an accurate account of Arjuna on the battlefield facing his enemies who are also his cousins. Krishna is the god Vishnu who is acting as charioteer and adviser to Prince Arjuna who is a brave warrior caught up in the war between two princely families.   *(5)*
b) The reply forms basic Hindu teaching. Full marks will be given for an accurate summary of Krishna's teaching about the problems of war and life.   *(5)*
c) Essay type marking. Full marks will be given for a full, accurate account.

The Vedas	Foundations of revealed scriptures, brought by Aryans in the form of hymns sung by priests performing the sacrifices. *(5)*
The Mahabharata	Longest epic poem ever written, stories contained in it carried down for centuries by memory. Mention the Vyasas (editors) and role of Brahma and Ganesa. Most popular episode is the Bhagavad Gita which contains advice and discourses on every aspect of life. Great comfort to all who read it, no matter what tragedies they encounter.

Accept any accurate points.   *(5) (20)*

A STUDENT'S ANSWER WITH EXAMINER'S COMMENTS

QUESTION

a) Describe carefully the shrine or sacred place in a Hindu home.
b) Why is worship in the home important to Hindus?

(WJEC)

A room is set apart at the temple where the family will pray. There are statues of deities which respresent different Gods. A cover or roof of material is draped above, behind and by the side of them. The deities were beautiful clothes and flowers all round them. There is a bowl of sweet foods (which are offered to them) in front of them

Worship is so important because it puts the Hindus in the right frame of mind to think about God, and to believe him, and it calms them and enables them to live their life better. Also they can pay their respects to God through worship.

Comments

The answer is only partly correct. You do not include sufficient details about the shrine room. Note that the shrine in the *home* includes a picture or statue(s) of the favourite family deity, or one particularly connected with the family. You should refer to the other symbols (lights and incense) that may also be part of the shrine.

There are other important aspects of worship in the home – it shows devotion (loyalty) to the deity; meditation creates inner calm and unity with the deity; worship in the home includes prayer (the gayatri mantra), is a focus of unity for the family; is an opportunity to hear the scriptures, to instruct children and to pay homage to elders.

PRACTICE QUESTIONS

1 Describe the main features of a Hindu shrine. Note whether you are describing a shrine in a home or a Mandir. It may be useful for you to use illustrations or diagrams to assist your description. *(Knowledge – 10 marks)*

2 Explain the meaning and/or purpose of at least five objects on the shrine. You must show clearly what the objects reveal about Hindu beliefs and practice. *(Understanding – 10 marks)*

3 Consider the importance of the daily Puja for members of the family and the effect this daily act of worship might have on their thoughts and actions during the rest of the day. *(Evaluation – 10 marks)*

(SEG)

GETTING STARTED

Islam made its appearance in the early seventh century in Arabia, where God revealed its essence to his prophet. Islam means 'submission' and one who 'submits' is called a Muslim. Its main strength is in the countries of the Arab League but there are Muslim communities elsewhere in the world. Islam is a dominant religion which claims to have about 900 million followers.

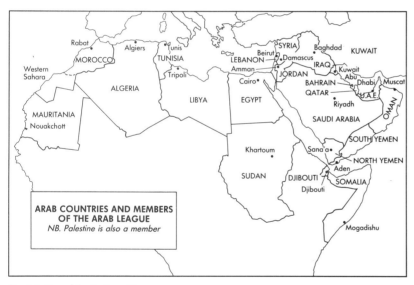

Fig. 8.1 Map of the Arab world

It is a universal religion and classless creed. It embraces the whole life in its submission to the will of God. Faith and life, religion and politics, the material and spiritual merge in obedience to the divine will. Islam is a guide for complete living and Muslims believe it to be true for all times. It is, they say, God's final revelation to which nothing further needs to be added. It is not a new religion but God's last word, revealed at a particular time and applying for all time. It does not change, because God does not change. The Muslim stands in relation to God as a slave to his master. The slave has no rights, except to obey his master's will. The slave who does this receives his master's favour and feels no longer a slave, but privileged to share his master's kindness and mercy.

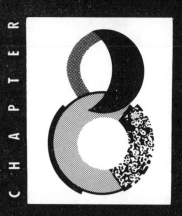

ESSENTIAL PRINCIPLES

1 ▷ THE MOSQUE

Wherever there are Muslims, you will find a mosque. The sound that haunts the Muslim in any part of the world is the call to prayer that is chanted by the *muezzin* from the minaret of the mosque. He calls them with the words:

> God is the greatest.
> I bear witness that there is no God but Allah.
> I bear witness that Muhammad is the messenger of God.
> Come to prayer.
> Come to security.
> God is the greatest.

On Friday at noon male Muslims are called to attend the mosque in accordance with the instructions of the Qur'an:

> In the name of God, the Most Beneficent, Most Merciful.
> O believers when you are called to prayer on Friday,
> hasten earnestly to the remembrance of God and cease your trading.

Mosque (*masjid*) means 'place of prostration' and its architecture is an aid to this. The approach is along a courtyard, where there are facilities for worshippers to wash themselves ceremonially before they enter the sacred place. In Britain, however, modern purpose-built mosques may not have the washing place outside but just at the inside. There is also a place for shoes to be left.

The main part is the central prayer hall and the great dome which gives a sense of space and light. There are no pictures or statues, so that nothing may distract from the worship. The walls are covered with beautifully decorated ceramic tiles and geometrical figures and texts from the Qur'an. Coloured glass is also used to decorate the prayer hall. There are no seats and the floor may be heavily carpeted. Around the mosque there may be arches of a distinct style and in the wall facing Mecca the *mihrab*, a niche that directs attention to the *ka'aba*, the most sacred symbol of Islam. To the right of this there is a pulpit (*minbar*) and nearby a lectern (*kursi al-Qur'an*) with a copy of the Qur'an.

FRIDAY PRAYER

If you were to attend a mosque by invitation for Friday prayer, you would find that only men enter the prayer hall. There are special places for the women. You would hear the men chanting in Arabic their profession of faith which is notable for its sound:

> Laa – ilaaha – il – lal – lah; muhammad rasoo – lul – laah.

that is

> There is no god but Allah; Muhammad is his messenger.

The Muslims recite this with determination and conviction. The ritual prayer (*salat*) is made with a deliberate act of will. This prayer follows a rhythmic sequence as the worshippers are in ordered ranks facing towards Mecca. There is no set ritual, but the worshippers follow the actions of the imam. Each movement (*rakah*) involves the whole body as a gesture of complete submission to God. The hands are raised and the worshippers bow, stand upright, prostrate themselves so that the forehead touches the ground, sit back on the heels, turn to the right and the left and greet their neighbours with the words:

> Peace be upon you and the mercy of God.

During the *rakahs* the worshippers recite the creed to witness to the greatness of God and give thanks. Each bodily movement is a symbolic act of submission. The sequence, which is repeated several times, is the symbol of the rhythm and discipline of prayer, and of human virility and alertness. The greeting at the end reinforces the unity and solidarity of all Muslims.

A mosque is not a consecrated building and is used as a school and for social gatherings. All matters relating to the Muslim community may be discussed in the mosque and in non-Arab countries classes to teach children Arabic are a regular feature.

IMAM

The imam is not a priest, but one who leads the Friday prayer. He stands in front of the congregation and ensures that they face Mecca and follow the *rakahs*. He may deliver a sermon during Friday prayer, which varies with the Muslim calendar, but it may be on any matter political, national or social that concerns Muslims, as well as being a religious utterance.

2 ▷ MUHAMMAD

Muhammad was born in 570 CE in Mecca. His father died before Muhammad was born and his mother died when he was six. For a time, his grandfather took care of him until his uncle Abu Talib became his guardian.

Mecca was an important religious centre, with shrines to many gods who were worshipped by the people of Arabia. At this time many Arabs were animists who believed in the existence of many spirits (*jinn*) who were either friendly or hostile. Among the many gods they included Allah and revered him along with others. Mecca housed the *ka'aba* which was the centre of worship. This was a cube-shaped shrine which contained the Black Stone, a meteorite said to have fallen from the sky thousands of years earlier.

According to tradition, when Muhammad was twelve he and his uncle were travelling together in Syria when they met a monk who greeted him as God's messenger. During his travels he met Jews and Christians, as well as followers of the native religion. This opened his mind to new ideas and enlarged his experience of the religious scene. He married Khadijah and managed her commercial affairs; he saw his marriage as a blessing and he did not take another wife whilst Khadijah was alive. Later she supported him in his teaching.

CALL

Little is known of Muhammad's activities until in 610 he claimed that the angel Gabriel had visited him with a message from God. At the time he was meditating in a cave, when Gabriel appeared holding a piece of silk cloth with 'Recite' written upon it. He asked three times, 'What shall I recite?' and then the angel began to recite the words on the cloth.

> Recite in the name of thy Lord, who created man from a clot of blood.
> Recite! The Lord is wonderfully kind who taught by the pen.
> Taught mankind what they knew not!

The account is recorded in the Qur'an, but Muhammad reported what he had seen and heard to his wife. As time went on he received further revelations and believed that God called him to be the messenger of his word to the world. Muhammad believed that God spoke to him directly and made him his *rasul*, or messenger, to declare before the world:

> There is no god but God (Allah),
> Muhammad is Allah's rasul (one who is sent).

The revelations which Muhammad received are written in the Qur'an. He claimed to recite the words of the revelations as they were delivered in *surahs* (= chapters). He believed that God had called him to declare his words and direct people to him. He was supported by his cousin and his friend Abu Bakr and at first he shared his message only with a small circle, but eventually with all who were ready to listen.

THE MESSAGE

The core of the message was that there is but one God and everyone must submit to him. Others, such as Jews and Christians, believed in one God but now God declared his final message to the world. God had sent other prophets from the time of Adam who were given a message for their own time, but now he sent his final and perfect message through Muhammad. God's revelations were complete and everyone must surrender to his will.

Hijrah

The people of Mecca were not prepared to receive Muhammad's message. Members of his tribe, the Quraysh, the strongest in Arabia, were hostile and they reacted with amusement and ridicule at first, and then with the threat of persecution. They saw the message as a threat to the traditional religion and to their trade in idols. Mecca was a wealthy city on the main caravan route and many pilgrims came to visit the *ka'aba*. Travel between the Yemen in the south and Gaza and Damascus in the north was brisk and the Meccans gained from this trade. But the social life was corrupt and the widows and poor were oppressed. Muhammad called the merchants to respect the old standards of justice and kindness and declared that everyone must appear before God, to receive reward or punishment. They were not prepared to listen, but a turning point came in 622 when some of the people of Medina were ready to receive his message.

Muhammad left Mecca for Medina, where he set about bringing together a community of those who were ready to submit to God. This not only marks a turning point in his career but also the beginning of the Muslim era. Muhammad did not find it altogether easy to win all the people of Medina to his teaching. There were certain Jews who were prepared to accept him as a prophet, but rejected whatever was contrary to their own prophets. Others believed that he restored the pure religion of Abraham that had fallen into disrepute. Muhammad was intent on preaching his message to the whole of Arabia. Although he had left Mecca, he did not give up the hope of returning. He was determined to purge the *ka'aba* of its heathen connections and make it the shrine of Allah. He taught his followers to pray in that direction as a focal point of their faith and hope. He had withdrawn strategically from Mecca, but his absence was only temporary and he could not desert the city for ever. He prepared his followers for the time when they could return to Mecca. In the meantime, it was their sacred duty to attack the Mecca caravans and any who stood in the way of his dream of capturing the *ka'aba* for Allah. A number of battles were fought against the Meccans and Muhammad won notable victories at Badr when a small army defeated the Meccans. Later, they were also defeated on the slopes of Mount Uhud. The way now seemed open to return and take possession of the *ka'aba*. Muhammad called the Muslims to prayer, giving the call (*Adhan*) a special significance for those who submitted to Allah. By now, a number of the tribes of Arabia had accepted his message and slowly Arabia was being united by his teaching. The *ka'aba* was established as the central shrine of Islam and its most sacred point.

Muhammad engaged in a variety of activities, including politics. He proved an effective political leader who succeeded in making an alliance between the Muslims and surrounding tribes. This laid the foundation of the Muslim state. He also negotiated a settlement between Christians, Jews and Muslims, and he himself was more readily received as God's prophet. The two cities of Mecca and Medina, which had played a significant part in his career, were now subject to his influence. Mecca received the status of being the spiritual centre of Islam.

DEATH

Muhammad died in 632 in Medina. The day after his death he was buried in the house in which he died, which later became the first mosque. His death was announced with the words:

> Let him know, whosoever worshipped Muhammad, that Muhammad is dead;
> but whosoever worshipped God, let him know that God lives and never dies.

The crusade for winning the world for Islam continued and within a century after Muhammad's death Islam had taken root as far west as Spain and as far east as India.

ACHIEVEMENTS

Muhammad never claimed to be other than a human being who was charged with a special mission from God. He did not claim to have supernatural powers, or to work miracles. The only miracle Islam recognises is the Qur'an, the mouthpiece of God's revelations. But Muhammad had a number of supernatural visions which imply that he was specially favoured by God. Muslims regard him, therefore, as an ideal person, and because he taught about the final destiny and judgement some call him an 'eschatological' (someone who teaches about the ultimate state) figure. One modern Muslim writer has said of Muhammad:

> He was before all, his name the first in the Book of Fate; he was known before all things and all being, and will endure after the end of all.

There are three notable achievements that you should consider:

1 Muhammad gave the Muslims their self image, as he stamped his mind on the religious practices, making them an essential part of the Muslim's 'submission'.
2 Muhammad established a community (*umma*) on the basis of kinship and submission to God. This became the model for Muslim solidarity and unity.
3 Muhammad gave his people a new sense of nationhood by blending faith, justice and political destiny.

3 >	THE FIVE PILLARS

Every Muslim who submits to God also submits to God's law. The command to do this is implicit in every revelation from God. It lays down for the believers the direction God intends them to follow. At the same time, God makes it possible for those who surrender to him to live according to his law. Islam is a present way of life, as well as an ideal to be achieved. So there are precise rules to be followed. These are the Five Pillars. The opening *surah* of the Qur'an contains the prayer:

Guide us in the straight path, the path of those upon whom your favour rests.

> **The Five Pillars and their importance in Islam.**

The Five Pillars are:

- Shahadah (creed or profession)
- Salat (ritual prayer)
- Zakat (almsgiving)
- Saum (fasting)
- Hajj (pilgrimage)

SHAHADAH

The creed is the essence of God's revelation and the prime profession of Islam:
There is no god but God and Muhammad is the messenger of God.

Note how this profession shows awareness of God as 'one'. It is a sin (*shirk*) to associate any other being with God. God has no partner, nor does he incarnate himself in any form. God is not defined, but his 'oneness' is deliberately affirmed. The creed professes Muhammad as God's messenger – the bearer of his final revelation. In this sense he is unique and so is held as an ideal before the eyes of the Muslim. God is given ninety-nine beautiful names in the Qur'an, but they all relate to his 'oneness' (*tauhid*) – the one who creates, is all knowing, all present, merciful, judge, and who determines all that is. Muslims repeat the 'beautiful' names maybe by using a string of beads (*misbaha*) as a rosary.

SALAT

Muslims practise two types of prayer – one is *du'ah*, which is a prayer of petition (asking) and invocation (pleading) that may be said anywhere, and at any time. It expresses the Muslim's complete reliance on God. The other is *salat*, that Muslims are required to perform five times a day – at dawn, noon, in the afternoon, at sunset and at night. *Salat* is a ritual prayer that may be offered anywhere, but always in the direction of Mecca. Before *salat* the Muslim must wash in the prescribed manner and stand on clean ground. Hence many Muslims carry a prayer mat for this reason. *Salat* must be performed for the right reason or intention (*niyyah*). This must express the earnest desire of the Muslim, and before commencing on the ritual, the number of '*rakahs*' (gestures or movements) to be performed must be stated. At the end of each pair of '*rakahs*', and at the end of salat the *shahadah* must be said. *Salat* is obligatory for men and women, and children from the age of twelve are also expected to observe the times of prayer. If possible, prayer should be said in company with other Muslims, and if the prayer time is missed it may be made up later.

ZAKAT

The Muslim is taught:
Give something of the means which God has given you.

Almsgiving is an act of charity, not a tax or a freewill offering, but a gift made to God. Only the person who has surrendered to God can pay 'zakat', as it is a religious duty. In practical terms it is a gift of a proportion of a person's disposable income, but the amount differs according to circumstances. *Zakat* must be paid every year and has the significance of showing solidarity and kindness towards the poor, the means of helping the spread of the faith, of assisting those in debt and prisoners of war. *Zakat* must always be given willingly and with sincerity. No-one should refuse '*zakat*' or feel a sense of shame at receiving it. Muhammad showed generosity during his lifetime and the offering and receiving of *zakat* expresses the same spirit.

SAUM

During Ramadan, adult Muslims must refrain from eating, drinking, smoking and sex between dawn and sunset. After sunset, fasting is not allowed. Fasting inevitably involves some personal discomfort and inconvenience, and whereas it is a religious duty, it is also left to the individual conscience. Those who fast must declare their intention willingly:

> I intend to fast on this day in order to perform my duty toward Allah in the month of Ramadan of the present year.

For the Muslim, fasting is a joyful act and develops self discipline. Those such as the sick, the pregnant or the elderly are exempt, but if the fast is broken intentionally it may be undertaken later. Fasting is an act of sacrifice but Muslims make it together in solidarity. It is also a way of identifying with people who are deprived, or who suffer from famine or drought. Those who observe *saum* will receive their reward.

HAJJ

Once during their lifetime Muslims are expected to make a pilgrimage to Mecca and the *ka'aba*, providing that they are in good health and can afford it. It is important to express the intention to make the pilgrimage by saying:

> O Allah! I intend to perform the hajj. Make thou the same easy for me and accept it from me. I have conceived the intention (niyyut) for hajj.

Pilgrimage is full of ritual performance and heavily symbolic. During the *hajj* the Muslim is at the disposal of God and must be ready to observe all the conditions and ritual. (You will find these described under the section on 'pilgrimage'.)

4 ▷ THE QUR'AN

Qur'an means 'to recite' and is the name of Islam's sacred book. *In what way is it so special to a Muslim?* It is given the most sublime status and is treated with the utmost respect. When it is being read or recited, everyone is silent and may not eat, drink or make any noise. It is lavished with care and no other book may be placed on top of it. Technically, it is not translated for the original is laid up in heaven and there are only copies of this on earth. Those copies in the mosque are beautifully bound and decorated as an expression of reverence for the spoken word.

The Qur'an is written in Arabic and wherever Islam is practised it is read in Arabic. Arabic is a living language but not all Muslims are able to speak it. Many may learn the language for the sake of reading the Qur'an. It is difficult to convey the beauty and power of the original language in translation. Many Muslims learn the Qur'an by heart, so as to be able to recite it at will. They say then that the message of the sacred book is enshrined in their hearts. The Qur'an is a binding force between Muslims all over the world.

INSPIRATION

From beginning to end the Qur'an is the direct and unaltered revelation of God. It is not composed, or compiled, as other books. Muhammad was inspired to recite what God spoke to him. He did so in a state of *wahy* (inspiration) and in this state he communicated exactly what God told him. Nothing was altered by the prophet, or interfered with in any way. It is believed that the Qur'an existed in heaven from the beginning and was then revealed to Muhammad and later recorded in the exact way in which he received it. The work of recording the revelation commenced during Muhammad's lifetime and continued after his death. An authoritative version was produced by Caliph Uthman in 650 and this has never been altered.

THE MESSAGE

The Qur'an consists of 114 *surahs* of different lengths. At the head of each surah there is a heading that assigns it either to Mecca or to Medina, but sometimes these surahs merge into each other. The text is in rhymed prose, which is excellent for chanting aloud and is full of impressive pictures and vivid metaphors which reflect life in Medina and Mecca. This helps the Muslim to learn and remember the content as each surah carries a descriptive title such as 'cow' (surah 2), 'iron' (surah 57), 'afternoon' (surah 103), 'elephant' (surah 105), and 'dawn' (surah 113).

Here, within 114 surahs, is the totality of Islam, all that it teaches about God and human life, the world and how to behave within it. The teaching is directed to the individual and to society and regulates life in every aspect. It initiates the Muslim into what is Islam and how to live in accordance with it. All that a Muslim must do and avoid is prescribed within its pages. Here is the testimony of a modern Muslim to the impact of the Qur'an:

The Holy Qur'an teaches me to worship Almighty Allah, him and him alone, to obey his orders contained therein, to follow the teachings and examples set by the Prophet Muhammad, to do good to others, especially to my parents and relations, and to be honest and truthful in all my actions and dealings; in short it gives me a complete code for rightful guidance of my life.

HADITH

Hadith means 'saying' or 'statement', which refers to traditions about the Prophet Muhammad that circulated among Muslims after his death. These sayings are a body of tradition which grew up in different parts of the Arab world and became precious to followers of Islam. They tend to idealise the prophet in every way and to marvel at his many roles. He is portrayed as a very courageous and generous character who showed exceptional kindness to the needy and dejected. The earliest traditions are probably the most reliable and they are used to reinforce the Qur'an, but *never* to verify it.

In the 9th century Al-Bukhari set about trying to distinguish between true and false traditions. The most reliable became known as *sunna* (custom) and the way of action for orthodox Muslims. Here is an example of one such tradition reported by Abu Dharr:

I came to the prophet and found him asleep in a white dress. I came a second time and found him sleeping. On the third time he was awake. When I sat at his side he said: Whoever says, there is no god but Allah, and dies in this belief will enter paradise.
I replied: Even if he is an adulterer and a thief?
He said: Even if he is an adulterer and a thief. (The question was asked and replied to three times.)
The fourth time Muhammad added: Even if Abu Dharr were to turn up his nose.

The Hadith has been described as 'popular Islam'. In order to appreciate this it is important to remember how the Muslim places great stress on imitating the character of Muhammad.

5 ▷ FESTIVALS AND PILGRIMAGE

Muslims follow a lunar calendar of twelve months and date their era from the year 622 when the Prophet Muhammad emigrated from Mecca. *Eid* or *id* (the Muslim name for a festival) is an enjoyable and pleasant time. Everyone takes part and engenders a spirit of friendship, goodwill and solidarity. Visitors and strangers are welcomed and special provision is made for the poor and less fortunate.

NEW YEAR FESTIVAL

New year's day falls on the first of Muharram and is particularly important for Shi'ite Muslims. Extra time is spent in prayer during the first ten days of the New Year and in recalling events in the life of Muhammad. Shi'ites commemorate the martyrdom of Caliph Ali and Husain, the true successors of the prophet. They spend the day in mourning for the martyrs of the faith and in Shi'ite towns symbols are set up in the streets and members of the sect dress in black. They hold gatherings to recall stories about Muhammad and Ali and Husain. It is an emotional time, when the Shi'ites eat the 'food of sorrow'. At the end of the ten days a passion play may be performed to tell the story of Husain and the massacre at Karbala.

On new year's day, special mention is made of Muhammad's departure from Mecca. He had expected to settle in Taif to the south, but opposition from the leaders of the old religion proved so strong that for safety he went to Medina, which became known as the 'city of the prophet'.

MUHAMMAD'S BIRTHDAY

On the twelfth day of the third month (Rabi'ul-Awwal), Muslims celebrate the birthday of Muhammad (maulid an nabi). Naturally, this is an important occasion and it may be marked with lectures and celebrations and the whole month may be kept as the 'birth month'. The celebrations date from the time when the Abbasids of Baghdad were the rulers of Islam. Stories of the prophet are told to encourage Muslims to think about his importance and achievements. They are exhorted to extol his character and example. The day is a public holiday, bright clothes are worn and homes are decorated. There may be processions and feasting but the religious purpose is not overlooked. There are readings from the Qur'an and prayers are said and throughout, the praises of Muhammad are sung.

THE PROPHET'S NIGHT JOURNEY

On the 26th day of Rayab (the seventh month) Muslims celebrate the Hadith, which concerns Muhammad's journey by night from Mecca into Jerusalem. From the remains of Solomon's temple Muhammad is said to have ascended into heaven and shown many wonderful signs by God. It was on that night that God revealed to him the times for daily *salat* which every Muslim must perform. The spot of Muhammad's ascent is marked by the mosque called the Dome of the Rock. During the celebration there are readings from the Qur'an and prayers. Stories are told about the life and work of Muhammad, especially the tradition that the angel Gabriel came to take him from Mecca to Jerusalem on a winged horse. Whilst Muhammad was there, all the prophets before him joined in prayer until eventually he ascended through the seven heavens to paradise. Before he passed into paradise he spoke to each of the prophets and then received his reward from God as the human medium through which his message was recited before the world.

BREAKING THE FAST

Eid ul-Fitr celebrates the end of the fast of Ramadan on the first three days of Shawal (the tenth month). It is a joyous occasion when the family gives thanks that the fast has been made and is now ended. The day starts with a bath and morning prayers and then everyone dresses in new clothes and attends the mosque for special festival prayers. The prayers give thanks for keeping the fast and for living according to the rules of the Qur'an and the joy of living as a Muslim. There is a sermon in the mosque on the theme of generosity and the duty of caring for the needy and of helping them to share in the joy of the festival. As an act of kindness, the head of the family pays a kind of welfare tax on behalf of the family. During the day visits are paid to relatives and friends, and children are given gifts with the greeting 'Happy Id (Eid)' or 'the peace of God be with you'. It is a time for renewing pledges to Islam and the Muslim community and strengthening social bonds. The words of Muhammad are recalled:

> When Eid ul-Fitr comes, the angels stand at the doorway and call upon Muslims: 'O company of Muslims, go to the generous God, who gave you the good things and grants the great reward . . . and when they prayed the angels called upon them saying: Indeed your Lord has forgiven you: return to your home following the good way.'

DAY OF ARAFAT

On the 9th day of the last month of the year (Dhul-Hijja) Muslims commemorate the final revelation of the Qur'an. This happened on Mount Arafat shortly before Muhammad's death. The Day of Arafat brings together all Muslims who perform the *hajj* (pilgrimage) to examine themselves, to spend time in prayer and meditation on God's revelations and his will. The following day they complete their pilgrimage with the festival of sacrifice. On the Day of Arafat they recall the revelation to Muhammad:

> In the name of God, the Most Beneficent, the Most Merciful:
> This day have I perfected your religion
> For you, completed
> My favour upon you,
> And have chosen for you
> Islam as your religion.

FESTIVAL OF SACRIFICE

This marks the end of the annual pilgrimage to Mecca. It is also known as the Great Feast and the Festival of Sacrifice. It recalls how Abraham was willing to sacrifice his son as an act of complete submission to God. As a symbol of their own willingness to submit completely to God, Muslims traditionally sacrifice a sheep or other animal and then enjoy a meal together. They do not forget the poor and share at least one third of the animal with them. There are also special prayers. During the celebration Muslims remember Muhammad's final sermon, which exhorted Muslims to follow the Qur'an and the Hadith:

> O people. Understand my words. I have left you something with which, if you hold fast with it, you will never fall into error: the Book of God and the practice of his prophet.

PILGRIMAGE

As you saw, pilgrimage (*hajj*) is one of the Five Pillars of Islam. Today many pilgrims make the journey by air but checks are made on everyone before they enter Mecca. After making the pilgrimage they are known as *kajji* or maybe *Hassan hajji* or *Yasir hajji*. Male pilgrims traditionally wear a simple one-piece garment which covers the whole body. This creates a sense of equality and unity between the pilgrims. They do not cover the head but they wear backless sandals. Women are not expected to wear any special clothes. Everyone is expected to follow set rituals, and guides ensure that this is done:

1 They walk around the ka'aba seven times and kiss or touch the Black Stone and say 'Here I am present before you'. In this way they make contact with the roots of Islam.
2 They move to the hills Safa and Marwa in the centre of Mecca and recall Hagar's agonising search for water for her son Ishmael, and then they drink from the spring (Zamzam).
3 They visit Mount Arafat on the 8th day of the hajj where they worship God in penitence and confirm their loyalty to the Muslim community.
4 On the 10th day they stone the three pillars at Mina where they believe Satan tempted Ishmael to rebel against Abraham. The stoning symbolises the rejection of evil and the works of the devil. Afterwards they sacrifice a sheep and enjoy a feast together.
5 The last two nights are spent at Mina and some may visit Muhammad's tomb in Medina or the Dome of the Rock in Jerusalem.

The pilgrimage is a moving experience, especially mixing with fellow Muslims from all over the world, and you should take account of these five reasons why *hajj* is so important to Muslims:

1 It symbolises their equality – they all wear the same simple clothes and perform the same rituals.
2 It creates a sense of unity and community.
3 It kindles the flame of faith at the Hearth of Islam.
4 It is a focus of spirituality.
5 It strengthens individual faith and identity with the universal community.

6 ▷ RITES OF PASSAGE

Muslims look upon the family as the living symbol of Islamic society. It is its most basic institution, where the values and ideals of the faith are preserved and practised. The Qur'an provides guidance about the family and how to maintain its unity and happiness. The family must be united for the sake of the children, who are the pride of their parents. The parents have responsibility for the nurture of their children and setting them on the path to full personal development. They must show the children great kindness and, most importantly, care for their spiritual well-being.

In return, children must be loyal to their parents and show obedience. Parents deserve their children's love and the children must be patient and compassionate towards their parents as they grow older. The care of parents is a good and beautiful thing and children must give them support whenever they need it. The male is the head of the family, but the woman is its heart. The father provides for the material needs of the family, but the mother is expected to create a truly Islamic home in which the principles of Islam are faithfully followed. The Muslim family is an extended family and all occasions in life involve all its members.

BIRTH

A new life is a gift from God to the family. In recognition of this, the family gives thanks in a practical way by giving food and clothes and money to the poor. God's name and the *Adhan* is whispered quietly into the ear of the new-born child and on the seventh day it is named and its head shaved. This removes the uncleanliness of birth and encourages the hair to grow more thickly. A feast (*aqiqa*), to which relatives and friends are invited, is held at the naming ceremony.

Traditionally, two goats or a sheep are sacrificed in the case of a boy, or one in the case of a girl. The meat is then cooked in accordance with Muslim law, while a third animal is given in charity. Parents may follow the ancient custom of seeking the help of religious leaders in choosing a name for the child. Muhammad is reported to have said that God favours names such as Abdullah (the servant of Allah) or one of the ninety-nine beautiful names for a girl. Names which are just trendy are avoided, since the name is thought to influence the child's personality and character.

At the age of four (although this varies), the ceremony of *bismillah* takes place. In the presence of guests and children the father asks the child to repeat the formula: *In the name of Allah the gracious, the most merciful*, and then follows verses from the Qur'an. So begins the child's education into Islam. All who are present share sweetmeats, but there is no elaborate feasting. Male circumcision is done early, preferably on the seventh day, but some Muslim tradition leaves it until a later age. Circumcision (*khitan*) is generally practised even though it is not mentioned in the Qur'an. It is looked upon as an act of initiation which is thought to have been commended by Muhammad. For this, the child is dressed in his best clothes and there is usually a celebration meal. Presents are given to the child but it is not usual to make this a very elaborate occasion.

MARRIAGE

In principle, marriage is a commitment to God and to a dignified way of life, which is necessary for the survival of the race. The creation of a family is a social necessity and a righteous act. It is commended in the Qur'an as a natural state, from which nobody is barred. Marriage is not a sacrament but a step towards a fuller and richer life. The consent of the woman and her guardian must be obtained and in marriage she has her own rights and duties. She should be a good partner and contribute to the happiness and stability of the family. She must be attentive to her husband and not hurt his feelings. His expectation is conveyed in this way:

> Our Lord: Grant unto us wives and the offsprings who will be the joy and comfort of our eyes, and guide us to be models of righteousness.

The husband is expected to treat his wife with kindness, honour and patience. He must keep her in a good estate and not cause her harm or grief. In some cases, a husband may have more than one wife and where this happens he has the same responsibility towards each of them. In general practice the Muslim does not have more than one wife and in Britain the law does not allow this. Sex before marriage is disallowed and is punishable according to the sacred law (*shariah*). Divorce is permitted, but is never advocated. The ideal is a life-long union; there are no trial marriages, and frequent change of marriage partners is frowned upon. Only if the marriage contract fails completely should it be broken, and then it should be terminated with honour and kindness. Should this happen the wife's rights are safeguarded by Islamic law.

The marriage ceremony is happy yet solemn, simple yet beautiful. It may take place in the bride's home or in the mosque in the presence of the couple's parents, friends and relatives. The bride and groom dress in their best clothes and the ceremony may be conducted by any knowledgeable male Muslim. The *qadi* (legal official) reads from the Qur'an and the Hadith and announces the amount of the dowry (marriage gift). Whatever the dowry, it belongs to the wife. Husband and wife do not necessarily hold property jointly. The husband is expected to provide for his family with the help and service of his wife. The couple exchange vows and hear from the Qur'an the duties of husband and wife and the religious basis of marriage. At the marriage feast dates are shared and afterwards the bride and groom leave for their home. The following day, relatives and friends gather for the *walima* (marriage celebration).

DEATH AND BURIAL

There is natural grief at death, but it need not be a sad occasion. Islam teaches clear views about resurrection and life after death. Death is faced without fear and in a spirit of hope. The soul enters into eternal life and blessedness and reunion with departed friends. As death approaches the Muslim recites the creed (*shahadah*) and prays for forgiveness. Friends and family join in reciting passages from the Qur'an, and the last profession before death is, *'There is no god but God and Muhammad is his messenger'*.

After death the body is washed in scented water and dressed in a white robe. A male is dressed in three robes and a female in five. Rich and poor are treated alike. The body is taken to the mosque or an open place where friends gather for the funeral prayers. The prayers may be led by a member of the family or the *imam*. Afterwards the body is taken in procession to be buried in a cemetery. There are no strict rules as to how long a body should be kept before burial, except that it should not be kept in a house too long. There is no coffin and the grave is dug to the size of the body, which is buried facing Mecca and the *ka'aba*. Prayers are said for the family of the deceased and friends offer their sympathy. But there should be no weeping for the life has returned to God to whom it belongs.

7 > LAW AND SOCIETY

❝❝ The relation between Islamic law and society. ❞❞

Islam has a special way of conveying what it means by relating the commands of God to everyday human activities. The word *shar'iah* can mean 'canon law' *and* guidance for what Muslims must and must not do. They share common ground about the things their faith allows and the things it forbids. So they have a common understanding of good and evil, hence their religion becomes a way of life as much as a set of beliefs. *Shar'iah defines the day to day moral and social aspects which are the human side of the religion.*

The 'sacred law' (*shar'iah*) is declared through the Qur'an, which is compulsory and universal and governs the activities of every Muslim. It reveals God's will for all times. But the world today is very different from the time when the Qur'an was revealed. *How do Muslims apply or accommodate the law to new situations or when new problems arise?* There are two answers given:

i) Muslims draw 'Analogies' (comparisons) from the Qur'an. For example, they may say 'this situation today may be compared with that in the Qur'an and the Qur'an tells us how to deal with it.'

ii) Muslims may reach a 'Consensus' (agreement) about how to act. For example, they may say 'we must consider together how to deal with this problem and act on the consensus.' Muhammad once said: *'My community will never agree upon an error.'*

You may regard the 'sacred law' (*shar'iah*) as an amalgam of the Qur'an + the Hadith + Analogies + Consensus.

Shar'iah assigns activities to five categories:

1 Compulsory (*fard*), e.g. the Five Pillars.
2 Commendable (*sunna*), e.g. actions which add to the quality of life such as hospitality, courtesy.
3 Allowed (*halal*), e.g. kindness to animals, especially those to be slaughtered for food.
4 Discouraged (*makruh*), e.g. divorce.
5 Forbidden (*harem*), e.g. intoxicating drinks, meat sacrificed to idols.

INTERPRETING THE LAW

The interpreters of the sacred law are the *ulama*. They are learned in the law and custodians of Islam's teaching. They elaborate the law and how it applies to the whole of life. The law gives Islam stability as a religious and a moral system and guidance for political and civil action. It defines how, ideally, an Islamic society should be organised and the obligations of individual Muslims towards it. No Muslim can contract out of the duties of living in society and ensuring that it operates according to the law. The ideal has to be worked out in practice and every Muslim has a part in this.

SOCIETY AND POLITICS

Like everything else, politics is under the sovereign rule of God. He makes his will known through the *shar'iah* and it is the obligation of the political leaders to see that this is fulfilled. The head of the Muslim state is responsible for the good order and defence of the state, in accordance with the principles of the law. Islam must be kept strong and united and Muslims must be ready to defend their ideals. The *jihad* (holy war or striving) is laid down by the Qur'an as a duty. It is the duty of the Muslim to fight in order to defend and propagate the faith. Any 'holy war' must be properly defined in accordance with the *shar'iah* and led by the head of state.

The law prescribes the way of dealing with social rights and with social evils. It is applied whenever political action is called for, especially in such matters as the provision for the poor and socially deprived, upholding the rights of women and orphans, property rights, and the treatment of criminals and prisoners.

EDUCATION

The mosque is a place of education and there is no barrier to learning as part of the Muslim way of life. It leads to wisdom which is summed up in the Qur'an:

'He gives the wisdom to whomsoever he will, and whomsoever is given the wisdom, has been given much good.'

Education cultivates attitudes and trains pupils in the spiritual and moral values of Islam. All knowledge comes from God and, whereas no-one can achieve perfect knowledge, worthwhile knowledge produces goodness, righteousness and harmony. The ideal is to train children and others in a planned way, so that they will learn to acquire and practise Islamic ideas and manners through sound intellectual training. In recent times many new developments have taken place in education in Muslim countries such as Saudi Arabia, where many new primary schools have been established and the education of girls is supervised by the Girls' Education Administration. However, Muslim education faces the challenge of how to operate a system of education in the modern world that also retains identity with the traditional values of Islam.

WOMEN IN SOCIETY

Basically, Islam teaches that women are equal with men but have different responsibilities. Men and women are the children of Adam and Eve and are equal before God. They are equal, but dissimilar in the functions they perform. Women have the right to own property and to dispose of it as they may choose. They may take part in all appropriate activities and enjoy male company in the normal course of life. The Qur'an decrees that a woman should dress modestly and behave decently in society. Devout Muslim women follow the rule of covering the whole body and only expose the hands and face. The clothes are loose, so as not to show the shape of the body. The extent to which this custom is followed differs from country to country. The custom of wearing a veil is a social one and is not mentioned in the Qur'an. Women may attend the mosque but have their own quarters. The Qur'an places the woman in charge of her husband and husband and wife must live in mutual support. On marriage, a woman has the right to expect that she will be provided with a home, clothing and health care. She has the right to be treated as an equal.

One problem which Muslim girls face in Britain concerns whether or not they should be educated in single sex schools. In Muslim countries, boys and girls are educated in separate schools. Consider the case of two Muslim girls who were given places in a co-educational school but their fathers refused to allow them to attend. The question was whether the girls should wear *shalwar* rather than short skirts, should they have a special diet of food cooked according to Muslim law, should they be exempt from swimming lessons, from PE lessons, from the school assembly? The Muslim parents were concerned to protect their daughters from current social trends in Britain. *Why was this?*

DIET

Apart from food that the Qur'an declares to be unlawful, Muslims are permitted to eat all foods. The foods that are not allowed include pork and pig meats and blood products. Other meats are allowed, providing the animal is killed in the prescribed way. This is *halal* – cutting the animal's throat with a single stroke and then draining its blood. As this is done the *bismillah* (in the name of the merciful Lord of mercy) is pronounced to show that the animal is being sacrificed for a genuine purpose.

Alcohol is not allowed at any time, as it is harmful and wasteful and destroys the individual's relationship with God. It must not be used in the preparation of food or as a medicine. Neither must it be kept in the home to give to guests from other religions.

8 ▸ SECTS AND MOVEMENTS

Islam did not have a natural leader after the death of Muhammad in 632. He did not give any instructions about his successor as leader. He had created a Muslim state and it now needed a leader. Who was he to be? How was he to be chosen?

There was a difference of opinion between two parties. One declared that the leader must be chosen by God, just as he had chosen Muhammad to be his prophet. The other party said that the community must choose the leader. They could not agree and so there was a division. The first party believed that God intended Muhammad's son-in-law, Ali, to be the leader, but the other party chose Abu Bakr as the successor (*caliph*). The followers of Ali became known as the Shi'ites, and the followers of Abu Bakr as the Sunni.

 The emergence of the sects of Islam and their present role.

SHI'ITES

The Shi'ites are a fundamentalist sect committed to the belief in a spiritual succession of *caliphs* (successors), who are the direct descendants of the Prophet Muhammad. As the true successor the Shi'ites gave authority to Ali as leader.

They abide by the authority of the Qur'an as a direct revelation from God and interpret every word in a literal way. They observe the Five Pillars as the absolute rule for the Muslim. They differ from the Sunni in the way that they interpret their history. After the two sects had emerged, Ali's son Husain tried to snatch the leadership from Yazid. He was unsuccessful and was murdered in the attempt. This had a profound effect on the Shi'ites, who saw the death of Husain as an act of extreme barbarism. The Shi'ites interpreted the death of Husain as a sacrifice and this turned their attention to questions about suffering. *What is suffering? Why do innocent people suffer?* They saw that life involves suffering and began to teach the virtue of suffering for the sake of others. They extolled innocent suffering as a supreme virtue. They observe the anniversary of Husain's massacre by performing passion plays (*ta-ziyahs*) and visiting the scene of his murder at Karbala.

Shi'ites call the true leaders *imam*; they have authority to guide and interpret the eternal truths of the Qur'an. The imam also has authority to show how the teachings of the Qur'an must be applied. One of their teachings is that a 'hidden imam' will one day appear and make complete the salvation of Islam. He will be a descendant of Ali and the coming of the 'hidden one' will bring peace and justice to all humankind. The Shi'ites are important communities in Iraq and Iran, the Lebanon and Bangladesh. They have been responsible for the more active role of fundamentalists in Iran and the Lebanon in recent times. They are prepared to engage in a 'holy war' (*jihad*) to defend their beliefs, and believe that to die in its cause is a guarantee of a place in paradise. On the whole, the Shi'ites have been the poorest classes and often uneducated. But in the Lebanon their position has changed in recent years and some of them hold key positions in the country. More than half the population of Iraq are Shi'ite Muslims, who saw the recent war with Iran as a crusade on behalf of the Arab world.

SUNNI

More than ninety per cent of Muslims are Sunni. They too are traditional in the way they interpret the Qur'an and also the Hadith of Muhammad. They are devoted to the community of Muslims and its authority to make decisions on their behalf. The 'consensus of the community' (*ijma*) is binding. They teach firmly that God's judgement is inevitable and that everyone must appear before him to account for their actions. They regard themselves as the orthodox sect. But the differences between the Shi'ites and Sunni are not easy to explain. One recent Muslim has written:

> The distance that divides them is very small. They don't differ on the key concepts such as the Koran, Muhammad, God, the acts of worship – not on any fundamental theological issue at all. The only difference of any fundamental value is how the Muslims run their estate (i.e. apply their teachings and put them into practice).

KHARIJITES

Like the Sunni, this group disputed the claims of Ali to be the leader. They too said that the community must choose the leader, but also have the right to depose him. The Kharijites are more narrow in their outlook and more puritanical in their ways. They condemn all who sin and do not repent as infidels or unbelievers. Such persons are no longer members of the community. They place great stress on works and the paramount importance of defending Islam by means of the 'holy war' (*jihad*). They oppose Arab aristocracy and today they survive in small communities in Oman, Zanzibar, Algeria, and southern Africa.

SUFIS

The Sufis are the mystics of Islam. They became active in Iraq in the 8th century and have enriched Islam with their poetry and works of wisdom. They derive their inspiration from the Qur'an and the Hadith.

All mystics follow a simple way of life, practise fasting, self discipline, self denial and asceticism. Sufis view Muhammad as a mystic and, like him, they aim to focus their whole life on perfecting their relationship with God. The Muslim who does this experiences paradise here and now. Therefore, for them the constant remembrance of God (*dhikr* Allah) is of prime importance, it means devoting time to meditation, prayer and reciting the litany. They use expressions like 'living in God' (*baqa*), 'self denial against the world' (*fanah*) to convey their complete devotion.

The Sufis follow a characteristic life style. They do not believe that politics and material things can satisfy the desires of the heart, but charity given freely and following the instructions of the Qur'an can'. They have their own style of education and literature and have produced notable thinkers. They use allegories to interpret the Qur'an, but their chief aim is to live in union with God. Their teachers or elders (*sharykh*) warn constantly against relying on human systems of salvation.

9 > ISLAM THEN AND NOW

❝❝ The spread and dominance of Islam. ❞❞

The spread of Islam is a record of spiritual fervour, zeal for God and territorial conquest. During the time of the four caliphs (632–661), Islam strengthened its hold on Arabia and spread to Syria, Lebanon and Africa. In 611, *Mu'awiyah*, the ruler of Damascus, became the leader and he organised Islam on the lines of the Byzantine empire. Damascus, not Mecca, became the centre of the Muslim world. He introduced the principle of hereditary succession and linked Islam more closely with the state. Political leaders began to play a more forceful part in the affairs of Islam which developed as an international political movement.

Early in the 8th century Islam dominated Spain and spread to India. This opened the way for close contact between Arabia and India and trade in crafts and textiles. By the middle of the 8th century the dynasty of the *Umayyad* came to an end and Islam entered upon a golden age. In 762 Baghdad became the centre of Islam under the *Abbasid* dynasty. Baghdad was a centre of commerce and culture with links with Greece, Rome, Persia and India. It was a centre of wealth which cultivated and sponsored developments in mathematics, medicine, science, philosophy and the arts. In other parts of the Islamic world, elaborate mosques were built, including the famous Cordova mosque, notable libraries and centres of learning sprang up, and in general Islam society became more open. However, an important question arose about the *interpretation of the Qur'an*. Must it always be interpreted in a traditional way? Or should it be interpreted in the more modern way, so as to meet new requirements? There were two main views – one the 'traditional', and the other the 'creative' interpretation.

THE MONGOLS

In 1258 Baghdad fell to the Mongols and within fifty years they accepted Islam. The centre now became Cairo and the Al-zhar university a centre of learning for Islam as a whole. The unity in culture and learning was strengthened, but the old international political movement faded into memory. There was a strong allegiance to tradition and the Five Pillars, and under the Ottoman Turks, Islam reached another pinnacle.

THE OTTOMAN EMPIRE

Under the Ottoman Turks, Constantinople (Istanbul) became the new centre as Islam strengthened its hold on the Middle East. In the 18th century Islam felt the challenge posed by modern science and new ideas about the origin of the world. Islam declined for a time in India but a succession of active leaders worked to revive it. In the 19th century a national movement arose in India which sought to win middle class Indians to the Muslim way of life. Early in this century the Muslim Congress was founded with the aim of establishing an independent Muslim state in North West India. Today, 85% of the population of Bangladesh are Muslims.

THE ARAB LEAGUE

In the last fifty years Islam has seen many changes. In 1954, the Arab League was formed in the attempt to create greater unity between Muslims. The solidarity of Islam is a dominant issue in the Muslim world at the present time. Muslims often ask the question: *'Can Islam continue to provide a point where people of all classes can meet, find guidance and a common life style?'* To answer this question is Islam's mission in the world today.

SAUDI ARABIA

Saudi Arabia has a special responsibility for preserving and propagating Islam. Here Muhammad was born and here Islam is said to flourish in its purest form. Here are the two most sacred places of Islam (Mecca and Medina) and the Saudi Arabians feel an obligation to operate the 'sacred law' (*shar'iah*) in the most literal way.

It is usual for women to wear a veil and be segregated. They do not drive cars, although there are signs of changing attitudes. The objection to girls being educated is less rigid and they may be educated by male teachers, although this is done via closed circuit television.

Gradually women are being allowed to make a greater contribution to society and the state provides the means for them to do so. Nevertheless, Saudi Arabia continues to follow the Qur'an to the letter when punishment is administered. Thieves may have their hands severed, murderers are executed, drunkards are flogged, adulterers are beheaded in public, alcohol is forbidden, gambling is outlawed, public cinemas and pornography are illegal.

THE IMAGE OF ISLAM

The situation of Islam in the modern world is complex. The process of change has to go forward and Islam claims to be a unifying force. The main issues that it faces are: the importance of tradition to Islam; how to adapt to changing social attitudes; the influences and pressures of international life; and the survival of religious values in a time of rapid social change.

MUSLIMS IN BRITAIN

Estimates of the number of Muslims in Britain vary, but the number is likely to be nearly two million. They live mainly around the larger cities, London, Birmingham, Bradford, Cardiff. Many male Muslims come here in advance of their families and rely upon friends and relatives to find them work. They come mainly from India and West Africa.

Muslims, like other minorities, have to face the challenge of living in a different culture. It is not easy always to retain their identity or follow the strict practices of their faith. Conflict and misunderstanding cannot be avoided completely, and sometimes it is difficult to observe the Muslim rites of passage in a traditional way. Likewise, there are difficulties with regard to the complete observance of Islamic customs at festival time, such as sacrifice, and from time to time there is confusion about the use of Muslim names, regulations regarding dress and diet, hygiene and education. Language is another problem, as the Muslims come from different language groups, but in the mosque (there are about three hundred in Britain) the language is always Arabic.

APPLIED MATERIALS

BENNETT, O. (1986). *Ramadan and Eid ul-Fitr.* MacMillan.
BRUCE, R. (1984). *Muhammad.* Holt, Rinehart & Winston.
IRVING, AHMAD, AHSAN (1979). *Qur'an – Basic Teaching.* Islamic Foundation.
McDERMOTT, M.Y. & AHSAN, M.M. (1982). *The Muslim Guide.* Islamic Foundation.
NASR, S.H. (1982). *Muhammad, Man of Allah.* Muhammad Trust.
TAMES, R. (1982). *Approaches to Islam.* Murray.
TAMES, R. (1984). *Islam.* Batsford.
ULLICH, M. ZIA (1984). *Islamic concept of God.* Kegan Paul.

EXAMINATION QUESTIONS

QUESTION

a) Name **two** Muslim sects other than a mystic sect. *(4)*

b) Is it strength or weakness for a religion to be divided into separate sects? Give reasons for your answer. *(6)*

c) Describe the main activities and teaching of **one** of the two sects you name. *(4)*

d) Say whether or not you agree that the existence of many sects makes co-operation between religions difficult. *(6)*

(WJEC)

**OUTLINE
ANSWER**

a) Either Sunni or Shia or Sufi.

b) The reasons may include: it affirms strength by showing variety and variation; it consolidates groups; increases zeal and fervour; to be divided means: being fragmented; creates discord; leads to competition; appears disunited . . .

c) The description should refer to the origin, the main stance, the practices, organisation, influence of the sect.

d) It may create confusion . . . rivalry . . . makes it difficult to achieve understanding . . . may not be fully representative . . .

A STUDENT'S ANSWER WITH EXAMINER'S COMMENTS

QUESTION

a) Say what you mean by the word 'almsgiving'.   *(2)*

b) i) Give **two** reasons why almsgiving is important to a Muslim.

    ii) What are the other Pillars of Islam?   *(6)*

c) Explain **two** of the Pillars of Islam, other than almsgiving.   *(4)*

d) i) What does Islam mean by 'duty'? Give examples.

    ii) What happens to Muslims who fail to fulfil their duty?   *(8)*

                                                                                      (WJEC)

a) Almsgiving is one of the Muslims Five pillars of faith, known as Zakat. It is collected as two and a half per-cent of a Muslims total moveable wealth.

b) Almsgiving is important to a Muslim because Muhammad taught that people should be generous to the poor at all times. It may be one day that they will be poor, and be grateful recipients of Zakat. The other pillars of Islam are the creed - Shahada; Praying five times a day - Salat, the Muslims tax - Zakat; Fasting during Ramadan, and to go on to a pilgrimage to Mecca once in their lifetime.

c) The creed of Islam is called 'shadaha' and says 'There is no god but god and Muhammed is his prophet'. This is the most important pillar. Muslims are also expected to pray five times a day, which is called Salat. Many do this at the mosque, but the most important thing is that it is done facing Mecca.

d) Islam means by 'duty' about their duty to god (Allah). It is their duty to obey the laws of Islam, especially the five pillars of faith. It is a duty of a Muslim to be kind to fellow Muslims. It is also the duty of a Muslim to spread and defend the Islamic faith.

Comments

This answer is along the right lines. One weakness is that you do not develop any of the points or give evidence in support of them. Your definition of 'almsgiving' is apt but note that it is referred to in the Qur'an. In b) you should mention how it shows solidarity and refer to the special occasions for giving alms. The other pillars of Islam are correct but pay attention to the *way you present them*. Try to give a neat presentation. The two pillars selected are quite alright in c) but you have not done what the question asks and write an *explanation* about them. Think again about the meaning of these. In d) part i) duty is derived from the Qur'an and the shar'iah. You must explain this more carefully. The two points of duty you mention are good but you do not give any *reasons* for choosing them. You have not answered the last part of the question.

QUESTION

a) Why do Muslims say their prayers facing Mecca? (4)

b) State what a Muslim would say is the importance and purpose of prayer. (6)

c) Describe **three** aspects of prayer that are common to most religions. (6)

d) Explain why Muslims pray to Allah (God) as Gracious and Compassionate. (4)

(WJEC)

> Muhamed told them to. It was the holy place. They go there to pray. They pray for peace and lay on the ground. They have a praying mat they take it with them sometimes they stop in the road and lay on the floor. Religions pray because it makes them feel good and when they go to the church they need to prayer and then say amen. The muslims call God Allah it is their name for him they say he does everything they ask.

Comments

This is a poor attempt even though you have included some correct points. You should show which part of the question you are answering, so use a), b) etc for each part. a) is too brief and you should say *why* they pray facing Mecca. In b) try to imagine what a Muslim feels when praying and take note of the words 'importance and purpose'. They are different. c) asks you to describe aspects . . . you should refer to prayer as thanksgiving etc. In d) the last two words should be *explained*. You must read the question with care and then answer what is asked.

JUDAISM

GETTING STARTED

Judaism is an umbrella term to describe the beliefs and practices of religious Jews. They number about 14 million today but there is a close connection between Judaism as a religion and the Jews as a race. Everyone born of a Jewish mother is born into the Jewish race, but not all Jews observe the religion of Judaism. Religious and non-religious Jews belong to the same race but we shall use Judaism to describe the religion of those Jews who *practise* its beliefs and customs.

The word 'Judaism' was first coined by Jews who wanted to describe their way of life as being different from their neighbours. It is not a unified religion today and Jews follow different traditions and customs in different parts of the world. Their homeland is the state of Israel, but those who live in the lands around the Mediterranean have different customs from Jews who live in other parts of Europe and America. You will also learn about the division of modern Judaism between Orthodox and Reform Jews. They all practise the Jewish faith and belong to the Jewish race.

ESSENTIAL PRINCIPLES

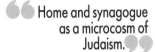

1 > FAMILY AND RELIGION

> " Home and synagogue as a microcosm of Judaism. "

The Jewish home has always been a bridge between religion and race. It is a focus and microcosm of Judaism. It has been the backbone of the observances and customs of the faith and preserved its essential features when these have been under threat. No-one can study Judaism without taking account of the importance of family religion.

The *mother* is the queen of the home. She plays a supreme rôle in preserving the faith and ensuring that it is practised regularly. She is responsible for the preparations for religious celebrations and seeing that the traditions are faithfully kept.

THE SABBATH

The Sabbath is a weekly festival that centres on the home as well as the synagogue. It runs from sunset on Friday to sunset on Saturday. The mother makes the Sabbath preparations for the family. She prepares the *kosher* food in accordance with the regulations, uses special dishes for meat, and observes the laws of personal hygiene. In a religious home there may be morning and evening prayers, and a blessing said at the beginning of every meal:

> *Blessed art thou, O Lord our God, King of the universe.*

The mother is the first to introduce children to the observances of Judaism. She sets them on the 'spiritual paths', but the father takes seriously the religious education of the children. It is important for children to learn about their faith so that they can practise it intelligently. It is said that '*an ignorant man cannot be pious*'. Jewish children receive their first lessons in moral values in the home, where they are given rules for life. Members of the religious community generally share in the religious and moral training of the young, in the hope that they will grow up to be good members of their race and religion. One sign of a religious home is the *mezuzah* – a small metal container with a tiny parchment scroll – placed on the right side of the door or in one of the rooms. The scroll has on it the words of the *shema* (*Hear, O Israel, the Lord our God is one Lord*). Every child is taught this first, and pious Jews recite it twice a day as an act of faith in God and in his chosen people. Their Bible instructs them to teach the shema to their children and to repeat it when at home or away. As the members of the family pass the *mezuzah* they touch it as a mark of dedication to God's laws (*mitzvot*) and his presence.

2 > THE SYNAGOGUE

The synagogue is Judaism's main institution. It is usually a purpose-built building which is the focus of Jewish community life. Its primary use is for worship, but it is also used for education and for social gatherings. Orthodox, Reform and Liberal Jews have their own synagogues but each has the same basic furnishings and symbols. These include the Ark, which houses the scrolls, near which is the perpetual flame (*ner tamid*) that reminds the Jews of the light that burned night and day in the temple in Jerusalem. At the front, there is a platform (*bimah*) and a reading-desk where the *Torah* is read and the cantor conducts the worship. All Jews are free to attend the synagogue services although a quorum of ten males has to be present. In the Orthodox synagogue, men and women are separated but in the Reform synagogue families may sit together. There is an eve of Sabbath service in the synagogue to welcome the Sabbath as a bride:

> Come, my beloved, with chorus of praise,
> Welcome Bride Sabbath, the Queen of the days.

TORAH

There is a regular Sabbath morning service whose central feature is the reading of the Torah scroll. The Authorised Daily Prayer Book is used (there is an English version) and the service need not be in Hebrew, the sacred language of the Jews, if this is not understood. The service, or parts of it, can be in the language of the people. Males cover their heads with a prayer cap (*yamulka*) and the elders sit in the front. They usually wear a prayer shawl (*tallit*) as a token of obedience to the Law, and a small leather case, or phylactory (*tephilin*), attached to the left arm or the forehead as a sign of devotion of heart and mind to God. The *Torah* scroll is removed from the Ark and read from the lectern. This (the Sefer Torah) is written by hand in Hebrew and decorated with various silver ornaments and small bells. As it is removed from the Ark, all eyes are fixed on it as the ornamental curtain decorated with verses from the Bible is drawn aside.

The Torah is arranged in the form of a lectionary, so that a part is read every Sabbath. Over a cycle of three years it is read from beginning to end. A Midrash (commentary of the Bible) describes the Torah in the synagogue service:

> God says to the Jews: I have given you the Torah, I cannot separate myself from it . . .
> Therefore wherever you go make me a home to dwell in. As Scripture says, 'And you
> shall make me a sanctuary, and I will dwell in their midst.' (Exodus 28.5)

The scroll is carried through the congregation, who stand in its honour. They can see and touch it for themselves, but the Torah itself is not worshipped. Hymns and psalms are sung, and in a Reform synagogue these may be led by a choir and organ. Set prayers are said and there is time for private prayer. The reading of the Torah is supplemented by a reading from the Prophets (*Haftorah*) from a printed Bible. Any member of the congregation may be called upon to read, and in a Reform synagogue this may include women. When the Torah is read, a special pointer is used. The service may include a homily given by the rabbi which is probably a commentary on the reading. The rabbi is not a priest, but the chief elder of the synagogue. Trained as a teacher, he is supported by the congregation.

The service is more informal than in other religions, and the atmosphere more relaxed. Worshippers may join or leave at any time, they may talk to each other and children may wander around the synagogue. It is a congregation, not a consecrated building (synagogue = gathering), but first and foremost it is a meeting with God and not simply a place. So worshippers radiate a sense of homeliness and pleasure at being able to meet and greet each other with the words 'Shabbat Shalom' (a peaceful Sabbath).

PRAYER

Prayer in the synagogue is a set rule and worship an act of obedience. Prayers need not be confined either to the synagogue or the home, since prayer and worship may be offered anywhere. But the same rules apply – God must be approached in a spirit of reverence and humility. Freedom to worship God at any time or place implies that all life is sacred and that everything good in life is God's gift. So the pious Jew remembers God after leaving the synagogue or when away from home and as he or she engages in the ordinary things, such as eating, washing, travelling, meeting friends, receiving and giving gifts. The final prayer in the synagogue is a joyful offering of praise:

> And the Lord shall be King over all the earth:
> In that day shall the Lord be one, and his name be One.

The Jewish year is regulated by a cycle of festivals and commemorations. They are central to Judaism and are observed faithfully as an integral part of the religion. They fulfil the regulations (*mitzvot*) which Judaism observes. There are *four* main reasons for saying that the festivals are a central core of Judaism:

1. **They forge a link between Judaism past and present.** Every major festival is an act of remembrance which relives in a dramatic way some event from the past, so present and past are brought together and also point Judaism to the future. Judaism today identifies with the triumphs and sorrows of its past.
2. **They focus on the central beliefs of the faith.** All festivals are religious occasions which serve to deepen the experience of the faith. Many celebrations centre on the Torah and other religious teaching.
3. **They are communal acts.** Families and communities of Jews celebrate the festivals together in the home or the synagogue. They keep the community identity alive and confirm the bonds of unity.
4. **They form a pattern of celebrations.** Each festival links with the other in its intention and purpose so as to give a sense of coherence to religion as a whole.

THE JEWISH YEAR

The Jewish year is a lunar cycle of twelve months, or 345 days. The year begins with the seventh month (*Tishri*) and is celebrated by Jews all over the world. For everyday purposes they may use the calendar of the people, as they do in Britain, but their celebrations follow their own calendar (*luach*).

THE JOY OF THE SABBATH (SHABBAT)

The weekly Sabbath is prepared for gladly and joyfully. It is a day of joy and rest, and not of sadness. Preparations to welcome the Sabbath begin in the home on the Friday with an evening service (*Kabbalet Shabbat*) to celebrate the climax of creation when God finished his work. Psalms are sung in praise of the Creator and his presence in the world and human life. The day of the Sabbath (Saturday) is chosen by God and laid down in the ten commands. You have seen how the mother prepares the Sabbath meal. At this, the father praises the virtues of his wife:

'*A woman of worth is more precious than rubies. For her children rise up and call her happy.*'

Parents bless their children and the father recites the prayer of sanctification (*kiddush*). One ritual observed before the meal is washing the hands in the prescribed way. Special loaves (*hallot*) are broken and handed round. Since they are in the shape of a plait they symbolise the unity of God, the Torah and his people. Salt is sprinkled over these loaves as a sign of the dignity of human labour. During the meal the family remember past events and their present faith. Between the courses (the meal lasts a long time), songs (*zemirot*) may be sung and thanks given for the joys of the Sabbath. Before it ends they look to the future and their hopes as God's people.

After attending the morning service in the synagogue (see the earlier account of this), the family enjoy a midday meal (prepared in advance) and spend the afternoon quietly. At the end of the day the act of separation (*havdalah*) merges the Sabbath with other days. A cup of wine is drunk to symbolise the carrying of the joys of the Sabbath into the other days. A song about the coming of the messiah (deliverer) is sung when the joy of the Sabbath rest and peace will be enjoyed universally.

THE NEW YEAR (ROSH HASHANAH)

New year's day is a solemn day of quiet reflection when Jews take stock of their lives and achievements. It is not a time for revelry, but for thinking about God's mercy and judgement. At the same time, greetings are exchanged such as the simple 'Good year', or more traditionally 'May you be inscribed in the Book of Life for a good new year'. It is time for new beginnings and Jews dress in their best clothes, or wear white as a sign of purity. Special bread in the shape of a crown or a ladder is baked in the home and eaten as a symbol of God's sovereignty and of the link between God and the home. Apples dipped in honey and pomegranates, the symbols of sweetness and fertility, may also be eaten.

In the synagogue on new year's morning a special service is held (*musaf*), based on the *Rosh Hashanah* Prayer Book. The service revolves around praise to God as king and the uncertainty of life. The story of the birth and binding of Isaac is read and hymns and prayers in remembrance of God's goodness are included. At the service the *shofar* (a ram's horn trumpet) is blown as a reminder of the sacrifice by Abraham of a ram in place of his son Isaac.

In the afternoon the family may visit a river or a well when they say more prayers and empty their pockets into the water as a sign of shedding sins. In religious terms the new year ritual centres on *creation*, *judgement* and *renewal*. Jews remember how at the beginning, God created the world. They reflect on his judgement on evil and by casting off their sins they begin the new year by submitting to him. The *shofar* heralds the call to a new beginning and a new life of justice, peace and goodness.

THE DAY OF ATONEMENT (YOM KIPPUR)

Ten days into the new year the Jews observe a day of religious observance called the Day of Atonement. It is a day of repentance, that is, turning away from sin, and making a fresh start. Sins are confessed directly to God and prayers are said for forgiveness for personal and private wrongs. This includes asking others to forgive them for any hurt done.

Yom Kippur is a fast day kept to show sincerity, self discipline, dedication and compassion. It is a day for helping people in need and for reciting memorial prayers for the dead. On the Day of Atonement the Ark is covered in white and a solemn prayer (*Kol Nidrei*) is sung as a memorial to Jews who have suffered persecution. The account of the ritual of the temple in Jerusalem is read, which tells how the high priest made a sacrifice on behalf of the people on the Day of Atonement. The reading from the Prophets is on the theme of fasting and purity and right attitudes. The closing service of the day is called Neilah, and the first line of the *shema* is recited before the *shofar* is blown before the open Ark.

FESTIVAL OF LOTS (PURIM)

On the fourteenth day of Adar (February/March) a festival of thanksgiving is held to commemorate the victory of Esther over the oppressor Mordecai. It recalls the courage and stand Esther took in defence of her own people when they were threatened by the villain Mordecai. She led them in their struggle for freedom and independence and eventually saved them from destruction even at the risk of her own life.

A Purim service is held in the synagogue in the morning and evening. During this the story of Esther (which reads like a novel) is read from the Megillah scroll. The congregation join in the reading and respond with shouts of joy and hand-clapping when Esther's courage is mentioned and with shouts of anger at the mention of the tyrant. The mixture of praises and booing creates an uproarious atmosphere which everyone present enters into. The worshippers greet each other by saying, '*Be happy! It's Adar*.' A festival meal is held which may last for several hours. Candles are lit, gifts are exchanged, and there is entertainment to add to the carnival atmosphere of Purim. Plays may be performed which portray the story of Esther, while effigies of the tyrant are burned. There may be processions, with children dressed in fancy dress. But the serious purpose of the festival is never forgotten.

PASSOVER (PESACH)

Passover is a spring festival held during Nisan (March/April). Preparations are made in the home in advance. All ordinary food (*harmetz*) is eaten or removed so that the special passover meal (*seder*) may be prepared. Dishes and cutlery are ritually prepared as well as the food. The family gather for the passover meal and usually guests are invited. On the table there is unleavened bread (*matzah*), bitter herbs (*maror*), and a piece of lamb (*pesah*). In the centre of the table is the *seder* plate, with bitter herbs, greenery, a shankbone of lamb and a boiled egg. Also on the table are four cups of wine and the 'cup of Elijah'. The head of the family presides at the meal, which begins with the invitation:

> 'Let all who are hungry come and eat. Let all who are in need come and celebrate Passover.'

First, the boiled egg is eaten with salt water. As the symbolic foods are eaten, an explanation is given of their meaning for the benefit of the younger members and guests. Between drinking the four glasses of wine the youngest member asks four traditional questions:

> Why is this night different from other nights?
> Why do we eat unleavened bread?
> Why must we eat bitter herbs?
> Why must we dip vegetables into salt water and bitter herbs into sauce?

The answer given is either '*We were slaves*' or '*Our ancestors worshipped idols.*'
Or the words of the ancient text may be spoken:

> And according to the understanding of the son, his father instructs him. He begins with the disgrace and ends with the glory; and he expounds from: A wandering Aramean was my father . . .

As the 'cup of Elijah' is filled, the door is opened to welcome the prophet who is expected before the messiah comes.

Father and mother may tell the story of the release of the ancient Jews from slavery in Eygpt. As they come to the part about the plagues, everyone spills a drop of wine as a mark of sorrow for the suffering of the people. After the meal they greet each other, '*Next year in Jerusalem*', and in the state of Israel the greeting is, '*Next year in Jerusalem rebuilt*'.

The passover is a celebration of freedom and deliverance from slavery. It is celebrated with great emotion, especially by Jews today. They relive the experiences of their ancestors and say, '*We have come out of Egypt*.' The bitter herbs remind them of the slavery, the unleavened bread of the hasty flight from Egypt, and the egg and salt of the new life after suffering. The four cups of wine symbolise the four stages on the journey: the release from slavery; the entry into the promised land; becoming God's people; and being redeemed. The name of Moses is not mentioned, as the story is told so that all the praise is focused on God who made the delivery possible.

TABERNACLES (SUKKOTH)

This is an autumn festival which lasts for seven days in Tishri (September/October). It is also known as the 'Season of Rejoicing'. It is a harvest festival and on the first day a service is held in the synagogue which includes the prayer:

> May it be your will, O my God, and the God of my fathers, that you cause your divine presence to live among us, and may you spread a covering peace over us.

The service includes a procession of waving *lulav* branches to the four points of the compass to symbolise God's universal blessings. The whole service is joyful and psalms of praise and thanksgiving are sung. During the festival, Jews may make a tent or booth (*sukkah*) as a temporary home and set up small booths in the synagogue. These are a reminder of the time when the early Jews lived in tents on their journey to the promised land. The booths are intended as a symbol of God's provision and care. If Jews live in them for seven days, this is seen as a symbol that their whole lives are blessed by God. The booth is a simple structure which may be made of any material. It is not blessed or consecrated but blessing comes to those who live in them. On the final day of the festival (the Great Hosanna or Hoshana Raba), a willow branch may be shaken until all its leaves drop off and prayers are said for rain.

REJOICING IN THE TORAH (SIMHAT TORAH)

Immediately after the Feast of Tabernacles comes the Festival of Rejoicing in the Torah. Although the one is connected with the other, they are also different. Rejoicing in the Torah is a very joyous festival. A special service is held in the synagogue and the Torah scroll is paraded around the synagogue seven times. Children as well as adults join in the procession and this creates great religious fervour. At the beginning the scrolls are removed from the Ark by the cantor (*hazzan*), who leads the procession. Psalms and popular songs are sung and the refrain is repeated in Hebrew:

> Please Lord, save us. Please, Lord, make us succeed.

The children wave flags decorated with motifs and they may also form dancing parties by linking hands with their elders. After completing one cycle, the scrolls are handed on to the worshippers so that everyone has the joy of carrying them. The procession passes under a canopy (*chuppah*), which is specially erected as though a marriage is taking place. The Torah is often compared to a bride. The canopy may be formed simply by holding upwards the four corners of a prayer shawl (*tallit*). The procession may pause under it and hear parts of the Torah read. In modern Israel, Jews gather at the western wall in Jerusalem on Simhat Torah carrying scrolls under small canopies. They then read them as an act of rejoicing and to show solidarity with Jews everywhere.

WEEKS (SHAVUOT)

The Festival of Weeks is a harvest festival which is held seven weeks after passover in the month Silvan (May/June). Homes and the synagogue are decorated for the festival and summer foods are eaten. In the special synagogue service there are readings about the giving of the ten commands and from the Book of Ruth. The latter is connected with the harvest and with David, the ideal of the expected messiah. According to tradition, David was born during this festival. The Prayer Book calls it 'The Season of the Giving of Our Torah'.

During this festival special emphasis is placed upon the education of children. In the past it was usual to take children to the synagogue for their first lesson on this day. Those who had made progress in school may be honoured by being allowed to take part in the synagogue service or joining in the procession of the Torah scroll. The Torah is studied closely and usually there is a celebration meal for family and friends.

In earlier times, Jews used to make an offering of the first fruits to God and each night between passover and the Feast of Weeks a measure (*omar*) of barley was brought into the temple in Jerusalem. The decorations in the home and synagogue are a reminder of how Mount Sinai was covered with vegetation when the ten commands were given. In modern Israel the festival has a close connection with the land and future prosperity and productivity.

FESTIVAL OF LIGHTS (HANUKAH)

This festival is held on 25th Kislev (December) and the following seven days. Its central ritual is kindling lights in the home. A *hanukah* lamp is lit and placed in the window or open door. It is lit in the presence of the whole family, immediately after sunset. It is an eight-branched lamp – one lamp is lit each night of the festival as these words are spoken:

> These lights are holy and we are not permitted to make use of them, but only to see them in order to thank your name for the wonders, the victories and the marvellous deeds.

By the end of the week all the lights are burning and during this time there are family gatherings, gifts are exchanged and games are played. In the synagogue, the service includes a reading from the Book of Zechariah about God's Holy Spirit.

The Festival of Lights celebrates the victory of the Jews against the Greek tyrant Antiochus Epiphanes in 175 BCE. He had tried to force the Jews to conform to the Greek way of life and to worship the Greek gods. He set up an image of the Greek god Zeus in the temple, but the Jews were so incensed that they rose up against him. They lit a light to symbolise their defiance but the lamp only had enough oil for one day. But, miraculously, the lamp burned for eight days. This encouraged the Jews and, led by their priest, Mattathias, they were determined to rid their land of the tyrant. When Mattathias died, Judas Maccabeus led a series of guerilla attacks against Antiochus, and ordered the temple to be rededicated to God. On 25 Kislev in 164 BCE the rededication began and lasted for eight days. Judas then decreed that this should be celebrated by every future generation.

FESTIVAL OF INDEPENDENCE (YOM HA'ATZMAUT)

Independence day commemorates the return of the Jews to Israel in 1948. It is held on 5th of Iyar (April) with public gatherings, parades and various celebrations. During the parade twelve torches may be carried to symbolise the twelve tribes of Israel and Jewish unity. Religious Jews say special prayers for national unity and the redemption of the people. In modern Israel the Jews observe Holocaust Day (*Yom Ha-Shoah*) on the 27th Nisan, as a memorial to the victims of Nazism. It is a day of solemn remembrance:

> 'We remember with reverence and love the six millions of our people who perished at the hands of a tyrant more wicked than the Pharaoh who enslaved our fathers in Egypt . . . they slew the blameless and pure, men and women and little ones, with vapours of poison, and burned them with fire.'

There are no public gatherings on this day, nor are there any entertainments or celebrations. It is a day of quiet reflection. As they remember the holocaust, they pledge their opposition to all forms of oppression, tyranny and racism.

PILGRIMAGE

Judaism does not include pilgrimage as an essential obligation but Jerusalem attracts Jews from all over the world to visit sites associated with their religion and race. The most sacred is the mount of the temple and the ruins of the first temple built by Solomon. These remains are called the 'wailing' or the 'western wall'. Here, religious Jews gather to read the Torah and to grieve for the destruction of the temple by the Romans in 70 CE. They are often overcome by grief at the very sparse remains of the temple and pray near the wall and kiss the stones. They look forward to the time when the temple will be built again. They also remember the times when they were not able to visit the sacred place, but since the capture of the old city from the Arabs in 1967 the Jews are able to visit it once again. Pilgrimage is therefore a bitter-sweet experience for pilgrims.

4 ▶ MAJOR BELIEFS AND ETHICS

You will find a considerable variety of beliefs and opinions among religious Jews. Many prefer to speak of Judaism as a *complete way of life* rather than *a set of beliefs*. They have no formal or structured creed. The essentials of their faith are derived from their Bible and the *covenant*. This word is central to their beliefs. It means 'solemn agreement' or the covenant which God made when he chose them of his own free will to be his 'elect' or 'chosen' people. He chose them for a special purpose:

> 'But you, Israel (Jews) my servant,
> you are the people that I have chosen,
> the descendants of Abraham, my friend.'

GOD

Judaism takes the existence of God for granted and it offers no proof of this. God has no form or beginning or image. He is present everywhere and is eternal.

The nearest thing to a statement of faith is the *shema* and whenever it is recited the Jews declare four beliefs about God that are fundamental to Judaism:

- *God is one.* The whole being of God is in his unity and he has no agent or incarnation of himself.

- *His name is Jehovah.* Jews do not pronounce the sacred name, instead they use the word Lord or God. Their word *Yahweh* (which gives the English Jehovah) is of a spiritual being who is beyond human ability to name.

- *God reveals himself.* God enters into the experience of his people to reveal his will and nature.

- *God is personal.* He is the God of Abraham, Isaac and Jacob. His character is holy; he is separate from all other beings; he is loving and merciful; he shows favour to whoever he chooses; he is faithful; he keeps his covenant with his people.

HUMAN LIFE

God created the first human being in his image. This does not mean in a physical sense, as there can be no physical likeness between God and any other being. The image of God is a spiritual quality that makes every human being unique.

Body and spirit

Human life is a unity of body and spirit. The spirit pervades the whole of life. When God created the first human being he breathed his spirit on him and he became a 'living soul'. Being created in God's image implies that the human being has a special status in the world. Judaism describes this as 'being a little lower than the angels'. The human being is given dominion in the world by God and the status of representing him before the world. Therefore human life can reflect the justice, goodness, love and compassion of God before the world.

Individual and community

Judaism does not view the individual in isolation from other individuals. Everyone is born into a family, a race and a nation. Everyone is part of the social 'whole'. No-one can contract out of the corporate whole. The destiny of the individual is bound up with the destiny of humankind. This unity between the individual and humankind extends to the past, shapes the present, and points forward to the future. The social and religious practices of Judaism are rooted in the past and the individual is identified with this. Jews refer to themselves as the 'children of Abraham'. No-one acts in the present entirely alone for all the activities of Judaism are notably communal. God is a God of a 'people' and every individual belongs to this 'people'.

THE NATURAL WORLD

The natural world is God's creation or his 'handiwork'. He is not identified with nature, but he controls it and acts within it. The natural world is made for the good of humankind and to serve God. Judaism does not teach self withdrawal from the natural world, but self fulfilment within it. It believes that nature is God's gift and that its resources can be used for the benefit of humankind and for his glory. The development of the physical life is seen to be good and proper, celibacy is not advocated, nor does it set up monasteries to withdraw from the world.

In the 18th century the *Hasidim* movement known as the 'pious' or 'godly' became well known throughout Judaism. Its purpose was to teach a life of complete devotion to its faith and practices. Besht, one of the movement's prominent members, called Jews to remember that salvation is for the *whole* of creation and for the *whole* of life, physical, moral and spiritual. He laid before his fellow Jews the ideals of love, charity and compassion which should be practised through immersing themselves in the affairs and concerns of life in the natural world.

The *Zionist* movement of recent times has focused attention on the realisation and fulfilment of national hopes and ideals in the 'here and now'. The movement claims that Jews do not have to wait for the appearing of a promised deliverer sometime in the future, who will usher in the new age of justice and peace. By acting in the right way in the present, humankind can help forward the process of salvation. Human life can find its rightful fulfilment through commitment to right action in the natural world.

THE AFTER LIFE

What happens when a person dies? A modern Jewish writer has summed up the attitude of Judaism to death:

> 'Heaven and hell, garden of Eden and judgement day or resurrection we can accept in a very broad symbolic sense only. Frankly, we do not know how man survives. But we trust that he survives, in accordance with the compassionate decree of the Eternal One.'

Jewish beliefs about life after death have developed in a fluid way. In Bible times there was a belief that the soul entered *sheol* (hell) where the good and wicked survived as shadows. Later, this gave way to a view of heaven and hell as two distinct places. The departed entered one or the other to be punished or rewarded.

The soul is thought to survive in union with the body. A body is necessary for the survival of the soul. So there developed a belief in a general resurrection of the good and wicked. God does not desert a person at the point of death, but holds the hope of entering a state of blessedness. This implies a hope of immortality as God himself is immortal. This makes belief in an after life logical, inasmuch as i) *God is eternal*; he created the human being as a 'living soul' and so it is reasonable to believe that the soul lives a life of eternity with him; ii) *faith and godliness will be rewarded*; faith and love will not end with physical death.

Many religious Jews say it is idle to speculate about immortality, as no-one can demonstrate what it will be like. Yet it is not unreasonable to hold to a belief in immortality, but in terms of defining it the words of the rabbi are clear: *'Frankly, we do not know how man survives.'*

ETHICS

When a religious Jew asks the question, *'What must I do?'* the answer given might be, *'What God requires'*. One of their prophets introduced his moral teaching with the question, *'What does the Lord require of you?'*

The ethics of Judaism rooted in religion.

The ethics of Judaism are not a set of rules or regulations, but a response to this question.

The ten commands

The ten commands are Judaism's pattern for moral living. They were given to a religious (covenant) community to give its moral action direction and unity. Without this, individuals would 'do their own thing' and the social and moral order would crumble.

First, note that the ten commands are set in a faith context: *I am the Lord your God*.

Second, note that they are set within the context of the covenant: *I brought you out of Egypt where you were slaves*.

The commands therefore are rooted in faith in God who led his people out of slavery.

Read the commands against this background:

Worship no god but me;
do not make for yourselves images;
do not use my name for evil purposes;
observe the Sabbath;
respect your father and mother;
do not commit adultery;
do not steal;
do not accuse anyone falsely;
do not desire another man's house.

Having read the ten commands ask these questions:

  i) which commands apply only to individuals?
  ii) which relate to a generation gap?
  iii) which refer to those who seek to control others?
  iv) why do they cover so many aspects of life?
  v) are they a prescription for a complete way of life?

Three requirements

Judaism teaches three ethical requirements which are laid down in the 'Ethics of the Fathers' (*Pirke Aboth*):

> By three things is human society sustained, by the Law, by worship and by deeds of kindness.

The three (Law, worship and kindness) show how closely linked religion is with kindness.
Law (Torah): the Law (Torah) is a basis for right living, it instructs in religion and morals.

> The rabbis wondered who would sit at the right hand of God. One of them said: 'It is they who come before God because of their knowledge of the Law, and because of their good deeds.'

The Law must not be confused with legalism. The prime purpose of the Law is to instruct the Jews to answer the question, *'What does the Lord require?'* Torah means 'instruction' as well as Law.
Worship: in the teaching of Judaism, worship is the response of the *whole* life (body and spirit) to God. It is not simply a spiritual act but one answer to the question, *'What does the Lord require?'* It is the dynamism for moral action, or the 'sanctification' of God's name in work and worship.
Kindness: the Pirke Aboth does not define the deeds but clearly grounds them in positive behaviour. They derive from the Law (Torah) and find their inspiration in worship. Kindness therefore is following the instructions of the Law in justice; providing for the weak; showing respect for the aged; caring for servants; showing hospitality. The *shema* requires Jews to love God with heart, mind, soul and strength *and* to love one's neighbour as oneself. Love is not speculation but action, it is not private but social, it is one of the 'duties of the heart'. This is summed up by Rabbi Hillel:

> The pious man is he who loves the world and hallows life in such a way that his daily activities of eating, drinking, labouring, pleasure are raised to the highest level, so that all his acts are sacred and reflect the divine image.

5 ▷ RITES OF PASSAGE

Many of the customs observed by Jews during the life cycle have been handed down from the past and are marked with religious observances.

BIRTH AND CIRCUMCISION

The life cycle of a Jew.

There are no special birth ceremonies, but the naming of a child is associated with the rite of circumcision which takes place on the eighth day. This is properly called 'the covenant of circumcision'. It is a symbolic act performed according to God's covenant with Abraham. The physical act is infused with spiritual meaning which the Jews call 'the circumcision of the heart', that is, an act of obedience and consecration.

According to tradition, the rite takes place in the presence of Elijah and the chair used during the circumcision is called 'Elijah's chair'. Candles are lit and the rite is performed either at home, or in a hospital by a *mohel* (a person appropriately trained). It is customary to give the child a traditional Jewish name, and although this may not be used everyday it is always used on special religious or ceremonial occasions. The rite is one of initiation into the community and the father recites a prayer of thanksgiving:

> Praised be thou, O Lord, King of the universe, who hast sanctified us by thy commandments, and hast bidden him enter the covenant of Abraham our father.

The relatives and friends present give the child their good wishes and hope that he will live to study the Law and follow its instructions. The father may make a symbolic offering in the synagogue of five shekels as a sign of the child's dedication to God. The money is then given to charity. In the case of a girl, he may say a blessing for the child and her mother over the Torah scroll. Circumcision does not give the child a new status as he is already born into the Jewish race through having a Jewish mother. It is not a sacrament but an initiation into the faith.

BAR MITZVAH

Jews attach great importance to the *bar mitzvah* ceremony when the Jewish boy reaches the age of thirteen. He has now become a 'son of the Law'. You will discover how a young Jew feels when he reaches his bar mitzvah from this account:

It was seven-thirty on the morning of my bar mitzvah. My father woke me – the most important day of my life. I had studied for two months and still I was scared. In three hours' time I would be standing up there at the Bima (platform for reading desk), with all my relations, friends and congregation listening to me. I dressed wearing my new suit, polished shoes, and beautiful new silk cappel (cap). The family were rushing about in great excitement, and uttering quick words of confidence 'Don't worry you'll be just fine. In five hours it would be over, don't worry.' But still I worried.

At nine o'clock my father said that we would go, and my mother, father, sister and my grandmother and myself marched off to the synagogue. On arrival there we were met by the Rabbi, a large jolly man, whom I had grown to like over the years. He greeted us with a smile; he took me aside and gave me a few last hints, and much encouragement. The congregation arrived quickly. I was taken to the warden's box, where I sat. My consolation was that I had a very comfortable seat, but I still kept worrying. All the guests walked past the warden's box, shaking my hand. I thought that everyone was watching me, and I almost shrank. What cheered me most was when my great uncle gave me an old prayer book in a beautiful leather and gold covering. He said that it had been in his family for over five generations. It's almost unbelievable how good this made me feel; and I can never repay him for what he did. Then the Rabbi called out my name 'Binyamin ben Naphtali' (Hebrew Benjamin son of Naphtali). As I walked to the bima my legs felt like they were giving way. But I managed to go up the stairs, and stood at the reading desk. Then it was time for me to read from the Sefer Torah. I was still very nervous, but as I went on and I continued to read I felt much more confident, and until I recited the last word, I just felt wonderful. And then men were shouting 'Mazzeltov' (Good luck and happiness) and the women cried with pleasure. I stepped back – I was so happy – for I had done it well!

The boy has now become an adult and for religious purposes he is responsible for keeping the Law himself. You will see from the account how the boy is prepared for his *bar mitzvah* and is called up to read the Torah for the first time in the synagogue. He may at the same time receive a prayer shawl (*tallit*) and a prayer book (*siddur*) and may become a member of the *minyan* (the ten males who must be present when a synagogue service takes place). He may also receive a phylactery (tephilin) to wear as part of his dress. At the end of the ceremony he may recite the prayer over the scroll which begins:

Heavenly Father, on this sacred and solemn occasion in my life, I stand before thee in the presence of this congregation to fulfil my duty, to pray to thee every day and to keep thy Law that I may be a more worthy man.

Friends and relatives celebrate the bar mitzvah with a party. Girls today might have a bat mitzvah ceremony so that they too share in the religious community.

MARRIAGE

There is an old Jewish saying that an unmarried rabbi is not employed. He is not a complete person without a wife. Rabbi Akiba stated that, 'He who remains unmarried impairs the divine image.' From the religious point of view, an unmarried male Jew is unthinkable. The Jew is eligible for marriage after his *bar mitzvah*, and rabbis used to teach that no Jew should remain single beyond the age of eighteen.

The marriage service has changed over the years. In early times it took place in the bridegroom's home, and between the 16th and 19th centuries it was held often in the evening in the open air. Nowadays, most weddings take place in the synagogue. It was once forbidden to conduct weddings or funerals on the Sabbath. The ceremony is usually conducted by the rabbi, although any learned Jew may do so. It takes place under a canopy (*chuppah*), the symbol of the home and stability of marriage. The bride and groom stand here and drink a cup of wine (the symbol of plenty) and benedictions are said. The bridegroom speaks the words of consecration:

Behold, you are consecrated to me by this ring according to the law of Moses.

(In a Reform synagogue the bride repeats the formula, but in an Orthodox synagogue she remains silent.)

Customs vary, but the bride may wear a veil which is not removed until the ceremony is completed. The marriage agreement (*kethubah*) is read in the presence of two witnesses and a glass is broken. The agreement sets out how the husband will support his wife and how they will fulfil their spiritual and material responsibilities. The Seven Blessings of marriage are spoken and psalms 100 and 150 may be sung. The couple are toasted and greeted by everyone present. Generally, Jews view inter-marriage (marrying into another faith) with sadness, although it is estimated that thirty per cent of Jews marry outside the faith. They do not approve of marriage in a registry office. Divorce is permitted, but it is customary for the husband to obtain a document from the 'religious court' (*beth din*) signed by two witnesses. In Britain this can only be done after the civil divorce has been given. Even so, Judaism looks upon divorce as a tragedy and with sadness.

DEATH AND COMMEMORATION

In Jewish belief, death is a sorrowful parting when the life returns to God who gave it. As death approaches the Jew makes a confession (*niddui*) of faith in the life to come. The last words are the *shema*, but there is no set form of burial. At the funeral service a eulogy may be given, psalms sung, and the *kiddush* (a prayer in praise of God as sovereign over the whole of life) is offered. A Jew may tear the dead person's garment – but this (*keriah*) and other customs such as guarding the body, dressing it in a ritual garb, and observing a week's mourning are not now compulsory. A service may be held in the home of the deceased on the night before the burial, which may be by cremation or in a grave. Jews usually support a burial society to provide and care for a Jewish cemetery or an area for their own. A year after the burial a headstone may be consecrated at the grave, and a commemoration service may be held annually on the anniversary of a death.

6 SACRED WRITINGS

Judaism probably reveres its sacred writings above everything else. Every synagogue has an Ark which houses the scrolls of the Bible, and according to tradition the Torah scroll is a handwritten copy which is perfect in every detail. If a mistake is made in copying it, it cannot be used in the synagogue, but neither can it be destroyed. It is deposited in a *genizah* (burial place) to rot naturally.

TaNaKh

The letters TNK stand for the initial letters of the three divisions of the Jewish Bible: Torah; Nevi'im; Ketuvim (Law, Prophets and Writings). Altogether, there are thirty-nine books written by different authors and styles over a thousand years. They were handed down first of all in spoken form before they were set in writing, and then collected together in 90 CE to comprise the Jewish Bible. It covers about a thousand years of Jewish history and teaching.

The Bible is the core of Judaism and religious Jews say that they live by it and always carry it in their hearts and minds. They may have a *phylactery* as part of their dress, or a *mezuzah* as part of their home, both of which contain part of the Torah. Bible studies form about thirty per cent of the curriculum in Jewish schools, and in Jerusalem the Shrine of the Book (Bible) is a central symbol of the importance of the Bible. The Torah is believed to be perfect in every respect and need never be altered to meet new conditions. To do this would imply that there can never be a final Torah. Its teaching must not be altered and every part is literally of equal importance. Reform Jews, however, do distinguish between those parts of the Torah that are of 'value for all time' and those which are more 'temporary'. The part which says: '*do not deprive foreigners or orphans of their rights*' or '*do not cheat a hired servant*' are valid for all time; whereas, '*if a guilty man is sentenced to be beaten, the judge is to make him lie face downwards and be whipped*', is more 'temporal'. Reform Jews claim that as God spoke these instructions through a human agent, they may not be reported perfectly in every respect. The laws must be interpreted to show how they apply in different ages, just as God continues to reveal himself to different ways.

Nevertheless, the Torah is often said to be equivalent to the whole of Judaism. *To be zealous for God is to be zealous for the Torah*, and vice versa. Yet there have always been disagreements about how to interpret it. In early times the Sadducees (priests) and the Pharisees (progressive Jews) interpreted its teaching about the nation in a different way. In the Middle Ages the rabbis developed their methods of interpreting the Torah. Yet all Jews agree that the Torah has sustained them throughout history and they look forward to the time when its ideals will be universally received.

NEVI'IM

You will probably know the name of some of the prophets of the Jewish Bible, like Jonah or

Jeremiah. A prophet was someone who spoke God's message to the people, a message which might be about what was happening in the present or what God intended to happen in the future. God specially called the prophet and gave him his message to declare. These messages are written in the Books of the Prophets (Nevi'im) and form the second part of the Jewish Bible. They are often divided between major and minor books:

Major	Minor			
Isaiah	Hosea	Obadiah	Nahum	Haggai
Jeremiah	Joel	Jonah	Habakkuk	Zechariah
Ezekiel	Amos	Micah	Zephaniah	Malachi

The prophets were the great inspirers of religion and they interpreted it for the people. A reading from the Prophets is normally included in a synagogue service and they are still honoured as the moral and spiritual conscience of Judaism.

KETUVIM

The third part of the Bible is a miscellaneous collection of books. Some of them, such as the Book of Psalms or the Book of Proverbs, are widely used. Others contain stories which are very well known. Some, such as the Book of Ecclesiastes or the Books of Chronicles are not so widely used or well known. The Book of Psalms is used regularly in the synagogue services and in personal devotions. The psalms embrace human experience from birth to death, its joy and sorrow, its hopes and disappointments. Jews see the Book of Psalms as a mirror of what experience is.

Certain proverbs from the Book of Proverbs are heard every day, for example,

A labourer's appetite makes him work harder;
It is better to be patient than powerful;
Someone who is sure of himself does not talk all the time;
Intelligent people are always eager and ready to learn.

The Book of Ruth tells the moving story of Ruth and Naomi in a beautiful way. The Book of Job is both an epic and a powerful drama; it is one of the world's classics on the question of why do the innocent suffer.

A living book

Judaism looks upon the Bible as the foundation of its beliefs, but also the source of its inspiration and vitality. Some Jews regard it as a dialogue between God and his chosen people, which they believe continues whenever they hear it read or study it. The survival of Judaism is bound up with it. The guardians of Judaism are the teachers of the Bible.

Question: Who then are guardians of the city? Answer: The teachers of the Bible.

TALMUD

After the Bible, the Talmud is Judaism's most cherished book. Talmud means 'teaching' and it is a collection of teachings of many Jewish teachers over five hundred years. The teachings are about almost every subject under the sun and they reflect the practical spirit of Judaism. It is its 'Oral Law' and consists of two parts, the *Mishnah* and *Gemara*.

The Mishnah was completed in about 200 CE and provides guidance on a variety of subjects which range from agriculture to holy days, from hygiene to temple service.

The Gemara is commentary on the Mishnah as to how to interpret the laws. The Talmud also contains instruction on legal matters which is called the *Halachah*, and much teaching on moral issues given in parables and legends which is known as *Hagadah*.

The style of the Talmud is attractive and the teaching given in short graphic sayings, which are easy to learn and remember. Here are some examples:

Three things keep the world safe: truth, judgement and peace.
He who disciplines his own son will profit by him.
When a poor man stands at your door, God himself stands at his right hand.
A horse that is untamed will turn out to be stubborn.
Greatness runs away from him who runs after it; greatness runs after whoever runs away from it.
He who teaches his own son will make his enemies envious.
The punishment of the liar is that no-one will believe him when he speaks the truth.

Judaism maintains that the Talmud helps to keep it pure and protects it from error. Once a young man asked Rabbi Hillel:

'Teach me about the Jewish faith while I stand on one foot.'

Hillel replied:

'What is hateful to you do not do to your fellow man; that is the whole Law; the rest merely explains it – go and learn it.'

SIDDUR

The Jewish prayer book (*Siddur*) and the heart of its devotion is a treasury of spiritual experiences from the time of Abraham onward. It is an order of prayer for use in the synagogue. Orthodox Jews in Britain mainly use the Authorised Daily Prayer Book text.

The Siddur lays down what may be included in the services:

the shema; psalms and thanksgivings; the Amidah or Eighteen Blessings which include statements of praise, thanksgiving and petitions which the Jews recite standing; the Kaddish prayer which is recited at the end of each part of the services; readings from the Law.

The Siddur was compiled in the 9th century CE by Rabbi Amran of Susa, but there have been many prayer books compiled since. The first printed prayer book appeared in 1485. The form is always the same: morning, afternoon and evening prayer; the *hallel* psalms; prayers for the new moon; the *Kaddish*; the *Amidah*; prayers for holy days.

All the prayer books express the same spirit and unity. They also contain statements of doctrine, such as the thirteen principles of the Jewish faith formulated by *Maimonides* in the 13th century. Broadly speaking all Jews subscribe to these:

Belief in . . . God as creator and providence; his unity; his incorporeality; his eternity; him to whom alone is worship due; the words of the prophets; Moses was the greatest of the prophets; the revelation of the Law to Moses at Sinai; the immutability of the revealed Law; God as omnipotent; God as omniscient; retribution in this world and hereafter; the coming of the Messiah; the resurrection of the dead.

(You should refer these to the section in this Guide on the Major Beliefs of Judaism.)

JEWISH SECTS TODAY

The roots of modern Judaism are in the Middle Ages, but in the last century three divisions within Judaism became prominent and are still active: Orthodox, Reform and Liberal.

Orthodox

In the Middle Ages certain rabbis tried to create a closely-knit community of Jews based on their religion and culture. This pattern is followed today by Orthodox Jews, who adhere closely to the traditions of the past in their beliefs and practices. Their basic rule is the Written and Oral Law as an authentic guide for religious practices and practical living. In Britain the leader of the Orthodox Jews is the Chief Rabbi; he speaks on their behalf and usually represents them at public gatherings or in discussions with other religious leaders. He offers guidance about the observance of the Law and the rituals and customs of Judaism.

Reform and Liberal

In the early part of the 19th century certain Jews felt the need to reform the religion, so as to give it a greater appeal in the modern world. They saw the need to revise some of its traditional practices and use the language of the people in worship. The leader of the movement was David Friedlander (1756–1834), but the founder of the first Jewish reform 'temple' was Israel Jacobson. The movement spread to America and in 1840 the first Reform synagogue was established in England. At the time, traditional religious beliefs about the world were being challenged by the new science and some Jews felt the need to face the challenge openly. This must involve revising the narrow views of the Bible and the Talmud, the legal system of Judaism (*halakah*) and the traditional ceremonial rituals. The language of the services must be intelligible to the worshippers and not wholly in Hebrew, some of the restricted regulations governing the synagogue needed to be revised, and laws governing such things as dress and diet needed to be brought up to date.

The Orthodox and Reform Jews share more things in common than divide them. This was the view of a meeting of rabbis in London which made this pronouncement:

> We affirm that there exists a God who has made his covenant which we have freely placed into our lives. We affirm God out of our experience, out of the experiences of the Jewish people. We affirm God out of our doubts and our certainties, out of our past and out of all the possibilities of our future being.

7 > JUDAISM
THEN AND NOW

Judaism has always shown a passionate determination to survive and keep its identity. This is inspired by its profound belief that God has a special role for his chosen people in the world. The famous fortress at Masada in Israel is a symbol to Jews of the fanatical will to survive. Masada was a Roman garrison and armoury when the Romans ruled Palestine (Israel). In 63 CE the Jewish Zealot Menahem attacked Masada to seize arms for a major attack on Jerusalem. The attack was successful and the Zealots prepared for their offensive against Jerusalem. However, they were defeated and many Zealots killed. Some had taken refuge in Masada and put up a fierce resistance to the Romans. They made a pact with death and rather than yield they decided to kill themselves. Their leader addressed them:

> 'We revolted from the Romans with great pretensions of courage, and when, at last, they invited us to preserve ourselves, we could comply with them . . . let us go out of the world together with our children and wives, in the state of freedom. This it is that our laws command us to do.'

THE FOUNDING FATHERS

The origins of Judaism go back to Abraham (the father of the people) and Isaac and Jacob. *Abraham* received the covenant of circumcision and the promise that God would make his nation great and his descendants as the stars of heaven. Moses is the founder of the national faith of Judaism. Under God he led the tribes out of Egypt and eventually moulded them into a single nation. This was the first great act of liberation in their history which made them a nation. Jews always look upon this as the most significant religious event in their history.

God made a covenant with the whole people in the time of *Moses* and later renewed it under his successor *Joshua* when they entered the promised land. It took them nearly two hundred years to gain full possession of the land but they never lost the determination of the complete conquest.

UNITY AND PEACE

Through the skill and genius of *David* the whole land of Israel was brought under his rule. He made Jerusalem the capital of his kingdom and secured peace and prosperity for his people. He made Jerusalem the religious centre, but it was his son *Solomon* who built the first temple and made it the focus of the national religion. During Solomon's reign his father's empire began to break up and when he died it divided into two separate kingdoms, each with its own king and capital city. The kingdom of Israel in the north made its capital Samaria, but from the time of separation in 930 BCE until its collapse in 721 BCE, Israel was dogged by internal dissention and by attack from outsiders. The end came when the Assyrians made their final assault and carried the population into captivity.

The southern kingdom of Judah kept its independence for nearly two hundred years longer. The end came when Jerusalem was attacked by the Babylonians, who in 586 BCE made their final onslaught on the city and destroyed it completely. The temple was looted and then razed to the ground and the people were transported to Susa to begin their exile.

EXILE

For the next fifty years the story of Judaism is that of a people in exile. It was not a totally unproductive period for the Jews since they managed to keep their faith alive and to recall God's covenant. This gave them hope that one day they would return to their homeland. Their devotion to their race and religion sustained them until the time came for them to return home.

THE RETURN

The rise of Cyrus of Persia paved the way for exiles throughout the empire to return to their homelands. In 539 BCE, Cyrus issued an edict granting the freedom for Jews and other captives to return to their native lands, and in 536 BCE the first wave of Jews reached Israel. Others followed during the following years, but the sight which faced them was one of devastation. Jerusalem was a heap of rubble, the temple was in ruins and the land overrun by wild beasts. Yet they set about the task of rebuilding their life in their own country, inspired by prophets and others to put into action their will to survive. By 516 BCE the temple was rebuilt and dedicated, followed by the city of Jerusalem. Although they were under the domination of the Persians they were able to carry on the work of reconstruction without being oppressed.

OPPRESSION AND DISPERSION

The swift rise to power of Alexander the Great brought Israel under the rule of the Ptolemies and later the Seleucids. They were intent on making the Jews toe the line and conform to Greek laws and customs. They even tried to impose the Greek religion on them. This outraged some of the pious Jews, and when the Greek Antiochus demanded to set up an altar to the Greek god in the temple this sparked off a bitter struggle that lasted for three years. At the end the temple was restored to the worship of God and the Jews held a festival (*Hanukah*) in celebration of the event. But during this troubled period many Jews had left their homeland and settled in other parts of the world. So began the Jewish dispersion (diaspora). Communities of Jews came into being in many countries around the Mediterranean but they remained loyal to their race and observed the customs of their religion, but in an adapted form.

In 63 BCE the Roman occupation of Israel began, although the more extreme nationalists never accepted their rule. In 68 CE a major conflict broke out between the Jews and Romans and the temple was destroyed. The defeat of the Jews was decisive and they lost possession of their land completely. The history of the Jews from that time is of a people in dispersion, until they returned to establish the modern state of Israel in 1948.

LATER JUDAISM

The sack of Jerusalem and the destruction of the temple was a devastating crisis for Judaism, but the Jews refused to face total ruin. The two foci of their faith – the Torah and the synagogue – inspired them in their will to survive as a nation. Their rabbis not only encouraged them in their devotion to the Torah and the synagogue, but they also had a key role in teaching the Law and instructing Jews in the practices of their faith. A number of influential schools of rabbis came into existence for this purpose and these became important centres of learning. One consequence of this was that the Talmud was compiled in the two well-known forms, the Babylonian and the Palestinian.

In the Middle Ages, Jewish scholars were active in revising and redefining the beliefs of Judaism. They intended to present it as a reasoned faith that did not clash with knowledge or understanding. One of the most prominent leaders in this connection was *Moses Maimonides* (1135–1204) who joined the Jewish community in Egypt. He formulated the famous thirteen principles of the Jewish faith and wrote a famous work called 'Guide for the Perplexed'. Another important movement is the *Kabbala*, a movement of mystics that sought to stimulate and deepen the spiritual life of Judaism. It sought to direct attention to the promise of the Messiah or deliverer as a means of fostering greater spiritual fervour among the Jews. A number of messianic movements arose which received a popular following. Some of these are still active and come into their own in times of stress and crisis.

In the 19th century, as has already been shown, the liberal and reform movements arose. These radical movements have had a significant influence on Judaism in the modern world, but have still not broken their links with the past. On the contrary, they have sought to re-interpret the past in order to prepare for new developments.

THE 20th CENTURY

The two outstanding world events which have concerned Judaism during this century are the holocaust and the founding of modern Israel. The persecution of the Jews under the Nazis has sharpened the question of their survival in the modern world. More than half the Jewish population of Europe perished under Hitler and it faced its most severe test since the time of the exile in Babylon. The holocaust subdued the spirit of the people, but did not break it, and soon after the end of the Hitler war the Jews were making preparations to return to their homeland.

ISRAEL

The independence of Judaism as a faith was highlighted for the Jews when they returned to Israel in 1948. It gave Jews a new impetus as a race and a religion. Religious Jews see this event as the fulfilment of the promises of God. Some traditional and conservative Jews connect it with the messianic hope. Only the utmost extremists contend that the state should not have been set up because only the messiah can do this. The majority of Jews of every persuasion see the land of Israel (*eretz* Israel) as their historical, spiritual, cultural and geographical centre.

Today, Judaism exists in a state of tension, because, *firstly*, the Zionists (the political group) do not subscribe to it; and *secondly*, very conservative Jews question whether Israel should have become an autonomous state; *thirdly*, some Jews believe that the dispersion of their race is part of God's plan for them. The majority of Jews, however, have a special interest in the state of Israel as their native land. They say that God promised in the Torah to give it to their ancestors for an everlasting possession.

JEWS IN BRITAIN

There have been communities of Jews in Britain since 1656. Today, the Jewish population is about half a million. Many came here as refugees from religious persecution. There are numerous synagogues and a good many have been purpose-built. The best known is probably the London United Synagogue, which comprises eighty local congregations. The first synagogue was established in the City of London in 1701 and Queen Anne presented a rafter from one of her ships for the roof. The Chief Rabbi of the United Congregation is the leader of British Jewry.

The representative body of British Jews is the Board of Deputies that was founded in 1760. A Jewish rabbi occupies very much the same position as a Christian minister. There are colleges for training rabbis, and with the increase of Jewish immigrants in the 18th and 19th centuries, many Jewish schools were founded. Jews today have their own schools where a full range of subjects are taught, but the teaching is given in the atmosphere and style of the Jewish community. Jews often co-operate with other religious groups in Britain. In 1942 the Council of Christians and Jews came into being. Jews have also made substantial contributions to public life in Britain in politics, in literature, in the arts, in science, in medicine and music.

APPLIED MATERIALS

ALEXANDER, P.S. (1984). *Textual sources for the study of Judaism*. Manchester University Press.
CRAGG, K. (1982). *This year in Jerusalem*. Darton, Longman, Todd.
PALMER, M. (1984). *Faith and Festivals*. Ward Lock.
UNTERMAN, A. (1981). *Jews – their religious beliefs and practices*. RKP.
UNTERMAN, A. (1982). *Judaism*. Ward Lock.
WOOD, A. (1984). *Abraham and Moses*. Holt, Rinehart and Winston.

EXAMINATION QUESTIONS

QUESTION

i) Describe briefly a Sabbath welcome and Friday evening meal in a Jewish home.   *(4)*

ii) 'Observe the Sabbath day and keep it holy.'
'Remember the Sabbath day and keep it holy.'
What is the difference between these two sayings in the ways that Jews celebrate the Sabbath?   *(4)*

iii) In what ways is the Sabbath linked to the going out of Egypt and the release from slavery? How does it express aspects of God's nature: *(4)*

iv) What is the religious significance of the various features of the havdalah service? *(4)*

v) In the 20th century what benefit can you see in a day of rest for the whole community? Ought there to be one common day of rest in the UK? *(4)*

OUTLINE ANSWER

i) Four of the following points for one mark each: best clothes, food and tableware; prepared in advance; candles with blessings; greetings; blessing children; songs of welcome for the day; kiddush; hallot, salt; cover; table songs, grace after meals.

ii) 'Observe' – putting into practice
'Remember' – feeling
Two versions of commands (Ex. and Deut.) Physical and spiritual commandments.

iii) Two of the following (probably). 2 marks each up to 4.
Day of rest – antithesis of slavery, gratitude should lead to social justice for all.
Day of peace – harmony between people and with natural world.

iv) For each of the following, 2 marks for explaining significance (or 4 separate points):
Wine – 'I lift up my cup of salvation . . .'; b'Samim (sweet spice box) to smell and take spiritual fragrance of Shabat into week; plaited candle – permission now to 'make fire' so hold out hands to 'use' it; plait brings together 3 themes of Shabat (God, Torah, Israel).

v) God's nature – redemption, justice, peace etc. Evaluation at depth.

A STUDENT'S ANSWER WITH EXAMINER'S COMMENTS

QUESTION

a) Describe a Jewish wedding.

b) Comment on each of the following aspects of the ceremony.
   i) The symbolic marriage chamber (Chuppah);
   ii) The cup of wine;
   iii) The wedding ring;
   iv) The marriage settlement (Kethubah).

c) Why is marriage such a solemn ceremony in Judaism?

66 who? 99

a) The wedding takes place any day. There are flowers in the synagogue, the teacher waits for the bridegroom (he) wears a cap for prays and a shorl. The best man goes in first. They wait for the bride who has a white dress and bridesmaids. They have a place like a shelter and stands under it, they drink cups of wine and say (promises).

66 What are these? 99

b) i) this is like a house and is covered over

66 Why? 99

ii) this is red for good health or perhaps to make them happy.

iii) this is gold and he puts it on her finger to wear to show shes married.

iv) they say they will help together to bring up a family as soon as they can.

66 the question is about 'settlement'! 99

c) it is holy because it is in a synagogue and the teacher says prays and reads the Bible and puts his hands on them. They are happy then and everybody smiles at them.

Comments

You have followed the form of the question quite well but some of your ideas are confused. You do not cover any part in sufficient detail. You must include the part played by the rabbi and say more about the ceremony.

Part b) is very unclear. You need to learn about what the different symbols mean.

In part c) you must show that you understand the meaning of 'solemn' and be prepared to express an opinion about it.

QUESTION The following are some special words and ideas of the religion of the Jews:

       Torah; covenant; circumcision; bar mitzvah.

a) Choose **two** of these words, and say why they are so special. *(4)*

b) Suppose you were present at an act of worship or ceremony when the words you choose were used. Describe what you would see and hear. *(4)*

c) Usually in a Jewish ceremony the Shema is read or said. What does it say, and why is it so important to Jews? *(8)*

d) Explain any **two** other special words or teachings that you find help you to understand Judaism. *(4)*

---

a) Circumcision this is so important because god and Abraham had a bond and this is the outward sign of Jewish faith (circumcision is brit milah)

Barmitzvah this is so special to the boy because once he has had his barmitzvah he is classified as a man (Bar mitzvah means son of a commandment)

b) At the circumcision you would see a baby boy who is 8 days old and a group of men and women, and one man who is called the rabbi would be cutting baby boys foreskin on his penis and the rabbi would be saying he hopes this boy will follow the jewish faith and be healthy and the father would read a piece from the Torah.

The boy would be studying a piece from the Torah to read later today at his barmitzvah he would read it in Hebrew and later the family would throw a party for the family and friends and here the boy would be given very expensive presents and is then a man.

c) The shema is a prayer and some people take it as three commands it is three paragraphs long. They take each paragraph as a command.

d) Mishna which is the oral law; bat mitzvah this is the equivalent to a boy's bar mitzvah but it is for a girl and she has hers when she is twelve years old.

Comments

This is a confused and unsatisfactory answer. You have a sprinkling of knowledge but have not learnt how to use it. In a), whilst you show which words you select you are not very sure *why* they are special. Circumcision is a rite of dedication and you must refer to this. Bar mitzvah is special as a time when the boy assumes new responsibilities. You should refer to these and show that you know what they are. In b) you offer a very crude account of the ceremony. You do not mention the special person who conducts it or the symbols (e.g. the chair of Elijah). You should describe the action of the boy at his bar mitzvah in the synagogue. If he is a member of the reform synagogue the reading need not be in Hebrew. In c) you do not answer the question by stating *what* the Shema says. Neither do you say *why* it is important. Remember this expression is the basis of Jewish belief in God. Part d) is not answered as expected. You should explain (as the question asks) what is the Mishna. How do Jews operate the oral law? How does it help *you* to understand Judaism? You should do the same with regard to bar mitzvah. State and explain what happens in the synagogue and what the girl's father might do. Read again the relevant information to answer this question.

SIKHISM

GETTING STARTED

About seventy per cent of people who come from India to live in Britain are Sikhs. When you see people on the street wearing a turban you can be fairly certain they are Sikhs. For those Sikhs who wear a turban it is a symbol of their religion and social identity.

Sikh means 'disciple' or 'learner' and Sikhs belong to the religion founded by Guru Nanak in North India in the 15th century CE. The homeland of the Sikhs is the Punjab, a prosperous region sometimes called the 'granary of India' or the 'land of the five rivers' which once extended from Peshawar to Delhi, but since 1947 is much smaller.

ESSENTIAL PRINCIPLES

1 > GURU NANAK

Guru Nanak was born in Talwindi in 1469 and was a member of the Hindu warrior class (*kshatriya*). You can see from this chart the main events in his life.

1st Journey (1497 – 1509)
    To Eminabad and his meeting with the carpenter
    To Talumba and his meeting with Sajjan Thug
    To Tipalpur and his meeting with a leper
    To Hardwar and his encounter with Hindus
    To Rokilkhand and his encounter with Afghan
    To Assam and his meeting with an enchantress

2nd Journey (1510 – 1515)
    His journey to Sri Lankha and his meeting with Raja Shivvnabh

3rd Journey (1516 – 1518)
    His journey to North India and his meeting with Mansarovar

4th Journey (1518 – 1521)
    His journey to Mecca and his meeting with Jiwan
    His journey to Baghdad and his meeting with Bahlol
    His journey to Sind and his visit to the temple of Durga
    1521 his return to the Punjab and Kartarpur and the formation
      of the dharmasala.

Fig. 10.1 Chart of Guru Nanak's journeys

After his death in 1539 his followers collected a number of stories about him and wrote them in the 'Life Evidences' (*janam sakhis*). These stories are about how he received his message from God and why this is important. Although he was born a Hindu, Guru Nanak did not observe its customs and ritual, he did not wear the 'sacred thread' or any other Hindu symbols. Neither did he find satisfaction in the teachings of Hinduism or of Islam which had settled in that part of India and won many followers. Yet he was deeply interested in religion and searched for inner illumination and communion with God. His father was concerned about his unworldly outlook and tried to interest him in material things. He gave him money to start up a business, but instead Nanak gave it away to a group of poor Sadhus (holy men) and said it was more profitable to invest his money in feeding the poor.

> The foundation of Sikhism and the role of the guru.

When he was eighteen his father arranged his marriage, but when his first son was born Nanak refused to carry out the Hindu ritual of purifying his house. Birth, he said, is a natural event, and the only impurity is

the covetous mind,
tongue speaking untruths, eyes full of lust,
and ears accepting unreliable evidence as true.

CALL AND COMMISSION

In 1497 Nanak's life was changed through an unusual religious experience. He felt he was being carried to the divine court and into the presence of God. He was given a cup of nectar (*amrit*) to drink and told

Nanak this is the cup of my Name (*nam*). Drink it.

After this experience he remained silent for a day and then surprised his friends with the announcement:

> The Lord called me – a bard of no consequence – to his service – day and night I am at his beck and call.

After this he spoke words which are well known to his followers:

> There is neither Hindu nor Musselman, so whose path shall I follow? I shall follow God's path. God is neither Hindu nor Musselman, the path which I follow is God's.

From now on, Nanak devoted his life to teaching the message he received from God. He believed it was a new message which was neither a continuation of the teaching of Hinduism or Islam. God had called him to be a *guru* (holy man or spiritual teacher) and to declare his message before the world.

JOURNEYS

For the next twenty years Guru Nanak travelled widely in India and beyond, teaching his message. On his journeys he had some unusual experiences which help our understanding of Sikhism.

On his first journey he met Sajjan, the keeper of the Hindu temple and Muslim mosque in Talumba. Sajjan heard Guru Nanak sing some of his devotional songs and felt a strange desire to leave the ritual and observances of his own religion and follow the simple religion of the guru. He was ready to give up the profit he made from visitors to the temple and mosque and live a more honest life.

On his second journey Guru Nanak met a group of ascetics at Mansarovar. They had separated from the rest of the people and never did anything to help the poor and weak. By withdrawing they thought they could escape from suffering and evil. Guru Nanak told them that evil is trying to run away from real life, withdrawing from the world is a form of sickness, and caring only for themselves breeds selfishness. True religion is living a pure life in the world and not seeking to withdraw from it. It means helping and serving others. In order to do this, the religious person must practise self control and self discipline.

On his third journey Guru Nanak visited Mecca. He dressed as a Muslim and slept with his feet towards the *ka'aba* and the mosque. Jiwan protested that this was against the Muslim rule and he and the guru began to discuss the ritual and customs of religion. The Muslim Jiwan defended the way of Islam and Guru Nanak said that God read the heart and was not concerned with the outward signs of religion. He declared that God made no difference between a Hindu and a Muslim, the only difference that mattered is between right and wrong, and good and evil. God sees only the behaviour of those who believe in him and not the external acts.

KARTARPUR

Guru Nanak spent the last years of his life in Kartarpur. He collected together everyone who was ready to listen to his teaching. He did not dress as a religious teacher, but he did use a teacher's chair (*gaddi*), and everyone who accepted his teaching became disciples (Sikhs). They formed a community of disciples which was open to men and women and to people of any class or caste. This was not a religious order or organisation, but it extended friendship to everyone and opened a communal kitchen to feed the poor and needy. All members were equal in status and all shared the community's hospitality and generosity. The community was called the *dharmasala* and its members met together to sing sacred songs and to listen to the guru's teaching. One was Lehna, who had given up worshipping the Hindu goddess Durga to follow the teaching of Guru Nanak. Nanak was impressed by Lehna's devotion and humility and named him as his successor as leader of the community. Nanak changed his name to Angad (= a part or member of me) to denote a 'spiritual' succession, and as a sign of this he raised a canopy over his head.

Sikhs today speak with great affection of Guru Nanak and say they follow his teaching, which is basically:

1 In the sight of God all people are equal (Sikhs call this egalitarianism).
2 True religion is available to everyone.
3 True religion means devotion to God and right living in the world.
4 All people have equal rights – the weak and helpless as well as the strong and powerful.
5 Religious action is more important than religious theory.

As you saw, the community at Kartarpur met together to sing sacred songs and also to pray. Guru Nanak assumed that worship is a natural part of religion but it does not require elaborate forms or ritual. It is a spiritual and inward experience that relates the worshipper to God. Nothing must hinder this. Sikhs do not have a special holy day for worship, or any set form of ritual. They do not have priests or sacred personnel. Worship can be offered by individuals on their own, or in community with others. The core of Sikh worship is meditating on God through meditating on his Word.

FAMILY WORSHIP

> The Adi Granth and the patterns of Sikh worship.

Worship may be offered in the home, providing it has a copy of the Sikh sacred book (the Adi Granth) or a selection of sacred songs. A room may be set apart for worship. It is unlikely that many Sikh homes will have a complete copy of the Adi Granth and maybe only a small collection of the best known hymns (*gutka*). The family might gather together for worship at any time and may invite others to join with them. The purpose of family worship is always to call God to mind and to meditate on his Name.

If worship is offered in the morning, the Sikh rises early, takes a bath and then meditates on God before beginning the day's activities. The Sikh takes guidance from the work called 'The Sikh Way of Life' (*Rehat*) about the hymns that should be recited or read. This is:

  i) in the morning: Japji Sahib and Ten Swayyas of Guru Gobind Singh;
  ii) in the evening: Sodar Rahiras (a form of prayer);
  iii) before sleep: Sohilla (a form of prayer).

(*Japji Sahib* = a work composed by Guru Nanak for personal use; *Sodar Rahiras* = a prayer to focus the mind on the 'holy path'; *Sohilla* = a vesper prayer.)

CONGREGATIONAL WORSHIP

The *gurdwara* (which means 'the door of the Guru'), is the name of the Sikh temple. It developed from the *dharmasala*, which was the earliest name for the Sikh community.

The gurdwara has one central room for congregational worship. It is used for social gatherings as well as for worship. The main focal point is the Adi Granth or Guru Granth Sahib, which is placed prominently on a stool to symbolise a throne (*takht*) and the royal status of the Adi Granth. The sovereignty of the Word is supreme. There is a canopy over the Adi Granth and when it is being read a *chauri* (a fly whisk of feathers) is waved as though homage is being paid to a royal person. On the walls of the gurdwara there are pictures of Guru Nanak and the other gurus but there are no seats. Men and women are separated but there is no rule about this. Shoes are removed before entering the gurdwara and everyone covers the head.

The worshippers first walk towards the dais to pay homage to the Adi Granth by bowing before it and placing an offering of money or food for the communal kitchen. They then

Fig. 10.2 Reading the scriptures in a Sikh temple

move away, without turning their backs on the Adi Granth, to sit on the floor facing it. The worship begins when the sacred book is opened and read. Any member of the community may read the Adi Granth whilst the congregation sit and listen. Musicians sit near the dais and sing *gurbani* (hymns from the Adi Granth) in which the congregation joins and prayers may be said at any time. A sermon or explanation of the hymns may be given by a member of the congregation. There is no set time for finishing the worship but it always ends with a set prayer called *Ardas*. For this, the congregation stands and one member comes forward to address God on behalf of everyone present. The Ardas dates from the time of Guru Gobind Singh (the last personal guru) and is in three parts: a prayer to remember God and the ten gurus; a prayer for keeping the teaching of the Adi Granth; and a prayer for God's blessing on the Sikh community, for the sick and for other people. At the end of this the Adi Granth is covered with a silk cloth and then removed from the dais.

Prashad

At the end of the worship everyone shares *prashad*, a common meal which is prepared in the *langar* or kitchen, which is attached to the gurdwara. The meal is provided by members of the congregation. Eating together in this way is a mark of unity and a symbol of generosity. It follows the example of Guru Nanak, who opened his kitchen to everyone so that no-one leaves the gurdwara hungry or without sharing in its hospitality. Everyone receives the food with the right hand as a gift (*prashad*). This is another mark of equality and unity.

Sangat

The Sikh community at worship is called *sangat*. The whole community is responsible for the worship and everyone has a share in it. Anyone may read the Adi Granth, lead the prayers or deliver the sermon. The worship is arranged by a committee of the gurdwara but the committee never loses sight of the equality of all members of the community.

Nishan

Any building may be used as a gurdwara and it can be recognised by the flag that flies over it. The flag (*nishan sahib*) is saffron yellow in colour and has the symbols in blue of the Sikh religion. These are a wheel and two swords. The circle (*chakra*) is a symbol of the unity of God and the sangat (community). The swords are the symbols of the Sikh teaching and the willingness of the Sikhs to fight for it.

3 BASIC BELIEFS

GOD

The basic beliefs about God are conveyed in the *Mool Mantra* composed by Guru Nanak and which is the first part of the Adi Granth:

> God is One,
> He is the True Name,
> The Maker and All pervading Spirit
> Fearing nothing, hating no-one,
> A Being beyond time,
> Self existent beyond birth,
> Revealed by the grace of the Guru.

You will see that there are three main affirmations about God in this hymn: 'God is One'; 'God is Truth'; and 'God is Eternal and Self Existent'. The Sikh believes that these three aspects tell what God is 'in himself'. The hymn also speaks about God's actions: God is the Maker (creator); 'God reveals himself'. As creator, God is present everywhere and is in all things. Sikhism does not have any creation myths but has a strong belief in God as creator. He does not incarnate himself (take a human form) and yet he is present everywhere. The hymn refers to God in personal terms. He is a personal being who has moral qualities. He fears nothing and he hates no-one. His grace expresses who he is, and how he deals with human beings. Guru Amar Das conveyed this in the saying

> Through grace is the Lord attained and not otherwise.

You will notice that the Mool Mantra states that God is 'the True Name'. *Nam* (Name) is a synonym for God and so his name is in everything, or in the words of Guru Nanak: '*There is no corner without his Name.*'

Sikhism uses many different names for God, but there is only one God. There cannot be a God for one religion and a God for another. The Sikh symbol for God is the numeral one and the letter O. The True Name is the *Sat Guru* or the True God or God Himself. He is the *Waheguru* (the Lord of Wonder), but there is no formula or definition that can apply to Him:

> He has no quoit, nor mark, no colour, caste, or lineage,
> No form, no complexion, outline nor garb,
> No one can describe him in any way.

HUMAN LIFE

All life is God's creation, but no-one can tell what was in his mind when he created the first human being. Everyone is born into a state of transmigration and may be reincarnated after death. The goal of human life is to achieve freedom from the cycle of existence or the necessity of reincarnation. No-one can achieve this goal without God's help or by withdrawing from the life of the world. Guru Nanak taught a right attitude to worldly things:

> Do your daily duties with hands and feet,
> But concentrate on the Lord.

There is a spark of God in everyone and everyone is born equal. Human life consists of body, mind and soul. The three exist in unity and must be developed in harmony. True religion touches life at every point and provides the means for right living. The actions that people perform in this world follow them to the world to come. The body must be kept healthy by following the laws of good health and wholesome work. All action is important, but everyone has a free will and the right to choose. Everyone has the ability to reason and to know the difference between right and wrong. Everyone is endowed with wisdom that leads to making right choices. Whatever a person sows, he/she will also reap.

The three H's

Guru Nanak set out the conditions for achieving harmony in human life by defining the three H's:

i) knowledge of the *Hand* = the dignity of labour;
ii) knowledge of the *Head* = the search for truth;
iii) knowledge of the *Heart* = the higher self.

The goal is to achieve harmony between body, mind and spirit through achieving harmony with God. The result is then to achieve perfect freedom.

Virtues

There are five virtues that the Sikh is taught to cultivate: truth; contentment; service; patience; and humility. Those who follow the path of virtue hear God's voice and they do his will. The path of virtue leads to true freedom and union with God.

Vices

There are vices that should be avoided, but first it is necessary to know what vice is. Guru Nanak described it as 'dross' but it can turn to gold. Vice holds a person in the grip of selfishness which distorts human life. It builds a wall between the individual and God, it isolates a person from God and steeps itself in ignorance rather than knowledge of God. Egoism (*haumai*) is rooted in self love, is governed by desire for personal glory and shows loyalty to no-one. It requires constant spiritual effort to release oneself from the grip of vice which only deludes and keeps one a slave to false pressures. There are five cardinal vices that have their source in a false image of the self: lust; anger; greed; worldliness; and pride. Where these vices and egoism are present, God is absent.

Grace

No-one can achieve the reward of virtue through self effort alone. The reward is God's gift of grace (*nadar*). *Grace* is God's gracious gift which enables a person to achieve harmony with himself. Wherever God is, there is grace. He acts to assist people to achieve salvation and the 'state of grace'. This is described in the Japji:

> In the stage of grace a man is filled with spiritual power
> That nothing more can be added to him.

There are found very great warriors and heroes,
Whom the great Lord fills completely.
They are inextricably woven into the greatness of the Lord;
Such is their beauty it cannot be described.
They do not die, neither are they deceived.
Those in whose hearts the Lord abides,
There also dwell communities of bhagats (those who practise devotion to God).
They live in bliss, the True One in their hearts.

THE FIVE STAGES

On the path to union with God there are *five stages* which the Japji describes as:

1 **The stage of religious duty (Dharam Khand).** In this stage the Sikh observes God's law and lives by his providence, the signs of his grace and mercy.
2 **The stage of effort (Saram Khand).** Through effort and self discipline the Sikh maintains a right relationship with God. He responds to God and relies on his help.
3 **The stage of grace (Karam Khand).** The Sikh cultivates divine virtues and spiritual graces and is in a state of bliss.
4 **The stage of knowledge (Gian Khand).** The Sikh shows obedience and through wisdom attains knowledge of the world and its ways.
5 **The stage of truth (Sach Khand).** By showing knowledge of the truth the individual lives in complete harmony with God and a state of bliss. Then God and the individual are one.

THE GURU'S WORD

The sacred writings of Sikhism are known as the Word of the Guru (*gurbani*). Sikhs believe that the words of the Guru (God) come to them through the Guru Granth Sahib (the scriptures of the Lord God). In the Guru Granth Sahib God's Word is enshrined but the Guru is the Word. God revealed his Word and the Word will lead to God; the revealed Word leads to the revealer who is God. *The Guru Granth Sahib inspired by God is the Guru.*

Contents

Guru Arjan described the contents of the Guru Granth Sahib in a pictorial way:

In this dish are placed three things: Truth, Harmony and Wisdom.
These are seasoned with the Name of God who is the basis of all, whoever eats it and relishes it shall be saved.

The Guru Granth Sahib is a collection of hymns, most of them by Guru Arjan, but the hymns of Guru Nanak are particularly significant. It is said that as he was on his journeys he was inspired by God to sing these hymns whilst his companion Mardana accompanied him on a stringed instrument. As he did so, 'the Word descended on him'. But in addition to these the Guru Granth Sahib contains verses composed by Hindu and Muslim sages who belonged to the devotional (*bhakti*) tradition. Apart from these there are hymns by other religious mystics, such as Kabir, Farid, Namdev and Ravidas. Some believe that Guru Nanak was responsible for adding these, in order to show that his teaching had a universal appeal.

Divisions

There are thirteen divisions to the Guru Granth Sahib, divided according to musical regulations. Some are very joyful and others sombre, so that they express the whole of human experience. Some of the hymns are suitable for the morning and others for the evening. They cover a wide range of subjects, which include religious teaching and theology, ethics and practical guidance, philosophy and mysticism, personal and social advice. The Guru Granth Sahib is rich in imagery drawn from everyday life and there are many impressive pictures of nature and the seasons of the year. There is deep human interest and concern for humankind. There are many homely similies and proverbs:

As is the dream of the night, so is the world
As is the staff in the hand of a blind person
So is to us the Name of God.
The antidote for the poison of pride is humility.

In spite of its seeming divisions and variety of subjects there is a notable unity in the Guru Granth Sahib. Sikhs believe that it is a priceless treasure because it is the *Guru in their midst*. By following the direction of God's Word Sikhs believe they can obtain ultimate bliss. So they say

> The Guru is the Pool of Nectar,
> We are the swans on the bank,
> There is the sea of rubies and corals,
> Of pearls and diamonds of the Lord's praise.

Compiling the scriptures

Guru Arjan compiled the Guru Granth Sahib in its final form. He also established the order, and when this was done he installed the sacred book in the Harimander in Amritsar. The word *granth* means collection, and there was an earlier collection known as the Adi Granth. The hymns of Guru Nanak were included, although it is not certain whether these were collected by Guru Angad or his own disciple, Mansukh. There is a tradition that Guru Nanak arrived in Mecca carrying a book, a staff, a water pot and a prayer mat. The book may have been a collection of hymns. Guru Arjan compiled the Adi Granth by adding his own hymns, and the last of the *gurus*, Guru Gobind Singh, added the hymns of his father, Guru Tegh Behadur, and finalised the Adi Granth. He then enthroned it as the sole Guru. Henceforth there was no need of a human guru. *The Word is the Guru and the Guru is the Word.*

THE AUTHORITY OF THE GURU GRANTH SAHIB

After Guru Gobind enthroned the Guru Granth Sahib as the sole Guru in 1708 its content has never been altered. Every gurdwara has a copy, and every copy has the same number of pages. It is written in the gurmukti language (written punjabi). The hymns are set to music for use in worship, but the music is of a simple kind, so as not to detract from the words of the scriptures. The music is an aid to focusing the attention on the Word (Guru or God).

The Guru Granth Sahib is a visible sign of God's presence, hence it must be seen by everyone in the temple. The book itself is not worshipped, even though the worshippers bow before it. The Word alone is honoured and God alone is worshipped. The Word conveys who God is and whenever the words are read he is present. The Guru Granth Sahib is the source of knowledge, truth and wisdom, it exalts the worshipper as it is read. Everything a Sikh requires to live as a 'disciple' is contained in the Guru Granth Sahib. So, it is used when a child is named, at the initiation ceremony, at a wedding, and at a burial. It should be opened every day, but when it is not read it should be closed. Before it is removed from its dais in the gurdwara a prayer is said and everyone stands as it is being carried.

Dasam Granth

This is a work that some Sikhs use in their devotions, but it does not have the same status or influence as the Adi Granth. It was compiled by Bhai Mani Singh after the death of Guru Gobind Singh. It is a complicated work of 1700 verses on a variety of themes. Their intention is to inspire praise to God and patriotic fervour. Many Sikhs have copies of the Dasam Granth which is thought to contain the writings of Guru Gobind Singh.

Mohan Pothi

This is the earliest collection of Sikh writings supposed to have been made by Guru Amar Das. They were collected at a time when the religion was spreading and new members required instructions and guidance. It was necessary to preserve the teaching of the first three gurus and to hand it on. At the time, Sikhism was under attack and had to be defended against those who opposed its teachings. The Mohan Pothi (*pothi* = book) consisted of hymns by Guru Nanak and his two successors and warnings against false teaching and useless practices.

5 ▷ **RITES OF PASSAGE**

Sikh children learn the first things about their religion in the home. Guru Nanak and his successors desired the teaching to be passed on and that children should receive a grounding in its beliefs and practices. Guru Gobind Singh called upon parents to teach the Sikh faith to their children and to baptise them into the Sikh religion. Only in this way could they live noble lives and be given a firm moral basis for action in society.

BIRTH AND NAMING

Soon after birth a child is named in the presence of the Adi Granth. The book is opened and the first letter of the first word on the left hand page is taken as the first letter of the child's name. Names of girls and boys do not always seem very different. It is customary to place water and sugar on the child's lips and to offer prayers from the *Japji* and *Ardas*. These commit the child to God's grace and pray that he/she will live as a true Sikh, will serve other people, and be loyal to the Sikh homeland. The ceremony ends with sharing *prashad* as a sign that the child is received into the Sikh community. As soon as the child is old enough the child's religious education begins in earnest by learning the name for God (*Waheguru*) and the first hymn of the Adi Granth.

INITIATION

Not all Sikhs regard the naming ceremony as an act of initiation, but those who do consider themselves to be the only true Sikhs. They say it is necessary for following the teaching and living the life of a disciple to the full. The initiation ceremony dates from the time of Guru Gobind Singh, when it was quite elaborate. Today, a simpler form is followed, although many Sikhs wish for the full ceremony to be revived as a means of keeping the faith alive and ensuring the Sikhs devote themselves to it.

The initiation ceremony introduced by Guru Gobind Singh takes place in the presence of five members of the Khalsa (the Sikh brotherhood which includes women). They take their places before the Adi Granth and explain the principles and teaching of the faith. The person being initiated signifies acceptance of these and then one of the five recites a prayer for God's protection. The five now sit around an iron vessel full of fresh water and the person being initiated receives five handfuls of *amrit* (holy water) which is placed on the eyes and ears. The five members of the Khalsa repeat the Mool Mantra five times, and this is repeated by the candidate. Greetings are then exchanged and the candidate is received as a son or daughter of Guru Gobind Singh. They now become known as 'singh' or 'kaur'. Then everyone shares prashad from a common vessel.

MARRIAGE

A Sikh wedding may take place anywhere, providing it is public. Marriage is bliss (*Anand*) and the wedding ceremony is simple. Friends of the bride and groom come together around the Adi Granth and prayers are said. The Guru is a witness to the marriage and so makes it a sacrament and not just a contract. The couple bow before the Adi Granth and make their vows. The groom promises to protect his wife and the bride promises to accept her role. The person in charge of the ceremony speaks to the bride and groom separately about the duties of marriage and the scarf of the groom is placed in the hands of the bride. As they hold the scarf (*palla*) they walk clockwise around the Adi Granth four times and pause whilst four verses of a hymn are chanted to music. Then *prashad* is served to everyone and after prayers, gifts and greetings are exchanged. There is no formal betrothal before marriage, and marriage takes place only between members of the community. There are no child marriages and Sikhs are not allowed more than one wife.

DEATH AND COMMEMORATION

Sikhs believe that at death the soul leaves the body for a new dwelling. It ends the cycle of transmigration and enters upon eternal life. The soul (*jiva*) is immortal and lives for ever as part of God. This is the soul's reward for good deeds done in this life and through God's grace enters a state of everlasting bliss. After death the body is washed and dressed in clean clothes before being placed in a coffin. If the deceased is a member of the Khalsa, the Five K's are left on the body but no candles or lamps are lit. The body is taken to be cremated and on the way hymns are sung:

> The dawn of a new day
> Is the herald of a sunset,
> Earth is not thy permanent home.

The funeral pyre is lit by a near relative and afterwards the mourners return home, where for the next ten days they hear readings from the Adi Granth. When the four final passages are read the mourning period ends and the Adi Granth is covered with a silk cloth. Then the company share *prashad*.

You will recall that towards the end of his life Guru Nanak was asked by his followers to name his successor as the leader of the Sikhs. Clearly they felt the need of a human leader who would continue to lead the new movement and help it spread. Guru Nanak also wished the movement to continue and grow, but he wanted to ensure that it had the right kind of leader. For this reason he rejected his own sons and chose instead a spiritual successor. The Sikhs accepted this and each of the personal gurus was chosen as a spiritual leader.

THE SUCCESSION

In all, there are ten personal *gurus* including Guru Nanak. You should be aware of their names and know something of their importance within the Sikh faith.

1 **Guru Angad (1504–1552).** He was chosen by Guru Nanak and contributed to the religion by putting his hymns into writing and spreading them to other parts of India. He also took an interest in teaching the faith to children.
2 **Guru Amar Das (1479–1574).** He was a supporter of human rights and opposed all divisions based on caste. He protested against the custom of *purdah* (keeping women apart) and women wearing a veil. This *guru* also inaugurated some of the main ceremonies and centres of pilgrimage. He collected the hymns of the first three *gurus* and strengthened the unity of the Sikh community.
3 **Guru Ram Das (1534–1581).** His most important act was establishing Amritsar as the sacred centre of Sikhism. Here was built the famous Golden Temple of the Sikhs. Guru Ram Das also broke the remaining links with Hinduism and Islam. He thus finally secured the independence of the Sikh religion.
4 **Guru Arjan (1563–1606).** He built the Harimandir (House of the Lord) in Amritsar. The four doors of the Golden Temple are open to north, south, east and west as a symbol that the faith is open to everyone. We have already referred to his work as the compiler of the Sikh scriptures. He is also the first martyr of Sikhism. After the death of the Emperor Akbar in 1605 there was a movement to make Islam the dominant faith in India. The Emperor Jehangir turned on the Sikhs and arrested Guru Arjan and he met his death in 1606.
5 **Guru Hargobind (1595–1644?).** He marshalled his followers against the Muslims. He trained them as fighting men and defenders of the faith, if necessary by the sword. But he also cared for their spiritual life. He carried two swords – one the symbol of battle and the other of the spirit.
6 **Guru Har Rai (1630–1661).** He was a man of peace who won the respect of his followers by showing them kindness and generosity.
7 **Guru Harkrishen (1656–1664).** He succeeded his father when only five years of age and died at an early age. Before his death he announced that his successor would come from the village of Baba Bakala. For one so young, his wisdom was remarkable.
8 **Guru Tegh Bahadur (1621–1675).** During his time many divisions appeared among the Sikhs but he worked hard to maintain unity and to persuade them to unite with the Hindus against the Muslims. Sikhism took on a military aspect, but Guru Tegh Bahadur was killed in battle.
9 **Guru Gobind Singh (1666–1708).** He was an able and gifted leader. He dealt with the crisis of the Sikhs in a wise manner. He is best remembered as the founder of the Khalsa and also for enthroning the Adi Granth as the sole Guru.

KHALSA

The brotherhood of Sikhs founded by Guru Gobind Singh is the Khalsa (pure). Its members are the 'pure' or those who are completely devoted to the Sikh faith and way of life. It links together the ideal of spiritual and physical purity in a life dedicated to religion and human dignity. Ideally, the member of the Khalsa is a 'saint' *and* a 'worldly person'.

You have read already about the initiation ceremony, which was first held in the time of Guru Gobind Singh. During the Sikh Baisakhi festival Guru Gobind Singh and his followers met in Ananadpur. He stood before them and drew his sword and asked if there was anyone who was ready to die for the faith. There was a silence, so he asked again if there was anyone ready to sacrifice their life for the faith. After asking for the third time, one person came forward and said he was ready to give his life. The *guru* led him away out of sight whilst his followers waited in awe to see what would happen. Then they heard a noise as if a body fell to the ground and the *guru* returned with blood on his sword. He asked for another sacrifice but many of his followers left. Eventually another answered the call and was led away. Afterwards three others came forward and offered themselves. Everyone thought the five had been murdered until the *guru* led them back and announced that they had proved their love and loyalty to the faith. Only *they* were worthy of the name Sikh, so they were initiated into the community of the 'pure' and told to cry:

'To God be the victory.'

THE FIVE K'S

The symbols of members of the Khalsa are the Five K's. The five are a symbol of *unity*, *loyalty*, *devotion*, *purity*, and *enthusiasm* for God and the community. Every member is expected to practise self discipline and maintain the glory of the Khalsa. They accept a strict code of conduct by refraining from smoking, eating meat from animals killed according to Muslim ritual, and sexual intercourse with Muslim women. The Five K's are:

1 Kara – a steel band or bracelet worn on the right wrist to denote bondage to God and the Khalsa;
2 Kirpan – a small sword, the symbol of courage, confidence and readiness to defend the faith and the poor;
3 Kesh – long hair, the sign of holiness, saintliness, strength and virility;
4 Kanga – a comb, the symbol of cleanliness and inner purity;
5 Kach – short breeches or trousers, the symbol of agility, alertness and chastity.

The ideals of the Khalsa are precious to its members. They make all decisions in the presence of the Adi Granth. When Guru Gobind Singh installed this as the Guru he also declared:

Where there are five there am I,
When the five meet they are the holiest of the holy.

The Khalsa grew in numbers and within a few months more than eighty thousand Sikhs had received 'baptism by the sword'. It has been a focus of unity in Sikhism and its members believe:

So long as the Khalsa remains distinct, his glory and lustre will grow.

Sikhs in India use the same calendar as the Hindus, but their religious new year begins on the first day of Baisakhi. This is the only fixed festival in Sikhism and falls in April. Celebrations and festivals are divided between the anniversaries (*gurpurbs*) and the *melas*, which are closer to main religious festivals. We shall look first at the melas.

BAISAKHI MELA

Guru Gobind Singh baptised the first five members of the Khalsa in April 1699. Sikhs celebrate the anniversary of the founding of the Khalsa each April in a ceremony commonly called *Amrit* (the baptism ceremony of the Sikhs). It is held on the Sunday nearest the date of the initiation of the first members of the Khalsa. It is also the first day of the Sikh new year. In the homeland, Sikhs gather for community worship and listening to teaching from the Adi Granth. In the eighteenth century the main celebrations took place in Amritsar and they had a military flavour. Today, Sikhs may go on pilgrimage to the Golden Temple but there is no show of military power.

During the day, political meetings may be held in the morning and afternoon in a town near Amritsar and a market or fair is held at which animals are bought or sold. The day is one of activity and for showing solidarity. On this day also committees may be appointed for carrying out duties on behalf of the Sikh community and in some instances new members may be initiated into the Khalsa.

DIWALI MELA

The Sikh name is the same as the Hindu festival and is held at the end of October or early November to coincide with the new moon. This is a festival of light when Sikh *gurdwaras* are lit with lights to signify the coming of light to the natural world and of inner light to direct the believer to union with God. It is a time of rejoicing and exchanging gifts. Children have a prominent part in the festival and are given gifts. They are also told stories from Sikh history, especially the story of the courage of Guru Hargobind.

Guru Hargobind is one of the heroes of the Sikhs. He was put in prison in Gwalior for refusing to pay the fines which the Mughal emperor demanded from his father when he rebelled against him. When the Emperor Jehangir heard that Guru Hargobind had been put in prison he ordered his immediate release. But Guru Hargobind refused unless fifty two other prisoners were freed. The emperor agreed, on condition that each prisoner left the prison holding the guru's cloak. But the way out of the prison was so narrow that it was impossible for the prisoners to hold the cloak. So Guru Hargobind hit on the idea of having a larger cloak so that every one of the fifty two could take hold of it. So the emperor's condition was met and Guru Hargobind secured freedom for the prisoners and himself.

This story is told to children during the festival to teach them that the Sikh must defend the faith and the freedom to practise it. Guru Hargobind is known as the Great Liberator (*Bandhichor*) on account of his courage in standing up against tyranny and his struggle for political and religious freedom.

HOLA MOHALLA MELA

This is a spring festival which is held in February/March. In 1680 Guru Gobind Singh called his followers together to a celebration as a counter attraction to a Hindu festival. He wanted to make sure that every Sikh kept strictly to the observances and practices of the Sikh religion. At first, this festival had a distinct military aspect. There were military displays and demonstrations of military power. There were imaginary battles between two armies and a show of strength by Sikh fighters. In Guru Gobind Singh's time this lasted for two days, during which the *guru* himself took an active part. The climax came with an attack led by the *guru* on a stronghold that had been set up for the purpose. During the festival, wrestling matches and shooting competitions are held. Music and reciting poetry are also a feature and everything reflects the vitality and vigour of the Sikh community. Today, this festival is held mainly only in the Punjab, usually in the city of Anandpur.

GURPURBS

Turning now to the anniversaries or *gurpurbs* these are associated with the personal *gurus*. The anniversaries may not be kept by Sikhs all over the world, and many of them are local affairs. The most important are the birth of Guru Nanak and of Guru Gobind Singh, and the martyrdom of Guru Arjan and Guru Tegh Bahadur.

In the places where these anniversaries are celebrated – especially in India – the Guru Granth Sahib is taken in procession through the town or village. The procession is led by five members of the Khalsa dressed with the Five K's, a reminder of the first members of the Khalsa. A band usually leads the way and people throw flowers along the route. Afterwards, games and competitions are held for children and adults. It is usual for a rally to be held at the same time when a notable speaker is invited to address the gathering. Food is shared usually without cost to the people present.

The religious side of the anniversary is not forgotten. The Guru Granth Sahib is read from beginning to end, commencing two days before the anniversary and lasting for forty-eight hours. This is to make sure that the whole is read before the dawn of the day of the *gurpurb*. *Karah prashad* is prepared and served to everyone listening to the reading. More than one reader takes part and as time passes more and more people arrive to be present for the final ceremony. This commences with page 1426 of the Guru Granth Sahib and ends with page 1430. Finally, prayers (*Ardas*) are said and *Karah prashad* is served.

PILGRIMAGE

Pilgrimage is not a notable feature of Sikhism. In fact, Guru Nanak believed that visiting a special place for the sake of ceremonial washing and purification cannot make a person pure. This can only come about through a change of heart. So he declared:

> God's name is the real pilgrimage place which consists of contemplation of the Word of God, and the cultivation of inner knowledge.

Real pilgrimage is visiting the Guru, who alone can make a person pure and give inner knowledge. However, in the time of Guru Amar Das a kind of pilgrimage was introduced. The *guru* commanded his followers to meet at Gowindwal at the time of the festivals. He had an artificial pool made so that the pilgrims could bathe. He also erected sixty-four steps for them to get to the water. Guru Amar Das was keen on giving the Sikhs a central place for worship. Subsequently, Amritsar became the Sikh centre and many Sikhs visit the city and bathe in the pool and file past the Guru Granth Sahib. They also listen to continuous reading of the scriptures as the sacred book is carried to the Golden Temple in procession.

Guru Gobind Singh had little regard for pilgrimage. For him, visits to sacred places had no significance, apart from visiting the Guru. In this he followed the teaching of Guru Nanak:

Guru is the place of pilgrimage on the flowing river,
When the Lord showers his grace, the soul bathes,
In the pool of truth and becomes pure.

8 > COMMUNITY AND BROTHERHOOD

Sikhism has existed and developed as a community from the days of Guru Nanak. Sikhs are expected to support the community of Sikhs and always be loyal to its ideals. Every Sikh is expected to give some service to the community. Sikhism may be described as a practical religious community.

Among its main characteristics are the following:

1 **It is a caste free community.** All people are born equal and no-one enjoys a higher or lower status than others. It is human beings who make divisions, they are not decreed by God. Every member of the community has the right to life and freedom as God wills:

'The caste of all mankind is one and the same.'

2 **It is devoted to the ideals of Guru Nanak.** The teachings of the first *guru* are inscribed in the Guru Granth Sahib. The Guru Granth Sahib is the voice of God. God spoke to Guru Nanak and he speaks still through the Word that he gave him. As Sikhs hear the Word they also hear the teaching of Guru Nanak. This is their ideal for life.

❝❝Sikhism as a community and brotherhood.❞❞

3 **The community acts in unity.** Decisions which affect the community are made by the community as a whole. Once the community decides any action, every member is expected to abide by it. In this way Sikhs act as a community in unison. It is the community of the local *gurdwara* which mainly makes the decisions for the local Sikh community.

4 **The community is active in good works.** Good works bring the community near to God and into harmony with his will. Good works express the depth and sincerity of religious beliefs:

Words do not a saint or sinner make,
Action alone is written in the book of fate.

The practice of justice maintains the social moral order and gives everyone his due. Hospitality is to be extended to everyone. The communal kitchen (*langar*) must be open to everyone, especially the poor:

A poor man's mouth is the Guru's treasure chest.

Being generous with possessions and giving to charity are among the good works that help to keep the community pure.

5 **The community fosters honest labour.** Every Sikh is expected to earn his daily bread through honest labour. The *gurus* taught that each must earn a livelihood themselves. Work is a vocation, however humble it may be. By taking up honest work the Sikh is never idle. Idleness is frowned upon. So also is unfair practice or unwholesome ways of earning a living. A Sikh is expected to repeat the Name of God as he goes about his work and after work to offer prayers to God. Honest labour is never separate from true religion. All work is done for the benefit of others and every form of work that is honestly done is proper in the sight of God. The ideal is service, not self interest or self seeking.

6 **The community practises high moral standards.** Each member must maintain the good of the community. Each should always speak the truth, guard the tongue, show tolerance, be humble, act fairly and behave honourably to others. Stealing, gambling and adultery are frowned upon. To maintain the unity of the community at all times is doing God's will. He is the father of the brotherhood (this includes women) and all must follow his directions. The community that follows these ideals is described as *panth* – the corporate community that accepts the Adi Granth. This is tantamount to living by the Word of the Guru. No Sikh can practise his or her religion in isolation from the community. So they contribute a tenth of all earnings to support it.

9 > SIKHISM THEN AND NOW

You have seen from this account of Sikhism that it is a very active and virile faith. After the death of the last of the *gurus* in 1708 the religion passed through a very turbulent period. The conflict between the Sikhs and Muslims continued, although the Sikhs were able to hold on to their homeland in the Punjab. The faith did not expand much during this period, due chiefly to the English. In 1849 the Punjab was annexed to the British Empire.

The British allowed the Sikhs to preserve their religion and their own way of life. They recognised the Khalsa and permitted Sikhs to follow the Khalsa code. During this time the Sikhs held very firmly to the traditions of their religion and these were kept alive by introducing reforms to promote the practice of Sikh teaching. There were movements to reform education and society. At the same time, the gurdwaras came more and more under the control of political leaders, who made them centres of political influence and wealth. In the second half of the nineteenth century there was a movement to regain control of the gurdwaras for religious purposes. But the political and religious use of the gurdwaras was never completely separated. In the early part of the twentieth century a powerful political party called the Akali Dal came into being in the Punjab and this continues to be very active. The determination to preserve the Sikh way of life and the right to its own homeland is still part of the continuing struggle of the Sikhs to keep their identity and independence in the modern world.

During recent times many Sikhs have left their homeland and settled in other countries. You have heard already of the large number who have settled in Britain. It is estimated that about 300,000 have come to live in this country, and they have settled mainly in large cities. The greatest concentrations of Sikhs are found in Bradford, Leeds, Huddersfield, London and Cardiff. They can usually be recognised by their dress, and they follow many Sikh customs, especially in diet and religious observance and celebrations. There are many Sikh gurdwaras throughout Britain, the central gurdwara is in London, and the Shri Guru Nanak Sikh Sangat Sikh Temple in Huddersfield is well known. There was a considerable increase in the number of Sikh gurdwaras during the 1960s, when many more Sikhs came to live here.

The Sikhs who have come in recent times to Britain are mostly of the peasant classes, or Jats. They find work mainly in factories and public transport and in running small shops. The desire to maintain their identity can be seen in their association with the gurdwara and the Sikh community. They often show considerable religious fervour and they are encouraged in this by very devout individuals known as *sant*. These individuals visit gurdwaras from time to time to inspire and guide the members to be loyal to their faith and to observe it in their daily lives. The *sant* is regarded as a pure Sikh with a mission to uphold the religion in its purest form and to defend it whenever it may be eroded. In the wake of this, movements have grown up such as the Sikh Youth Federation and the Sikh Youth Movement to uphold and defend the Sikh identity and way of life.

A local gurdwara in this country may maintain contact with a corresponding gurdwara in India. This also helps to keep alive the concept of community and unity amongst all Sikhs. Where this happens there is an emphasis on spiritual religion and the honouring of the *gurus*. In such cases the Guru Granth Sahib is given a place of great honour.

It is important to point out that in spite of the desire among Sikhs to keep their identity there are also divisions among them, as in other religions. Some groups refer to themselves as 'pure Sikhs' and others as not. The different groups follow the lead of a variety of leaders who have striven to guide the community. This is why some Sikhs wear a turban of a particular kind and others may not. But whatever the groups may be, Sikhs show the same sense of keeping alive the beliefs and practices which have been handed down from the past. The Sikh Missionary Society helps young Sikhs with problems of life in Britain and in preserving their own values in a mixed racial society.

APPLIED MATERIALS

COLE, W.O. & SAMBHI, Piara Singh, (1980). *Meeting Sikhism.* Longman.
COLE, W.O., (1982). *The Guru in Sikhism.* Darton, Longman, Todd.
COLE, W.O., (1984). *Sikhism and its Indian Context.* Darton, Longman, Todd.
COLE, W.O. & MORGAN, P., (1984). *Six Religions of the Twentieth Century.* Hulton.
McHERD, M.W., (1980). *Early Sikh Traditions.* Clarendon.
SAMBHI, Piara Singh, (1979). *Understanding your Sikh neighbour.* Lutterworth.

E X A M I N A T I O N   Q U E S T I O N S

QUESTION

i) What is the name of the sword worn by Sikhs? Why is this sword important? What does it symbolise? *(3)*

ii) The gurus instructed Sikhs to give a percentage of their income to charity. What percentage did they instruct, and why did they do so? *(2)*

iii) State the five stages of spiritual progression in the Sikh faith. *(5)*

iv) What help do three of these stages give to everyday religious life? *(6)*

v) 'Love God and do what you like.' Would a Sikh be likely to agree with this statement? Give reasons for your answer. *(4)*

(LEAG)

OUTLINE ANSWER

i) Kirpan *(1)*

   originally for survival/self-defence; self-respect/dignity *(2)*

ii) One tenth *(1)*

   money service was an expression of love and a means of finding the way to God through unworldly attachment *(2)*

iii) Realm of Law; realm of knowledge; realm of beauty; realm of action; realm of Truth *(5)*

iv) Exposition of three stages (× 2) *(6)*

v) Reasons for agreeing or disagreeing with the *apparent* rejection of moral rules *(4)*

(WJEC)

A   S T U D E N T ' S   A N S W E R   W I T H   E X A M I N E R ' S   C O M M E N T S

QUESTION

a) Describe a Sikh wedding.

b) Explain the meaning of the symbols.

c) Do you agree or disagree with 'arranged' marriages? Give your reasons.

> A Sikh wedding takes place in a temple. It takes place in the morning. Their Bible is a holy book and they bow to it in the temple. They tie a scarf and walk round the book and sing hymns and they have gifts and then they have a feast.
>
> The symbol is the scarf it belongs to the man and is held by the woman. It brings them together and they feel as if their joined. Nobody else touches the scarf. They think they belong to each other and to the holy book that is God so they think.
>
> I don't agree with arranged marriages you should choose for yourself. Your parents dont always know best. I think if two people are in love they should get married and then ask their parents. Not many people do this today.

Comments

The answer is rather scrappy and not well expressed. There are some omissions. A Sikh marriage may take place in a home, and the parents then take a greater share in the arrangements. You need to give the *name* of the Sikh holy book to show that you understand that it speaks God's Word and makes his presence felt. You must also say something about the responsibilities of marriage. You are right in describing the scarf as a symbol of unity, but note how this extends to the whole of their lives, or union on every level.

CONTEMPORARY ISSUES

FAMILY AND PERSONAL RELATIONSHIPS

RACE AND PREJUDICE

WEALTH AND POVERTY

WORK AND LEISURE

LAW AND ORDER

WAR AND PEACE

HUMANKIND AND THE FUTURE

QUESTION

OUTLINE ANSWER

GETTING STARTED

The following grid defines seven topics that are common to the syllabuses of the examining groups on this option. You will see that the scope of each topic is wide and you should consult your syllabus for guidance on how you should deal with it. Each topic raises practical questions that are of universal concern and you must not be surprised if you find that Christians do not always agree about them. In dealing with such topics Christians make moral judgements and you must bear in mind that no-one can prove or disprove these simply by producing a logical argument. There are seldom clear-cut answers to moral problems that suit everyone.

However, you must remember that the same assessment objectives apply. You must *know* what the religious teaching about the topic is, and show that you *understand* this and are able to make a *reasoned personal response*. In making your response it is the *reasons* you give or the argument you put forward that will gain you the marks. Here we shall consider the topics from the point of view of Christianity.

THE TOPICS

	LEAG	MEG	NEA	NISEC	SEG	WJEC
Family and personal relationships	+	+	+	+	+	+
Race and prejudice			+		+	
Wealth and poverty	+	+	+	+	+	+
Work and leisure	+	+			+	+
Law and order	+	+			+	
War and peace	+				+	+
Humankind and the future	+	+				+

ESSENTIAL PRINCIPLES

THE ROLE OF THE FAMILY

The family is the basic unit of society. Everyone begins the adventure of life by being born into a family. It may be a two parent or a one parent family with other children. Here, everyone has the first experiences of living in a community and discovering their individual identity.

The traditional family in Britain is based on marriage as a life long union. The 'nuclear family' is the smallest family unit which consists of mother and father and a few children. It exists as an independent unit, with little reliance on the wider kin. Father and mother share responsibility for running the home and there is a strong bond of companionship between the members of the family.

A larger family unit is the 'extended family' which comprises other relatives, grand-parents, brothers and sisters of the parents, living together under the same roof. The members rely on each other for the support of the family but power is generally in the hands of the senior male.

The traditional pattern of the family is under strain today. Changes are taking place in the functions the family performs for its members, which include caring for the needs of children, providing a stable basis for social living, moral and religious development, caring for the health of children, and regulating sexual behaviour.

JESUS AND THE FAMILY

Jesus was brought up in the family home in Nazareth with his parents and brothers and sisters. He was the eldest child and probably had to help to support his younger brothers and sisters after the death of his father. His religion taught him that he must honour his father and mother. The penalties for not doing this were severe under Jewish law. Anyone who cursed father or mother, or despised them, could end up as 'a lamp that goes out in the dark' or to be 'eaten by vultures' or could be 'put to death'.

Jesus showed respect for family life and his parents. He counted families among his friends and often visited their homes in Galilee and Jerusalem. He was fond of children and dealt sharply with his disciples when they tried to protect him from them. The disciples believed that they were acting properly by protecting Jesus from being disturbed, but he challenged their attitude by saying: 'Let the children come to me: don't stop them.' He brought 'good news' to children as well as others.

PARENTS AND CHILDREN

According to the law, parents have certain duties to children. They must register their birth and send them to school. They should provide children with a home, food and health care. Child neglect is punishable by law and parents who abuse children can also be punished.

Parents have authority over children whilst they are growing up, and provide for the quality of life in the family. Parents give children their first experiences of human love and care and standards of behaviour and manners. Christianity teaches a clear message about parents:

> Parents – do not treat your children in such a way as to make them angry. Instead bring them up with Christian discipline and instruction.
> Parents – do not irritate your children, or they will become discouraged.

Notice the two positive aspects of this teaching: parents should bring up their children with Christian discipline; parents must instruct their children. *What do you think Christian discipline means in this context? What do you understand by Christian instruction?*

There are two other questions that you might consider: *Do Christian parents have duties to children that other parents do not have? Do you think that being brought up in a Christian family is different from being brought up in a non-Christian family?*

What about children? The fifth of the ten commands says:

> Respect your father and your mother.

In the Old Testament, duty to parents is the most important after duty to God. Children who show respect to parents are given a special promise:

> So that you may live a long time in the land that I am giving you.

Christianity confirms this respect for parents:

> Children – it is your Christian duty to obey your parents, for this is the right thing to do. Respect your father and mother is the first commandment.

Take note of how this teaching stresses the duty of *obedience* and *respect*.

GENERATION GAP

You will see that Christian teaching focuses on discipline, instruction, obedience and respect. *Why then is there a generation gap?*

These are some of the relevant questions that must be asked: Do children have any rights? To what extent should parents discipline and instruct their children? To what extent should children obey and respect their parents?

In earlier times it was usual for children to be ruled strictly by their parents until adulthood. Today, discipline is more relaxed. As they grow up children want to be free to choose their own life-style in dress, habits, interests, to have their own leisure pursuits. Christianity has no specific teaching on the 'generation gap'. But the principles already mentioned apply. You will notice that Christianity does not lay down specific rules, so you must consider how Christians apply the four principles when they deal with the question of relationships between younger and older members of the family.

MARRIAGE

Christianity teaches about marriage in a positive way. Read Mark 10.6–9. Ideally, marriage is a commitment of love between two people. Yet everything revolves around the meaning given to 'love'. Consider the following possibilities:

 i) Two people 'fall in love'. This is a matter of the emotions, affection and physical attraction; it arouses strong physical feeling and sexual passion.

 ii) 'Friends love each other.' This is a matter of enjoying each other's company, sharing common interests, admiring the same things, having the same outlook.

 iii) Two people 'commit themselves to each other in love'. This is a matter of complete and unselfish self giving, devotion to another person, showing deep caring and respect.

Read the following, and say which kind of 'love' is being portrayed:

> Love is now considered important to marriage in all parts of the world. But only in societies like ours is the idea of romantic love all powerful. From early childhood we are socialised into falling in love . . . (R.J. Coates, The Family)

Read the following, and say which kind of love is being portrayed:

> Love is patient and kind; it is not jealous or conceited or proud; love is not ill mannered or selfish or irritable; love does not keep a record of wrongs; love is not happy with evil, but is happy with truth. Love never gives up; and its faith hope and patience never fail.

DIVORCE

Divorce is one of the problem areas for families today and Christians are not agreed about how to deal with it. Divorce is the termination of marriage by legal means. Since 1984 the law allows people to sue for divorce one year after marriage. The dramatic increase in divorce can be seen from these statistics: in 1966 divorces in Britain numbered 43,000; in 1985 divorces numbered 160,000. More than ninety per cent of divorced people remarry. Does this imply that marriage remains a basic part of the structure of social life in Britain?

 The changing patterns of the family.

■ *What accounts for the increase in the number of divorces?*
 Here are some reasons which you may consider: people marry at an earlier age; women are economically more independent; there is a decrease in the birth rate; fewer people marry in church.

■ *What is the Christian perspective on divorce?*

Read the following law from the time of Jesus:
> Suppose a man marries a woman and decides later that he doesn't want her, because he finds something about her that he doesn't like. So he writes out divorce papers, gives them to her, and sends her away from his home. Then suppose she marries another man, and he decides that he doesn't want her, so he also writes out divorce papers, gives them to her, and sends her away from his home.

It is clear that a man had to have good cause for divorce. In this case he must write out a formal dismissal so that the divorce could take place. The matter probably went before an official although this is not stated specifically. There were two ways of interpreting this law: first, the school of Rabbi Shammai said that the only ground for divorce was adultery; second, the school of Rabbi Hillel said that any trivial fault in a wife was sufficient ground for divorce.

■ What was Jesus' teaching on this?
First read the following:
> I tell you: if a man divorces his wife, even though she has not been unfaithful, then he is guilty of making her commit adultery, if she marries again; the man who marries her commits adultery also.

Now read this saying of his:
> Man must not separate then, what God has joined together.

Did Jesus allow divorce on the ground of adultery? Did he disallow divorce when he gave the second teaching? The relevant considerations are:
  i) Jesus sets the question in the context of God's purpose when he created the two sexes;
  ii) he places the sexes on the same level;
  iii) he does not treat the question in a legalistic way;
  iv) he sets a standard for Christian marriage.
You can find out what this is if you read 1 Corinthians 7.10–11.

■ *What the churches say.*
All churches teach that marriage includes a pledge between husband and wife to remain united 'until death do us part'.

■ *What if the marriage fails?*
Here we find different attitudes. The Roman Catholic Church does not countenance divorce or remarry divorced people in church. If marriage breaks down, separation is proper and those who are separated may be admitted to mass. A divorced person who remarries whilst his/her partner is alive is excluded from mass.

The Church of England does allow divorced persons who have remarried to take Holy Communion, under certain conditions. It does not generally remarry divorced persons in church. If the remarriage takes place in a registry office it may be blessed by the church.

Certain Free Churches allow remarriage in church under some circumstances. One of the parties may be innocent and remarriage therefore is an act of compassion.

SEXUALITY

> ❝Christianity, personal relationships and morality.❞

Christianity teaches the Bible's view of the creation of two sexes for the procreation of human life. Human life is a threefold relationship of body, mind and spirit. The three are mysteriously interrelated so as to imply that sexuality is part of being human. No human being can develop fully in isolation from another. Every human being develops fully only in relationship with others. Sexuality expresses this relationship through physical, emotional and spiritual companionship with a single partner. It has the unique function of creating another human life.

Christianity views sexuality as the celebration of love in a fully consummated relationship. It is deep-rooted in human nature and must be satisfied like any other desire. But it is to be used for loving and not for self indulgence or self pleasure. Here is a decalogue of Christian teaching about human sexuality:
  i) it is God's gift through human creation;
  ii) it is fulfilled in a relationship of love with a single partner;
  iii) it is practised in a life of loving relationship with another person;
  iv) it is an encounter of the whole person (body, mind and spirit) with another;
  v) it respects the other person as a partner, not as a means of self gratification;
  vi) it is an interdependent relationship in which both partners are equal;

vii) it expresses the reliance of each partner on the other;

viii) it is fulfilment of love for the other as for oneself;

ix) it is a condition of lasting relationship within marriage;

x) it affirms the rights of each partner as a person, not as a thing.

The Christian ideal of human sexuality is often challenged by the more 'open' approach to sexual behaviour. Sexual behaviour within and outside marriage produces a variety of responses. *Is there a Christian perspective on this?* Read the story of the woman taken in adultery in the Gospel of John 8. The woman was guilty of sexual intercourse outside marriage or adultery. The law said that she should be stoned to death. Jesus was asked what he thought should be done. He did not call for the punishment, nor did he condemn the woman. He threw the question back to the accusers by challenging them to consider their own sexual behaviour. When this happened they had nothing more to say. *What then about Jesus' attitude?*

Consider these three points:

i) he did not condone what the woman had done;

ii) he told her not to sin again;

iii) he showed he was willing to forgive her.

Remember, in the teaching of Jesus, forgiveness is a sign of the 'kingdom present'.

ABORTION

Abortion is the termination of a pregnancy sometime after conception and before the child in the womb reaches maturity. Christian opinion and society at large is divided on their attitude to abortion.

■ *What the law says.*

Up until 1967 abortion was illegal, except in cases where it was known that the life of the mother was in danger. In 1967 Parliament passed an act which made abortion legal:

i) if the life of the mother is in danger;

ii) if the child might be born so severely handicapped that life would be intolerable.

The time limit for legal abortion was set at twenty eight weeks. In 1988 a bill was rejected by Parliament which would have cut the time limit for abortion to eighteen weeks.

■ *What the churches say.*

The question Christians face is whether it is right to abort a potential life any time after conception. There are broadly two points of view:

Life begins at the moment of conception; to abort the life is an act of murder; murder is forbidden by God; conception is of a human life not a foetus; sexuality is for the creation of life within marriage.	Christians must act out of love and compassion towards abortion; a higher good may be achieved by saving the mother's life and aborting the child; undue strain should not be placed on the mother who may give birth to a deformed child; the decision should rest with the mother; medical science should be used as God's gift to serve the good of the mother and unborn child.

What do **you** think?

A case study on abortion

Kate's story

You may think I'm bad. But listen to me, please. Jim and I hope to get married when he gets a regular job. We've been courting for three years. We didn't want to go the 'whole way' till then. But you know how things are. We just got carried away. Jim just wasn't able to withdraw quick enough. We couldn't help ourselves.

I kept it to myself as long as I could. Jim was very understanding and said that he loved me but he wasn't ready to marry me and couldn't support the baby.

So I went to the doctor and asked for an operation. He wasn't really in favour and I wasn't able to speak to anyone except Jim and he didn't want to advise me either. 'It's your decision,' he said. I thought about the life inside me, I felt awful, would it be murder if I had an abortion . . . ?

What do **you** think?

2 **RACE AND PREJUDICE**

People sometimes say things to shock us or make us think about a problem and do something about it. Consider this statement which a black South African made about Britain:

> I have been a victim of racism all my life in South Africa, but my most humiliating experiences have been with the church in Britain.

Is this a racist statement? Does it express prejudice?

" Christianity, race and tolerance. "

- *What is race?* Here is a working definition: *race is the dividing of human beings into categories according to the colour of their skin and their physical characteristics.*
- *What is racism?* Here is a working definition: *racism is hostility shown towards other human beings on account of their colour or physical characteristics.*
- *What is prejudice?* Here is a working definition: *prejudice is the prejudging of other human beings regardless of who they are.*

JESUS AND RACE

Jesus was brought up in a multi-racial country. Jews were a minority in their own country – probably not much more than half a million out of one and a half to two million. They were under Roman rule and there were many Greek communities. He lived in close proximity to people of other races. He had direct contact with them and they made contact with him. A Roman Centurion came to ask him to heal his servant and a Greek woman asked him to heal her daughter. He entered into dialogue with both of them and treated them on a personal level. He showed no respect for racial differences, nor did he enquire about their nationality. When he spoke about the growth of the Kingdom of God he said it would attract people from north and south, east and west.

RACE IN BRITAIN

Coloured people first came to Britain in the time of the Romans. Since the sixteenth century there have been communities of coloured people living here. In the eighteenth century the coloured population of Britain was about 10,000; in 1920 it was 20,000. Since 1960 the number of immigrants (people who have come to live here from another country or society) has doubled. Today there are over two million immigrants.

- *Is there a race problem in Britain?*

Immigrants have settled mostly in and around the large cities and there have been incidents of racial unrest and riots. The causes are complex but some are obvious: poor housing and unemployment; over-crowding in schools and poor performance; failure to integrate into the host society; social and political frustration; difference in life style, social habits and culture; feelings of inferiority and fear.

- *Prejudice*

This may come from the *host* community (i.e. the British) through feeling threatened by the influx of large numbers of immigrants; through fear of infiltration by immigrants into positions of authority in social, industrial and political affairs, through denial of rights, and through imposing its will on others. Prejudice may come from the *immigrant* community through showing antagonism, disregarding the customs and traditions of the host community, acting as agitators or in authoritarian ways.

- *What the law says*

In the past twenty five years there have been a number of acts passed to deal with the question of race in Britain:

   i) **1965** – The Race Relations Act made it unlawful to discriminate in any way between people on the grounds of race or nationality. It set up a Race Relations Board to investigate complaints.
   ii) **1968** and **1971** – The government passed laws about the rights of citizens of Indian descent to enter Britain and to reduce the number allowed to settle here.
   iii) **1976** – A Commission for Racial Equality was established and all forms of discrimination on grounds of nationality were abolished.
   iv) **1981** – The British Nationality Act created three categories of citizenship: those born in Britain; British dependent colonies; British overseas citizenship.

RACISM AS A WORLD PROBLEM

Take for instance the word *apartheid*. It describes the division of human races into separate racial and ethnic groups and the domination of one by the other. South Africa is an example of a country where apartheid is the official government policy. This policy determines that coloured people are compelled to live in their own townships; their rights are restricted by government legislation; they must receive work permits in accordance with state laws; the rights of workers are curtailed; education is limited to elementary level; schools are controlled by white people; coloured teachers are less well trained and paid smaller wages; coloured people who reach the stage of 'higher' education are cut off from the best universities; they have little say in government and fewer political rights.

Twenty five per cent of the population of South Africa is white and keep the best lands for themselves. The remaining seventy five per cent live in twelve per cent of the land space. Coloured people have few social services and are not allowed to travel freely. Men are forceably separated from their families by the 'Homelands Policy'. Every year 50,000 children die from malnutrition in South Africa (which is Africa's richest country). It is a criminal offence to fall in love with a person from another tribe.

RACISM IN PERSPECTIVE

1 In Islington

Mrs Anowara Johan is a Muslim who lives in Islington. She came to Britain from Bangladesh in 1967, she is married and has three teenage children. She speaks about her feelings:

'Loneliness and boredom are the worst problems, and they are much more acute among educated women. Women who have had good jobs back in the sub-continent, as teachers or social workers, feel really resentful when they come and find there is no chance of getting work.

Back home, social pressure against taking up jobs was acceptable for Muslim women. But somehow it is different here.

Husbands don't like their wives to work. I think they feel it threatens their manliness. Educated men often still cling to some very old-fashioned ideas about women. They can't stand the idea – "My wife is as clever as me". Among uneducated families there are some in Britain where the grown up girls are locked up. One woman I know locks her children up when she goes out.'

2 A minority group in Southall

'Southall is unique because the population is almost exclusively Sikh, fairly established and quite well off. Asians have the reputation for being quiescent and keeping within their own community. But in Southall last year things began to change. After the death of Gurdip Chaggar the young people started to express their anger. Older people are trying to contain the rebellion of the young people. But their rebellion is complicated. Partly they are angry at the way they are treated by the white society. They won't accept racism the way their parents did. But there's more to it than that. They are rebelling against the values of their parents, too. They don't want to accept the old ways.

Young people have come to me in despair, because one of them has had a marriage arranged by his or her parents, yet they are in love with each other, and want to settle down together. What can I tell them? I have on occasions advised them to elope. People want to make their own lives.'
(New Equals Nov/Dec. 1977)

What response do you think a Christian might make to these two accounts?

3 In the USA

'Rosa Parks was committed to the cause of civil rights. She led a 'bus boycott when a Negro woman was arrested and put in jail because she refused to give up her 'bus seat to a white person. On the decisive Monday morning the first 'bus came down the street, with headlights blazing in the December darkness. Normally, it would have been full of domestic workers on their way to white houses. The 'bus was totally empty, and so was the next. The third 'bus had two people on it, but they were white.

Almost unbelievably they had pulled off a virtually total boycott. The pavements were full of people walking to work, and in the roads there were people on mules, in horse drawn buggies and being carried to work by the specially arranged Negro taxis and Negro-owned private cars. For some who walked it was a round trip of twelve miles.

That day Rosa Parks was tried and fined.'   (From K. Slack, 'Martin Luther King')

Do you think that Rosa Parks acted in a proper social way? Is it right to cause other people to suffer innocently for the sake of upholding a personal opinion or prejudice?

A CHRISTIAN FOCUS

In general terms the Christian focus on race is centred in two sayings:

God created every race of men of one stock, to inhabit the earth's surface. . . .
There is no question here of Greek and Jew, circumcised and uncircumcised, barbarian, Scythian, slave and freeman.

The first saying focuses on all races being created by God. The second saying focuses on the belief in the unity of humankind.

Peter and Cornelius

Cornelius was a Roman centurion but also a good man. In a vision he was told to send for Peter and invite him to his home. Peter also had a vision that was exceedingly strange:

He saw the heaven open and something coming down that looked like a large sheet being lowered by its four corners to the earth. In it were all kinds of animals, reptiles and wild birds. A voice said to him, 'Get up, Peter, kill and eat.' But Peter said: 'Certainly not, Lord! I have never eaten anything ritually unclean or defiled.'

Peter received the message from Cornelius but normally he would not have entered his house, much less eat with him. He was not a member of the same race. But after meeting Cornelius and listening to him, Peter confessed:

I now realise that it is true that God treats all men on the same basis. Whoever worships him and does what is right is acceptable to him, no matter what race he belongs to.

(Acts 10.1–33)

You should ask the following questions: i) Why did Peter change his mind about Cornelius?; ii) why did God treat Cornelius on the same basis as Peter? iii) what is the meaning of the symbols of Peter's vision? iv) how does this incident focus on breaking down racial barriers?

ENCOUNTERING RACISM

Many individual Christians and Christian churches have spoken out against racism. Take for example the stand of the 'coloured' South African, *Allan Boesak*. He was born in 1946 in South Africa and studied to become a minister of the Dutch Reform Church. After three years as a minister in Cape Town he went to study in Holland and then returned to become chaplain of the university of the Western Cape. In 1982 he was appointed president of the World Alliance of Reform Churches.

Allan Boesak soon began to speak out against apartheid, even though he was a minister of the Dutch Reform Church which supports the government. He said:

It is morally wrong to accept for myself rights and privileges when such rights and privileges are denied others who are citizens of South Africa.

There was a smear campaign against him as a supporter of violence and about his having an affair with a white woman. In 1984 he was arrested on a protest march against a killing near Cape Town. After his release he was arrested again for attending the funeral of a young man who had been shot by the police. He was arrested a third time under the Internal Security Act and placed under house arrest. He continued to speak out against apartheid and the oppression of non-whites. He condemned the poor social conditions, low wages, bad housing, and the lack of any political rights. He asked, '*What does it mean to be treated as a Bantu or a coloured rather than a human being*?' Can a Christian be at peace and see his fellow human beings humiliated? Is this why God created all people equal? Must a person obey a government that makes unjust laws? Does a person have the right to resist?

In the summer of 1983 Allan Boesak and Desmond Tutu nearly lost their lives in an assassination plot. The plot was aborted but later Allan Boesak told his church:

If they kill us it is not because we have planned revolution. It is because we have tried to stand up for justice, because we have tried to work for true peace. It is because we have refused to accept cheap 'reconciliation' which covers up evil, which denies justice and which compromises the God given dignity of black people. It is because we love them so much that we refuse to let them continue to be our oppressors.

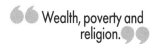

3 > WEALTH AND POVERTY

We hear people talk of the 'first world', 'second world' and 'third world'. The map shows a line dividing the world into these three 'divisions'. By the 'first world' we mean the countries of Western Europe, the USA, Australia, New Zealand and Japan. By the 'second world' we mean the USSR and the countries of Eastern Europe. By the 'third world' we mean most of the countries of Africa, South America and many parts of Asia.

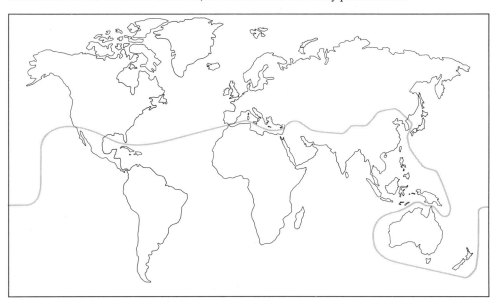

Fig. 11.1 Map of the North South Divide

The population is unevenly divided – 75 per cent live in the 'third world' and 25 per cent in the 'first' and 'second' world. The resources and income are also very unevenly divided – the 'first' and 'second' world enjoy 80 per cent of the world's income and the 'third' world 20 per cent. Does this mean that poverty is not a problem in the 'first' world?

66 Wealth, poverty and religion. 99

POVERTY

Poverty in Britain

These words were written recently by the Bishop of Liverpool:

> It has become appropriate to talk again about the poor; in Merseyside there are many areas where unemployment on a large scale has been present for years. There are areas where half the population are out of work. Side by side with working class families who may be earning large wages will be those who are properly described as poor. As you walk down a street two cars may stand outside No 12, where good incomes are coming in. No 14 has two incomes. No 16 a single parent family on Family Income Supplement.

Does this statement show that there are pockets of poverty in Britain? If so, where are they? What is the reason? Is 'wealth' and 'poverty' a way of comparing the position of people in the same society? Do ideas of wealth and poverty change from one country to another?

Poverty in the third world

> Lewis Nbobo is nine years old and lives in Soweto, a township in South Africa where a million people live in the same sort of conditions as in a big refugee camp. There's row on row of little tackboard houses, no electricity, no running water except what you can fight for at the overcrowded street tap at the end of the block. There are no trees or playgrounds, and there is nowhere to go. Lewis lives with his parents and four younger brothers, his aunt and her kids in one of the small houses. There's nowhere to play, so Lewis goes out and round the dusty streets to see what he can find.

How would you compare the two accounts of poverty? What is the contrast between poverty in Soweto and in Merseyside?

POPULATION

The poor in Britain are found mostly in large cities where the population is densest. Increase in population increases the demand on resources and makes it more difficult to make ends meet. The population explosion worldwide is one cause of poverty. Here are some facts:

- The world population increases by about 1,330,000 every week or 190,000 every day. The world population will double in thirty five years.
- The population of Britain increases by about a million every three years.

The majority of the world's population lives in cities:

- In 1985 the number of cities with one million or more inhabitants was 270 – an increase of 240 since 1900; 140 of these cities are in the third world.
- In 1985 the number of cities with ten million or more inhabitants rose to 18 – an increase of 16 since 1950; 10 of these are in the third world.

There is an avalanche of people abandoning the traditional village and rural life for life in the city. Every year the growth in urban population increases by ten per cent. The growth in population poses a grave moral problem: Must people limit the number of births?; can we stem the growth of population by voluntary or compulsory means?; should family planning be made legal?

RESOURCES

Resources are a key to survival, for if the growth in population outpaces the resources available for human life, disaster must follow. We may instance two basic resources for survival – food and water.

Food

When Jesus got out of his boat, he saw this large crowd, and his heart was filled with pity for them . . . When it was getting late his disciples came to him and said . . . Send the people away and let them go to buy themselves something to eat . . . Jesus told the disciples to make all the people divide into groups and sit down on the grass . . . He broke the loaves and gave them to his disciples to distribute to the people. He also divided the fish among them all. Everyone ate and had enough.

Christians take their cue for caring for the hungry from the example of Jesus who saw to it that the hungry people who followed him into the desert were fed. *He was concerned about their physical as well as their spiritual well being.* He also taught his disciples to pray *Give us today the food we need.* Christianity cares about food for the body, as well as food for the spirit. It was part of his mission to feed the hungry.

Hunger is one of the scourges of the modern world. Malnutrition is widespread and millions die every year from famine. There is unequal distribution of the food produced:

Half the world is starving,
Half the world is overfed.

You can see the difference between people in Britain and India from this table: the daily intake of calories in Britain for an average male is 3,300 and in India 1,600. The causes of this inequality are complex. In some countries it is due to lack of 'know-how' about how to produce food in sufficient quantity; fighting and war are factors which also affect the proper use and distribution of resources; political decisions also hamper development in some countries; alienation and discrimination are other factors which have to be considered; economics are also involved; human greed and selfishness may account for some people being underfed.

Changing attitudes: Jesus taught that the *attitude* towards wealth and poverty is the deciding factor. The same is true with regard to hunger especially when human factors account for it. The evil is not to possess wealth (which may be goods as well as money) but to lack responsibility to others. Read the parable of the rich man and Lazarus (Luke 16, 19–31); notice that the sin is *not* that the man is rich but that he ignored the need of the beggar at his door; the rich man took it for granted that some people were to be hungry and that he had no obligation to them; the rich man lacked compassion or sympathy; he assumed an attitude of 'I'm all right' which led him to leave the hungry beggar where he was. Jesus often spoke about *the need to change one's outlook or attitude*. Read the account of his meeting with Zacchaeus the tax collector in Luke 19, 1–10. After the meeting Zacchaeus was ready to repay what he had taken from others. *In what way does this teaching provide an answer to the problems of world hunger today?*

Water

This is a finite resource but a major factor in world poverty. The fresh water available on our planet today is the same as it was tens of millions of years ago. Yet the demand is infinitely greater. Can you imagine what it would be like if your home lost its water supply? Every home in Britain uses on average 568 litres of water every day. Contrast this with these two situations:

i) Drought regularly strikes parts of Brazil. The conditions of life change rapidly and the land becomes a semi-desert. During the drought many men leave their families in search of work and money to feed them. It is a desperate time. The women and children are left behind to fend for themselves. They are forced to sell or slaughter their goats and to eat bitter roots which give their bodies a little comfort from the agonising pain of hunger.

ii) There is little drinking water available for the people. In all six areas the farmers have lost almost their entire crop of beans and maize despite having planted two or three times. Although this year has not been declared officially as a drought year, the conditions are unavoidably those of serious drought and the effect on the population of the area is dramatic. (Report from Mozambique)

CHRISTIAN RESPONSES

Christianity has mounted a major onslaught on world poverty in respect of famine and drought. Two agencies devoted to this are Christian Aid and CAFOD.

Christian Aid

At the end of the Second World War the British Council of Churches set up an agency for helping the poor throughout the world. It aims to serve all people in need, whether or not they are Christians. Christian Aid is supported by many churches and the public. It gets most of its income from Christian Aid Week and voluntary groups. It provides aid through supplying food for people who are undernourished and who suffer from malnutrition, through health education, through providing medical supplies and dealing with people in times of disaster. An important part of the work of Christian Aid is educating and training people to understand the causes of poverty and injustice, to engage in schemes of agricultural training and ways of becoming more self supporting through the use of natural resources available. You can see how this works if you read this report from Sahel alongside the report above:

In the Sahel region of North West Africa – a semi arid belt of land on the edge of the Sahara desert – life has always been desperately hard. In the last ten years the Sahel has suffered recurrent drought and two devastating famines. The people are being pushed literally to the margins of existence.

But now farmers of the Sahel are fighting back. They are taking the initiative to improve their food production and raise themselves and their families out of desperate poverty, by organising themselves, making use of modern equipment and techniques, and adapting the centuries-old traditional methods of farming.

CAFOD

The Catholic Fund for Overseas Development was founded in 1962. It is the agent of the Roman Catholic Church in England and Wales for practical aid to the poor. Its aims are the same as those of Christian Aid. It works with local Roman Catholics who contribute to its funds. It has an extensive programme of educating people in poor parts of the world to help themselves and to make use of modern technology and knowledge in the production of food and other necessities.

Jesus and poverty

Jesus was brought up in a peasant home in Nazareth. He learnt a trade as a carpenter and it is improbable that he knew crushing poverty in his own home. He did not condone poverty or praise it for its own sake. He relieved poverty because it brings suffering and deprivation. It prevents people from living a full life. He gave special attention to people who were in need of help. Sometimes these were not people who were poor in a material sense or who lacked food and other physical essentials. They were in need of friendship and compassion or they were lonely or deserted or were treated unjustly. Poverty is not all of one kind, it can often make people aware of their spiritual and moral needs as well as of physical and material needs.

4 > WORK AND LEISURE

Work is said to be a blessing and a curse. Decide which of these statements presents work as a blessing:

> 'Work is good investment, and almost always pays!'
> 'My life is one dam'd horrid grind.'
> 'Our best friend is work.'

For some people work is the most satisfying part of life, they enjoy it and say that any job is better than none. *What makes for 'job satisfaction'?* Other people see work as a drudgery, the most miserable part of life, they cannot get through the working day quickly enough, they are always looking forward to the time when they won't have to work. *Why is this?*

 The dignity of work and the right to leisure.

People who enjoy work find it satisfying and it gives them scope to use their skills and abilities in a positive way. An artist, a designer, an inventor, an architect, a doctor or a teacher might all say that their work is creative and that they can use their special gifts and interests to the full. A person who only sits on an assembly line in a factory doing only one simple process in a mechanical way may find it boring because it allows no scope for initiative or enterprise of using personal skills or interests.

THE NECESSITY OF WORK

What is the value of work, whether it is of the first or the second kind? Work is necessary, for without it life would grind to a halt. Work was decreed by God at the time of creation to be necessary. He gave the first human being a command: 'In the sweat of your face you shall eat bread.' Bread is a symbol of the bare minimum essential for maintaining human life. It has to be earned or worked for (by the sweat of your face i.e. through human effort). Christians assume on this basis that God gives humankind the right to work and that it is also a duty. The two basic teachings of the Bible on work can be summed up as 'duty' and 'right'. Therefore:

- a person who refuses to work has no right to eat;
- there is nothing better than that a person should enjoy work.

Christians also believe that work is a good thing in itself. This is portrayed in the Book of Proverbs:

> Lazy people should learn a lesson from the way ants live. They have no leader, chief or ruler, but they store up their food during summer, getting ready for the winter.

You can see how this description teaches the necessity of work and why work is profitable.

Jesus the carpenter

Christians make much of the fact that Jesus was known as 'the carpenter'. He was a skilled craftsman who worked with his hands to earn his livelihood. He made essential equipment for the home and for agriculture. There is a legend that says that over the carpenter's shop in Nazareth there was a sign which said: *'The yokes which we make here will fit your animals well and comfortable.'* This must have given the carpenter a reputation for good work. Later in his teaching Jesus told his followers: *'My yoke is easy'*, that is, it fits well.

Paul the tentmaker

After Paul had become an apostle of Jesus he continued to work as a tentmaker. He once boasted of this being good and necessary work. He had no need to live off other people as he worked with his own hands to support himself. He didn't live as a parasite!

The Bible uses images of the workman to describe God – he is a creator, he works for his people, the Father works, God works in the believer, he works righteousness. God also involves people in being co-workers with him. Humankind shares with God the management of the world. The resources of the world are at the disposal of the workers.

Therefore the work of the electrician, the farmer, the physicist, the inventor, the scientist, is necessary for survival in the natural world. The inventions of modern technology, the nuclear reactors, the microchip, the computer and the operating theatre are the symbols of the will to survive. Without work there is no chance of survival.

Work and the common good

Work is a social necessity and essential for the good of society. All work has a social value and contributes either to the good or ill of society. You can put this to the test if you list a number of different occupations and ask what each contributes to the good of society. You may include, for example, a manual worker, a social worker, a policeman, a doctor, a priest, a debt collector, a housewife, and an entertainer. Consider the special features of their work and its value to others. Is it proper to describe some as 'ordinary' jobs of work? And others as 'up-market' jobs of work? Can some be classed as 'vocation' and others as 'doing a job'?

In Christian teaching, work is a social necessity: it is the way a Christian expresses responsibility to society. It also gives the worker a sense of dignity and self respect; it can be pleasurable as well as profitable; it is a means of forming social attitudes and nurturing attitudes of tolerance, patience, sympathy, affection and service. Work points beyond itself to its effect on others. You may consider how these points apply to the work of a tradesman, someone who works in public transport, a nurse, a social worker or a nursery teacher.

Furthermore, *Christianity condemns work that is not done for the benefit of others.* Selfishness is like someone who fights to destroy and not build up the life of society. It is as if 'a family divides itself into groups which fight each other'. The effects of work must not be divisive, but contribute to the common good. A further aspect of Christian teaching on work is that *work can be the means of changing the world.* Many people have helped to change the world through their dedication to their work, maybe as medical scientists, reformers, designers, inventors, pioneers. Every new invention is a means of changing the world, of influencing the quality of human life. Can you give reasons why the design of the internal combustion engine, the progress of medical science, the invention of satellite communication, the exploration of outer space, may be said to be world-changing events?

UNEMPLOYMENT

What about people who are denied the opportunity to work? This is a major question in many countries today. In the light of Christian teaching, the denial of the right to work goes against the natural order of life. Unemployment is not just the loss of earning power, but the denial of human dignity achieved through work. This is how the Bishop of Liverpool expresses it:

> It seems to me that the God I believe in, the Creator God who has given all people gifts to be developed and used, is indignant at a society which simply allows people to rot and says to them, 'There's nothing we need you for.'

A Christian response

Christianity aims to respond to unemployment in a constructive way. Here is an example:

> 'In Greater London the Tower Hamlets Bridge Projects Trust has provided Christians with scope for building a personal relationship of trust with people who are unemployed. They have been involved in helping unemployed people to be trained to set up small businesses as carpenters, window cleaners, drivers, car sprayers and others. They see this as a means of demonstrating positively the teaching of Christianity about work.'

In many places there are similar church-initiated schemes for helping the unemployed. Churches have worked together to set up advice centres or to inaugurate training schemes for young unemployed people. They have also called for a fresh approach by society to the problem of the unemployed. This could involve rethinking the distribution of work or work sharing and the effect of modern technology on employment. *Christianity enters these complex areas from the point of view of its belief that work is a means of serving God and fellow humans.* It believes that all work, however humble, has a positive purpose, that everyone should have the right to work in reasonable conditions, receive a just reward, not be exploited or work to the detriment of others.

LEISURE

As you have seen, the *Christian attitude to work is positive*. Work is good and represents the contribution to the welfare of the community. However, the worker is not a machine and needs a break from the 'daily round'. The need for rest from daily labour is recognised by the Bible. God rested on the seventh day of creation and gave the command that on the seventh day there should be rest from work for children, servants, and even animals. There is time for leisure on the Sabbath as well as worship; the command says that it is a day of rest from work; how Christians use the Sabbath (Sunday) today is often a matter of conscience.

It is difficult to offer a definition of leisure. If you try making a list of leisure time activities you will soon run into trouble. What is leisure to some may be a means of earning a living for others. Here are some relevant questions:

i) **Is leisure time for enjoyment?** Some may answer that what is enjoyment for them may be misery to others. A person may have a taste for a particular kind of music or sport that someone else may find very boring and dull.
ii) **Is leisure spare time?** Because work is the means of earning a living it rules out many people who work without being paid, such as a housewife bringing up a family.
iii) **Is leisure the opposite of work?** For some people work is their life and their enjoyment; take it away and they are miserable; leisure becomes stressful.
iv) **Is leisure doing what we like?** One person may choose to follow an interest or special activity but what may be open to some people may not be open to others for various reasons.

You may choose to answer these questions in your own way and then consider this working definition. *Leisure is the opportunity for doing things that give us pleasure outside the usual hours of paid employment.* This must include doing what gives us most pleasure and which is most relaxing.

CHRISTIAN PERSPECTIVES

There is no set Christian charter on leisure, so what are the principles or guidelines? Christianity takes a positive attitude to the use of leisure as being part of human welfare. The desire for pleasure and relaxation is natural and essential for personal well-being.

'All work and no play makes Jack a dull boy.' It makes him unbalanced; relaxation relieves stresses and gives opportunities for body and mind to recharge their energies; no-one can give of their best to work under conditions of fatigue or tiredness; no-one is expected to submit themselves to the care of an over-tired surgeon, or to play their best at a game when body and mind are tired. Christianity teaches a view of the body as the creation of God and therefore to be nurtured and cared for. Jesus cared about physical and mental health, and often told the people he healed to avoid the *cause* of their sickness. From these principles what consequences follow?

Leisure involves making choices. You will see what this implies if you make a list of the different ways you spent your leisure time during the past week. List things you did on your own, with your family, with your friends. Attempt now to *evaluate* (say what you think) your leisure time activities. Take a look into the future to the time when you will be in full employment. List some of the things you think you would like to do during your leisure time. Can you evaluate these? Finally, as you have been engaged in making choices, can you give reasons in each case for the choice you made?

Christians believe that Christianity involves them in making choices. They say choices have to be made in accordance with Christian teaching and principles. From your knowledge and understanding of Christianity, how does it relate to the choices Christians make about their leisure activities? Could you list some of the positive things? Are there any negative things?

Time and leisure

The Christian teaching on time can be expressed in this way. God created the world and divided it into days and seasons. Every living being is subject to time and God has given everyone all the time there is for living in the natural world. Time is the framework within which life is lived. The use of time is therefore of crucial importance to every human being. *Leisure is not activity outside or away from time; leisure is activity in time.* This makes the choice of leisure activity crucial in the light of Christian teaching. Increased time for leisure through shorter working days will widen the choice. The Christian principles for making the choice will not change but Christians will apply them in a new situation.

Law and order are essential for the working of society. *What is law?* Law is basically a set of rules which society makes to enable it to work in the best interests of its members. As such, everyone is subject to the law and is expected to live within it. This applies to the humblest citizen as to members of the royal family. Are there other kinds of law? Consider this list and say which of them are laws of the state and which are matters of social custom:

1 Everyone must stand for the national anthem.
2 People over seventy may have cheap fares on buses.
3 Speed limit for cars on motorways is 70 mph.
4 Gentlemen must give up their seats to ladies.
5 A policeman may enter any home if he has a warrant.
6 All children must attend school at three.
7 No-one must work on Good Friday.
8 Everyone must observe non-smoking laws on buses.
9 People travelling by bus must join a bus queue.
10 Everyone must clear litter from their own homes.

How do you rate those which are matters of social custom or practice? Do you think they are necessary to keep order in society? You may consider the rules you have to keep in school or if you belong to a club or organisation. What other kind of laws are there? Consider these:

1 You must not slander another person.
2 You must not encourage anyone to steal.
3 You must speak the truth before children.
4 You must not cheat at games.
5 You must not disobey your teacher.
6 You must not take time off from work.
7 You must not take another person's job.
8 You must treat animals with kindness.
9 You must not carry tales.
10 You must always respect older people.

You will see that these are *moral* laws and they may have a different authority from the laws of the state. If you break the state laws you may be punished by the state but the same is not the case with moral laws. *Does this mean that they are less important?* Society needs moral laws for its good order as well as the laws of parliament or of the state. The difference between these laws is: the laws of the state have the authority of the state legislation behind them; moral laws have the authority of conscience or religion.

JESUS AND LAW

What is the attitude of Jesus to law? Take his well-known saying: '*Pay the Emperor what belongs to the Emperor.*' Obviously this refers to the law of the state. It states that the Christian as a citizen must abide by the law of the state for the sake of good order of society. See how this is spelt out in this teaching of St Paul:

> Everyone must obey the state authorities . . . whoever opposes the existing authority opposes God . . . you must obey the authorities – not just because of God's punishment, but also as a matter of conscience. That is also why you pay taxes . . . pay then what you owe; pay then your personal and property taxes, and show respect and honour for them all.

Jesus did not lay down a body of rules which can be called 'Christian laws'. Instead, he gave a single ethic of love to show how his followers should behave. Consider this example:

> A Christian's neighbour creates a disturbance late at night through being drunk. He behaves in a violent way and attacks some of the neighbours. He also turns his home into an animal sanctuary which brings the neighbourhood into disrepute. The other neighbours protested and wanted to take revenge on him. The neighbours could not agree among themselves what they should do.

What do you think a Christian can contribute in this situation? Remember that Jesus did *not* teach a code of laws but a *motive* for observing laws. He left it to his followers to apply the principle according to their own conscience. This is why one Christian may act in 'good conscience', but another may act differently but also in 'good conscience'. Another point to note is that Jesus showed that law should be made to serve the good of human beings. Law should not be choked by tradition or repress human welfare. Law exists to serve human well-being and not vice versa. Notice too how Jesus taught that laws are not all equally important. Some laws can be trivial in comparison with the 'weightier matters of the law'. It is a mistake to confuse the lesser with the more important aspects of law. Can you think of laws that are trivial and laws that must be kept because they serve your highest interests?

BREAKING THE LAW

Laws are broken every day and rules are flouted. So what happens then? You may have your own views on the cause of law breaking or crime. Some of the causes (although not in any rank order) include: unemployment; boredom; too much money; thrill; greed; mob hysteria; jealousy; revenge; parent neglect; poor education; deprivation. Can you add to these?

Could you say whether any of these may lead to committing an offence or crime? Is there a difference? Suppose a person breaks the speed limit on a motorway. Is that an offence or a crime? If a person attacks a cripple and steals his/her money is that an offence or a crime?

The state distinguishes between an offence and a crime and has different law courts to deal with them . . . magistrates courts, crown courts, the high court, and the appeal court. A person who breaks the law is brought before one or other of these courts, depending on the charge. If found guilty, then the person is punished. The *purpose* of punishment is a matter of concern to Christianity. What is this?

Punishment as retribution

If anyone breaks the law, punishment is the payment (retribution) which society exacts. This means that the person is made to pay for what he/she has done. This may be a fine, or a term in prison, or community service. Then retribution is made. *What does Christianity teach about retribution?* It rejects retribution on at least three grounds: i) it runs the risk of being an 'eye for an eye' kind of punishment; ii) it does not take into account any personal circumstances connected with the law breaking; iii) it is too much like 'wanting to get your own back'.

Is retribution therefore fair or just? Consider the following incident:

> Billy, a cheerful and innocent boy, is pressed into service on HMS Avenger where the master at arms, Claggart, goaded by Billy's goodness, tries to bring about his downfall by accusing him of mutiny. Due to a speech impediment caused by his anger, Billy is unable to defend himself, strikes out at Claggart and accidentally kills him. Although all the officers want to acquit Billy, the captain points out that they must deal in law, not justice, and that mutineers must be discouraged from violence against their superiors. Billy is hanged.

Is it possible that society may be responsible for the offences or crimes that people commit? Who do you think is responsible for Billy's crime? Is there a conflict between 'justice' and 'punishment'? Or can punishment be too soft as to be worthless? Say what you think about 'retribution' as a form of punishment.

Prevention

If someone breaks the law we may say that something must be done to prevent it happening again. So the offender may be sent to prison for a long time, or even for life. The punishment can be the means of preventing society from having to deal with the same offender again. So it either keeps the offender out of the 'public eye' or else makes the punishment so severe that the offender will be prevented from ever committing a similar offence again. *How does Christianity view this kind of punishment?* One point to consider is whether this is a form of vengeance. Another point may be that society tries to wipe its hands of the offender and hopes not to have anything more to do with him/her. This would not be acceptable to all Christians. It may also be an admission of defeat by putting the offender beyond the reach of the offence.

Deterrent

A judge in a court of law may pass a sentence on an offender as a way of deterring others from committing similar offences. He says he must make an example of the offender, so as to deter others from doing the same thing. Is it a proper approach to law breakers? Consider this incident:

A gang of youths boarded a late night bus on Saturdays and attacked the passengers. This happened for a number of weeks until some plain-clothes policemen took action. They arrested the youths. The youths were brought to court and fined. The judge said he must make an example of them by imposing the maximum fine so as to deter others.

The attacks on passengers in that area ceased.

How does Christianity view this form of punishment? The relevant questions to ask are: Should each offence be dealt with in its own way and not for the sake of deterring others? Might the punishment be unjust if it is intended to deter others rather than be suited to the present offence? The three forms of punishment mentioned – *retribution, prevention* and *deterrent*, may not be strictly speaking alternatives. What do you think? Any form of punishment is meant to hurt. If anyone breaks a school rule or offends against society the punishment is intended to redress the wrong. A parent who punishes the child and says 'this hurts me more than it hurts you' knows at the same time that the punishment *is* intended to hurt. Is there any other way of punishing people who do not keep the laws or rules?

Reform

Can punishment be a means of reforming the offender? Sometimes an offender may be given work to do that will help him/her to contribute to the good of society. This helps the offender to live a useful life by doing some form of service that is constructive, such as learning a skill or working in a group and being supervised. *How does Christianity view this form of punishment?* The first point to consider is whether the offender has any rights. Christianity considers the *offender* as well as the offence. The basic rights of the offender as a person are paramount. A further point is that punishment as 'reform' places the onus on the offender as much as on society. The offender can learn from the reform measures and so develop a different attitude to law. Christianity acts on the principle that obedience to law is a matter of the right inner attitude. In all moral issues it is assumed that the individual is responsible for what he/she does. The Christian idea of responsibility is that we have free will so that we can either obey or disobey. The standard for this is set by God, who acts justly and shows love and forgiveness. The most important person to be considered in any case of offence or crime is the offender or criminal. This does not mean that punishment is ruled out but is viewed as a matter of action *and* attitude. The reason or motive for the action and attitude in punishing offenders should be guided by the truth and the ultimate good of the offender.

6 ⟩ WAR AND PEACE

For as long as anyone can remember there have been wars. The earliest peoples lived or died in a state of 'the war of all against all'. Only the fittest survived. After 'the social contract' and people begin to live in settled communities, the strongest sought to impose their will on others and used violence as a means of survival. *Is war therefore inevitable?*

Attitudes to war and peace divide society and religion. The majority agree that war is evil and there is wide disagreement about how to prevent it. On the one hand there are those who say that if we 'wish for peace we should prepare for war', that is, produce the means of defending ourselves or making ourselves so strong that nobody would dare to attack us. On the other hand, many people argue that the only way to outlaw war is by renouncing all the means of making war. The debate about this issue has dominated the world in recent times. *What is the Christian response to this pressing issue?*

Broadly speaking we are able to identify the following positions taken by Christians on the issue of war and peace.

THE CHRISTIAN PACIFIST

A *pacifist* may be defined as a person who is dedicated to peace and is against all forms of war as being the ultimate evil. Therefore they refuse to take part in producing weapons of war and see fighting a war as a form of murder. In the early centuries of Christianity most Christians were pacifists. They were persecuted, but they refused to use violence. A prominent Christian of the time, Origen said:

> For we no longer take a sword against a nation nor do we learn any more to make war, having become sons of peace for the sake of Jesus who is our leader.

Did Jesus teach pacifism?

In this context you need to study some of his sayings which Christian pacifists use:

a) *Happy are those who work for peace: God will call them his children.*

Pacifists see in this saying that Christ pronounced a blessing on the peace maker. The stress is on the work of *making peace*. Those who do this are called the children of God. What kind of peace making do you think he meant? Did he mean merely the absence of war? Or the absence of violence? Read this statement by Helda Camara, the Archbishop of Recife in Brazil:

> There is no doubt that Christ came to bring peace to men. But not the peace of stagnant swamps, not peace based on injustice, not peace that is the opposite of development. In such cases Christ himself proclaimed, he had come to bring strife and a sword.

What kind of 'strife' and 'a sword' does a Christian pacifist think the Archbishop meant?

b) *Love your enemies and pray for those who persecute you.*

Pacifists see in this saying a call to positive action. There is no command in the Bible to hate enemies but only to love one's neighbour. Love rules out doing any kind of harm to one's neighbour. Love in a positive sense means being active in doing good. Peace therefore involves working for a more just and fair society, for a world without violence, for the rights of all people to live in freedom. This is how love works, it does not create barriers or regard people as enemies.

CHRISTIAN NON-PACIFISTS

A Christian may be a non-pacifist for one of two reasons: i) it may be necessary to fight to preserve Christian values when these are attacked; ii) Christ did not teach an absolute pacifism.

A just war

After the Emperor Constantine gave Christianity legal status in the Roman Empire, many Christians were prepared to defend their new freedom by arms if necessary. They believed that under certain circumstances war could be justified. What were these circumstances?

One of the clearest statements on a 'just war' was made in the Middle Ages by *Thomas Aquinas* to guide Christians who were perplexed about being conscripted into the armed forces. He gave the following guidelines on fighting a just war . . . the *cause* must be just; the war must be *legally declared*; the *purpose* must be good; the *means* must be proper; the war must be *inevitable*; it must *protect* the innocent; it must *keep violence to the minimum*.

Did Jesus teach non-pacifism?

Christians who are not pacifists also appeal to some of the sayings and actions of Jesus:

a) *Do not think that I have come to bring peace to the world. No I did not come to bring peace but a sword.*

A sword is a weapon of destruction, it divides. So does the truth that Christ brings; it is more important than unity and it may be proper to use the sword for the sake of defending the truth and preserving the unity. Whilst Christ's ultimate purpose is to bring peace to the world, in the service of his kingdom it may be necessary to take sides and fight for the right.

b) *Jesus himself used violence when he drove out the moneychangers from the temple.*

There was probably plenty of scope for corruption and injustice in the dealings and Jesus reacted violently to these. There are occasions when it is right to show anger and use violent means in order to achieve a higher good.

CHRISTIANS AND NUCLEAR WAR

In the nuclear age it is said a 'just war' is not possible as the possession of nuclear weapons make complete destruction of life on this planet a distinct possibility. Today, bombs of the size of the one dropped on Hiroshima in 1945 are referred to as 'small tactical weapons'. An ounce of plutonium can kill 200 million people or if released as airborne dust can cause fatal lung cancer in over twice the earth's population. In the event of a nuclear war there can be no victors. This creates a dilemma for many Christians as you can see from these statements:

The Christian as citizen

If the Christian accepts the privileges of community life, he must not try to escape its responsibilities. Even if he tries he cannot altogether do so. The tax payer who pays for the atomic bomb is as responsible for it as the man who drops it.   (William Lillie)

The Christian abolitionist

Nuclear weapons are an offence to God and a denial of his purpose for men. Only the reduction of these weapons and their eventual abolition can remove this offence. No other policy can be acceptable to Christian conscience.

To possess nuclear weapons is wrong.   (USA Roman Catholic bishops)

The Christian negotiator

We must support the maintenance of a British nuclear force in order to fulfil our commitments . . . and to allow Britain to exert her influence in all future arms control negotiations.   (Church of Scotland)

The Christian defender

Governments cannot be denied the right to legitimate defence once every means of peaceful settlement has been exhausted.
                    (Roman Catholic document, Church in the Modern World)

A CHRISTIAN ALTERNATIVE

Christianity has always advocated an alternative to violence. It says little directly about whether a Christian should fight to defend his/her values. Instead it offers a vision of the world and how it should be run. It teaches a view of the future that involves humankind as well as God. It does not romanticise about the future nor is it disillusioned when the future is put at risk. *Its ideal is peace, but this does not present itself in terms of black and white.* It may be safely said that all Christians agree that anyone who engaged in war should do so only after all other means have been exhausted.

7 HUMANKIND AND THE FUTURE

What is the Christian perspective on the future? The TV programme 'Tomorrow's World' raises a curtain on the future. It is an optimistic world that raises hopes, even euphoria, in some people:

> We are living at the very beginning of time. We have come into being in the fresh glory of the dawn.

This is on account of the fact that the world is changing all the time. Some people equate change with progress – humankind is developing the skill and 'know how' to direct the future. They say progress is inevitable. If you consult your parents and grandparents, or an encyclopaedia about the changes of the past twenty five years, you may be staggered by the discovery. On the other hand, you may find those who say that it is *not* progress, nor is it right to equate progress with change. You may be able to compile a debit and credit table of the changes that have taken place in life in Britain during the past twenty five years. Many people are concerned about the future, especially those who have some responsibility for providing the means of livelihood of the world's increasing population. *What are the main concerns?* Here are four for you to consider.

PRODUCTION

An old Indian chief once said: *'The earth does not belong to man but man to the earth.'* Mahatma Gandhi once declared: *'Earth has enough for everyone's need but not for everyone's greed.'*

Production of enough food for the world is a matter of concern today. These are some of the concerns: the mass destructon of forests across the world causes a decrease in rainfall and a loss in the supply of oxygen and a sharp change in the climate which affects the production of food; more and more fertile land is being taken over by modern transport and building and the expansion of towns and cities; methods of cultivation and irrigation are frequently misapplied and produce waste land and cause soil erosion; the massive rate at which minerals and natural gases are being consumed; the danger that many animal species will become extinct.

These things are under human control. You may enquire how well this control has been used and how it affects the future of humankind.

ENERGY

The world is running out of some of the essential non renewable sources of energy. There are signs that world oil and gas supplies are likely to run out by the end of the century. Already there are moves in Britain to replace dependence on fossil fuels (coal, oil, gas) and to seek alternative sources of 'renewable fuels'. So 'energy parks' are being devised to harness natural energy from the winds and sea. Consumption of petrol is increasing all the time and scientists say that by the year 2020 the oil age will be over. A pressing problem is that industry, cars and aircraft are using up more oxygen and the plants which replace the vital oxygen are being endangered because of pollution and destruction of forests. Do you think that humankind needs a plan for survival? If so, in what way can religion contribute to such a plan?

POLLUTION

Read the following:

> Every day forty five factories, refineries and industrial plants release fifty two million gallons of trade effluent into the estuary (the river Mersey) . . . is this also a massive unflushed lavatory?

> (Jeremy Taylor, Polluting Britain)

Motor cars give out so much carbon monoxide that it reduces the oxygen we need to keep healthy. In some large cities of the world children have to wear gas masks to avoid breathing fumes polluted by waste gases. People who work regularly in dense traffic have to be relieved periodically because of dangers of pollution. Smog from chimney stacks, lead in the atmosphere, oil dumped into the sea, untreated sewage disposal, nuclear waste, are among the raw materials that pollute the natural environment and endanger life.

The rape of the environment in this way has given rise to a number of groups and organisations whose aim is to promote understanding of factors that cause pollution and which affect the quality of human life. They aim to educate about the conservation problems and to arouse public interest in the environment. You will find some of these mentioned in your syllabus including the Conservation Society, Friends of the Earth and other groups such as the ecologists and members of the Green Party.

What is the Christian response to this question? Consider the following points: God shares the care of the natural world with humankind; humankind should work with nature and not against it; humankind must show respect for natural laws; humankind must look to its lifestyle so as to show concern for others and the survival of all people. In this connnection you will find it helpful to read the following sources of Christian teaching: Genesis 1. 27–30; Psalm 8; Exodus 23. 10–11; Luke 10. 27–34.

HEALTH

Health is a matter of universal concern. The United Nations Health Organisation states that 70 per cent of the world's population is without any medical care and that 90 per cent of the illnesses in the world are the result of inadequate food, water, sanitation and living conditions.

Health implies more than the absence of disease. The task is to eliminate the cause of disease. How do you think the above causes of illness should be dealt with? The advances of medical science have brought many areas of human life under our control. This arouses strong emotional reaction and some difficult moral problems.

Consider how *contraception* allows sexual intercourse without the risk of conceiving a child. Does this imply human control over the beginning of life, and so is a means of controlling the population one also of eliminating disease? Or consider *euthanasia* (mercy killing). Is it kind to allow a person to suffer when the only prospect is further and worse suffering? Or is it better to allow people the means to end their life painlessly? What is your view? We know that everyone is dependent on medicines and drugs in one way or another. Those like tea or coffee, or medicines or tablets prescribed by a doctor are 'socially and morally acceptable'. But what about alcohol and tobacco? The case is more problematic and people are divided in their views on these. Here are some references that you may consider and apply to this question: Psalm 104. 15; Amos 2. 12; Matthew 11. 19; 1 Corinthians 8. 13; Ephesians 5. 18. Once you have read these then ask: What is the role or function of Christian teaching in respect of health? Is the work of a Christian doctor in any way 'special' in dealing with illness? How do you think Christians may see the relationship developing between themselves and others who are concerned in the general field of health?

CHRISTIANITY AND THE FUTURE

Christians are divided about how far they should be involved in practical issues like pollution and health. Some believe that Christianity declines when it becomes involved in such matters. Its role is spiritual. Others believe that only by taking an active part in dealing with such contemporary issues can Christianity show it is relevant to life.

You will discover that the majority of Christians believe that they should apply Christian teaching and principles to these issues as they affect the life of people in God's world. What can we conclude from this? There are four answers which Christians believe are relevant to the future of humankind in the natural world:

Firstly, at the beginning everything was created by God. To keep the world 'good' is a powerful motive for right action; this refers to the 'good' use of the world's natural resources and the control of exploitation and pollution.

Secondly, the natural world is an ordered world. Creation is a matter of order and different levels of life, functions and species. Using and controlling the advances of technology and serving the well-being of humankind go hand in hand.

Thirdly, humankind only achieves its potential in the natural world. To respect and control the natural world is part of human responsibility as delegated to humankind at the time of creation. Scientific, technical and industrial advances in this generation are the means given to humankind for perpetuating the human race.

Fourthly, Christianity holds that the natural world and the future of humankind within it as part of God's overall purpose.

APPLIED MATERIALS

BARCLAY, W., (1971). *Ethics in a Permissive Society*. Collins.
FIELD, D. & TOON, P., (1982). *Real Questions*. Lion.
FLETCHER, R., (1985). *The Family and Marriage in Britain*. Pelican.
GOWER, R., (1983). *Frontiers*. Lion.
PATEY, E.H., (1986). *Real Questions*. Mowbray.
TITCHER, R., (1981). *Religion meets the New Age*. Blackie.

EXAMINATION QUESTIONS

QUESTION

a) Describe two effects that unemployment has in each case on:
   i) those who have never been in paid employment. *(4)*
   ii) those who have been made redundant with little hope of further employment. *(4)*
b) What steps could the Christian churches in areas of high unemployment take to help unemployed people? *(8)*
c) How might an individual's faith influence his/her attitude to being unemployed? *(4)*

(SEG)

OUTLINE ANSWER

a) Points could include the following:
   i) Hopeless feeling for the future, lack of self-confidence, so many material things out of reach because of lack of money, eventual dependence on others to provide everything, no financial security or dependence, boredom, deterioration of abilities and enthusiasm. *(4)*
   ii) Worry about financial commitments, feeling that one is unwanted, all that has gone before has led to nothing, no appreciation of skill and conscientious work, life is over, boredom, anger and frustration, 'Why should this happen to me?' *(4)*

b) Basic underlying ideas could include:

make the unemployed people feel wanted, part of the brotherhood of man (or family of God). Each one is an important individual, God concerned with man's heart, not his job. To encourage and help in the search for work, using any known contacts. To provide opportunities for using the skills of the people in some constructive way e.g. study groups, dramatic production, sports clubs, visits, worship etc. It is hoped that answers will give imagination, practical, detailed suggestions. Give marks for understanding the function of the Church. *(8)*

c) Credit will be given for a negative response if good argument is used. Helpful points could include some of the following:

use of prayer and comfort of group worship, comfort of knowing one has one's fellow Christians to turn to for help and companionship; consciousness of one's dignity as a human being with God the Father etc. *(4)* *(20)*

QUESTION

a) Give two examples of groups of people who are working to preserve the world's wildlife. *(2)*

b) Give three reasons why it is important for the wildlife to be preserved. *(6)*

c) 'Man is free to destroy his world.' Discuss this statement from a Christian point of view. *(12)*

(SEG)

OUTLINE ANSWER

a) World Wildlife Trust. Greenpeace. Save the Whale. (Any known group.) *(2)*

b) Points could include three of the following:

Balance of nature; ecology; man's responsibility to God's creation and to future generations; prevention of extinction of species; prevention of such tragedies as the dust bowl in America; appreciation of beauty (2 marks each). *(6)*

c) Marks will be awarded for the points made and the quality of the argument. Points that could be made:

Man given responsiblity for the created world (Genesis); man also given free will to do as he wills; conflicting interests of the business world, manufacturing, effluent, poisoned rivers, acid rain, smog, big-game hunting, farmers' control of pests, use of nuclear weapons and others etc. *(12)* *(20)*

INDEX